Red Hat Linux 5.1

The Official Red Hat Linux Installation Guide

Red Hat Software, Inc.
Research Triangle Park, North Carolina

Revision: Inst-5.1-Print-MDP (5/98)

Red Hat Software, Inc.
4201 Research Commons, Suite 100
79 T. W. Alexander Drive
P. O. Box 13588
Research Triangle Park, NC 27709
(919) 547-0012
redhat@redhat.com
http://www.redhat.com

Contents

Introduction to the Macmillan Digital Publishing Edition

(**Editor's Note:** This manual is derived from the original Red Hat Linux 5.1 Official Installation Guide produced by Red Hat Software, Inc. This introduction has been added by Macmillan Digital Publishing to document features that are unique to our version of Red Hat Linux, or to stress issues of particular importance, particularly to first-time Linux users.)

Thanks for purchasing the *Complete Red Hat Linux 5.1 Operating System*! This award-winning operating system brings true multi-tasking and the power of a UNIX workstation to your Intel-processor PC.

Please Note: Linux is not an add-on to DOS. It is a complete operating system, so it's *very important* that you read this manual *before* installing the software. While Red Hat Linux is the easiest version of Linux to install, it is not like installing Windows or DOS on your machine. So if you've never installed Linux before, please take the time to read the installation-related chapters before starting to install Red Hat Linux.

Minimum System Requirements

Before you install Red Hat Linux, make sure your computer has the following minimum hardware and software requirements. Note that your experience using Red Hat Linux will be substantially more enjoyable if your system exceeds these minimum requirements, particularly in the areas of RAM and free hard drive space.

- IBM-compatible PC

- Intel-compatible '386, '486, Pentium, Pentium Pro, or Pentium II processor

- SCSI or IDE CD-ROM drive

- 8MB RAM (16MB or more highly recommended)

- 3.5 inch diskette drive (as drive A)
- 40MB hard drive space (character mode)
- 100MB hard drive space (with X Window System)
- Internet connection required for Internet software

Please Note: Red Hat Linux supports the widest possible range of PC hardware, including sound cards, video cards (and monitors), laser (and dot-matrix) printers, Ethernet network cards, and other specialized peripherals. To ensure compatibility with your PC's hardware, check the hardware compatibility list at
http://www.redhat.com/support/docs/hardware.html.

New to Linux?

Please Note: If you are new to Linux and this is your first installation, you should read this section; otherwise, you can skip ahead to the "Electronic Resource Library" section on page xi.

Many new users who install Linux the first time wonder, "Where are the .EXE files?" You'll find that Linux does not use file extensions like DOS or Windows does. All programs reside in the various bin directories on your hard drive (/bin, /usr/bin, and /usr/X11R6/bin are but a few of these directories). These directories contain the binary executables that run when you enter their name as a command. For example, the ls command runs /bin/ls, while the less command runs /usr/bin/less, and so on.

Another important item that confuses new users – Linux is case sensitive. For example, if you see a program called Lynx and you want to run it, you must type it exactly the way it appears – lynx, LYNX, or other variations will not work.

With MS-DOS, directories are separated with the backward slash character: \. For example, the System subdirectory of the Windows directory would be \Windows\System. However, with Linux, you must use the forward slash character: /. For example, the local subdirectory of the usr directory would be /usr/local.

When you need to read a CD-ROM, you must first *mount* the CD-ROM. The mount command makes the CD-ROM available to the Linux system. With DOS, Windows, and Macintosh systems, CD-ROMs automatically mount when you insert them in the drive. This manual and the electronic books contain more information on mounting CD-ROM and hard drives. However, here's a quick overview:

You must first have a directory that will serve as your CD-ROM's *mount point*. You can create a directory with the mkdir command. For example:

```
mkdir /mnt/cdrom
```

Next, you would issue a mount command to mount the CD-ROM on the mount point:

```
mount /dev/cdrom /mnt/cdrom
```

Please Note: The device specification /dev/cdrom used above may not correspond to your system's CD-ROM drive. If you have a SCSI CD-ROM drive, you should use /dev/scd0. If you have an ATAPI (also known as IDE) CD-ROM drive, your device name will be /dev/hdX, where X is a single letter (normally in the range a through d). You can use the dmesg command to see the device name given to your CD-ROM drive when the Linux kernel booted.

After you mount the CD-ROM, you can view its contents by looking in the mount point (/mnt/cdrom in our example). You'll need to use the umount command to unmount the CD-ROM in order to change discs (for example, umount /mnt/cdrom). Note that if you changed directory "into" the CD-ROM, the umount command will fail with a device is busy error. If this happens, simply change directory "out" of the CD-ROM (for instance, cd /).

Another hint that will save you time typing is to use the [Tab] key to automatically complete commands and filenames. For example, if the file you want to run is xloadimage, all you need to do is type the beginning of the filename, followed by [Tab]. If the system can unambiguously identify the filename, the complete filename will appear; otherwise, the system will beep at you, prompting you to enter more of the filename.

The X Window System

If you are new to Linux, your enjoyment of the operating system will be heightened by installing the X Window System. X is a graphical user interface that uses windows (not to be confused with Microsoft ® Windows®) that may be moved and resized on your screen. However, like Microsoft Windows, the X Window System allows you to operate in a graphical point-and-click environment. Red Hat Linux uses a version of X known as XFree86.

Please Note: While an X session looks similar to a Windows session, X does not act the same as Windows. For example:

- When typing in a text box, some X configurations will require you to first click on the window, while other configurations only require the pointer to be placed within the window.

- X, in general, does not support Drag and Drop operations, or associating file extensions with specific applications. Therefore, double-clicking on a spreadsheet file may not do what you'd expect.

Electronic Resource Library

The following Sams Publishing books have been provided in electronic format on CD-ROM 1. These books are in Adobe Acrobat format:

- Selected chapters of *Red Hat Linux Unleashed*, by Kamran Husain, Timothy Parker, et al

- *Teach Yourself Unix in 24 hours*, by Dave Taylor and James Armstrong

- *Apache Server Survival Guide*, by Manuel Alberto Ricart

Updated Information

Chapter 2 of the *Apache Server Survival Guide* is not applicable to Red Hat Linux 5.1. This chapter pertains to the installation and basic configuration of Apache. Red Hat Linux uses RPM (the Red Hat Package Manager). RPM allows you to pick and choose which linux "packages" (programs and associated data) that you want to add to your system. Therefore, you do not need to manually install Apache as detailed in the Survival Guide; RPM will do it for you.

Location of Electronic Books

The electronic books are available in the following location on CD-ROM 1:

- **Red Hat Linux Unleashed (selected chapters)** – /ebooks/redhatu.pdf

- **Apache Server Survival Guide** – /ebooks/apache.pdf (there are accompanying files from the original book's CD-ROM in /ebooks/apaches/cd).

- **Teach Yourself Unix in 24 hours** – /ebooks/24unix.pdf

Adobe Acrobat Reader

To view the Acrobat versions of the electronic books, you must install the Adobe Acrobat Reader, which is located on CD-ROM 1, in the file:

```
/ebooks/acroread_linux_30.tar.gz
```

After creating a temporary directory on your hard drive, use cd to change directory into that temporary directory, and issue the following command:

```
tar zxvf /ebooks/acroread_linux_30.tar.gz
```

Read the newly-created file INSTGUID.TXT, and follow the directions carefully to complete the installation. After you install the software, the reader will typically be named /usr/local/Acrobat3/bin/acroread. While running the X Window System, type the complete filename (with path) to start the reader.

Using the Acrobat Reader

If you haven't used Adobe Acrobat before, here are a few tips to help you get started.

The Acrobat Reader allows you to easily navigate through documents, search for words in the document, and jump from the table of contents to the area of interest using hyperlinks. The Acrobat buttons on the tool bar are there to help you control the reader's basic operation (See Figure 1).

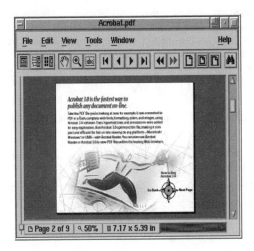

Figure 1: Adobe Acrobat Reader

You'll notice that the buttons are divided into six groups. Let's take a look at these button groups, from left to right:

- The first three buttons control the Acrobat Reader's screen layout. Only one of these buttons may be depressed at a given time. They produce the following layouts:

  - **Page image only** – The screen will contain the page image of the Acrobat document being displayed.

  - **Browser and page image** – The screen will consist of two panes: On the left, a hierarchical browser, allowing you to quickly find the desired section of the Acrobat document being displayed. The right-hand pane contains the page image.

  - **Thumbnail and page image** – The screen will consist of two panes: On the left, thumbnail images of each page in the Acrobat document being displayed. The right-hand pane contains the current page.

The next three buttons control how you can interact with the Acrobat Reader. Only one of these buttons may be depressed at a given time:

- **"Hand" scrolling** – When depressed, this button allows you to scroll (vertically and horizontally) using your mouse. Simply point at the part of the document you'd like to "grasp", press the primary mouse button, and drag. The document will scroll in the direction you drag.

- **Magnification control** – When depressed, this button allows you to set the magnification applied to the document. Simply point at the part of the document you'd like to magnify, and press the primary mouse button. The document will be magnified, with the point you selected at the center of the screen.

- **Text selection** – When depressed, this button allows you to select text for copying using the mouse. Simply point at the part of the document you'd like to select, and press the primary mouse button. Drag to the end of the text you'd like to copy, and release the primary mouse button. You may then paste the selected text into another window (Under X, this is most often done using the center mouse button on a three-button mouse, or by pressing both mouse buttons simultaneously on a two-button mouse).

The next group of buttons control navigation through the Acrobat document being displayed:

- **First page** – This button will take you directly to the first page of the Acrobat document being displayed.

- **Previous page** – This button will take you to the previous page of the document.

- **Next page** – This button will take you to the next page of the Acrobat document being displayed.

- **Last page** – This button will take you directly to the last page of the document.

The next group of buttons allow you to retrace your steps through the document:

- **Previous historical page** – This button will take you to the page that you had displayed last.

- **Next historical page** – This button will take you to the next page in your list of pages displayed. This button is only active if you've used the **Previous historical page** button at least once.

The next group of three buttons control how each page is to be displayed on your screen:

- **Actual size** – This button causes each page to be displayed at its actual size.

- **Fit page** – This button causes each page to be displayed at the largest size that can fit entirely within the Acrobat Reader's window.

- **Fit width** – This button causes each page to be displayed at the largest size that can fit within the width of the Acrobat Reader's window.

The last button (in a group of its own) allows you to search the document for the occurrence of any text you specify. A dialog box will appear allowing you to enter the search string, as well as to control case sensitivity, whole-word matching, and the like.

Additional help is available within the Acrobat Reader.

Using the Backup and Restore Utility (BRU 2000 PE)

The personal edition of BRU is included in version 5.1 of Red Hat Linux. BRU is a high performance, reliable backup utility from Enhanced Software Technologies, Inc. BRU 2000 PE does not support the following features that are available in the standard edition of BRU:

- Network-oriented backup operations, including:

  - Provisions for the backup of "raw" partitions/devices
  - Provisions for fifo-based controls (BRUTALK)
  - Double-buffered I/O

- File renaming during restore
- Tape overwrite protection

However, tapes created with other releases of BRU are fully compatible with the Personal Edition, and tapes created with the Personal Edition are compatible with the BRU's standard edition.

The following information will help you get started using BRU.

Here is a list of the various modes and options that BRU provides:

- -c – Create (backup) a BRU backup volume
- -x – Extract (restore) files from a BRU backup volume
- -t – Table of contents (file list) of a BRU backup volume
- -i – Inspect (verify) the contents of a BRU backup volume
- -e – Estimate the number of volumes a BRU backup will require
- -d – Difference (compare) the contents of a BRU backup volume with the original files on the system.
- -v – Verbosity level (up to four v's may be specified)
- -f – What backup device should be accessed

BRU's command line looks like this:

```
bru -(mode) -(options) -f (device) (path)
```

With these basic modes and options, all backup and restore functions can be performed. For example, to backup the contents of the entire system to the first SCSI tape drive, issue the following BRU command:

```
bru -cvf /dev/nst0 /
```

This will backup the entire system to the tape drive nst0.

To examine the contents of a tape made in this manner, issue this command:

```
bru -tvf /dev/nst0
```

Notice that it is not necessary to specify a file path to obtain a listing of the tape.

To restore the entire backup to its original path, issue this command:

```
bru -xvf /dev/nst0
```

This would automatically restore all files to their original locations.

To verify the contents of a BRU backup volume, there are two mechanisms available. The first is recommended, as it requires only the tape drive and BRU. This is the Inspect -i) mode:

```
bru -ivf /dev/nst0
```

This command re-reads each block written on the backup volume, and recalculates the 32-bit CRC (Cyclic Redundancy Check). BRU then compares the calculated CRC with the CRC that was written to tape. If the two CRCs do not match, BRU will warn you that the checksum is bad for the file in which the error occurred.

The second mechanism requires both the backup volume and the original data. This mechanism uses the Difference (-d) mode:

```
bru -dvf /dev/nst0
```

This command reads the data from tape, and performs a bit-by-bit comparison with the original data from your system. Of course, this command will report problems if files have changed on the your system since the backup was made. Introduction

Preface

Welcome! And thanks for your interest in Red Hat Linux. We have what we think is the best Linux distribution on the market today, and we work hard to keep it that way. Red Hat Linux 5.1 is the latest in a long line of software from Red Hat Software. We hope you like it, and that you enjoy using Red Hat Linux as much as we've enjoyed making it for you.

It's interesting to note that, while Linux is popular and well-known by a certain segment of the computer-using population, there are many people out there that are only now hearing about Linux. For this group of people, the following section should provide enough background to help you get acquainted with Linux and Red Hat Software.

What is Linux?

Back in August of 1991, a student from Finland began a post to the comp.os.minix newsgroup with the words:

```
Hello everybody out there using minix -
I'm doing a (free) operating system (just a hobby,
won't be big and professional like gnu) for
386(486) AT clones.
```

The student was Linus Torvalds, and the "hobby" he spoke of eventually became what we know today as Linux.

A full-featured POSIX-like operating system, Linux has been developed not just by Linus, but by hundreds of programmers around the world. The interesting thing about this is that this massive, world-wide development effort is largely uncoordinated. Sure, Linus calls the shots where the kernel is concerned, but Linux is more than just the kernel. There's no management infrastructure; a student in Russia gets a new motherboard, and writes a driver to support a neat feature the motherboard has. A system administrator in Maryland needs backup software, writes it, and gives it away to anyone that needs it. The right things just seem to happen at the right time.

Another interesting thing is that Linux can be obtained for absolutely no money. That's right, most of the software is available (at no charge) to anyone with the time and inclination to download it. But not everyone has that much time...

What is Red Hat Linux?

Enter a group of programmers based in North Carolina. Their goal was to make it easier for people to give Linux a try. Like many other such groups, their approach was to bundle all the necessary bits and pieces into a cohesive *distribution*, relieving "newbies" from some of the more esoteric aspects of bootstrapping a new operating system on their PCs.

However, unlike other distributions, this one was fundamentally different. The difference? Instead of being a snapshot of a hard disk that had a working copy of Linux on it, or a set of diskettes from which different parts of the operating system could be dumped, this distribution was based on *packages*.

Each package provided a different piece of software, fully tested, configured, and ready to run. Want to try a new editor? Download the package and install it. In seconds, you can give it a try. Don't like it? Issue a single command, and the package is removed.

If that was all there was to it, this distribution would be pretty nifty. But being package-based meant there was one additional advantage:

This Linux distribution could be easily upgraded.

Software development in the Linux world is fast-paced, so new versions of old software come out continually. With other distributions, upgrading software was painful – a complete upgrade usually meant deleting everything on your hard drive and starting over.

By now you've probably guessed that the group of programmers in North Carolina is Red Hat Software, and the package-based distribution is Red Hat Linux.

Since Red Hat Linux's introduction in the summer of 1994, Linux and Red Hat Software have grown by leaps and bounds. Much has changed; support for more esoteric hardware, huge increases in reliability, and the growing use of Linux by companies around the world.

But much still remains the same. Linux is still developed by people world-wide; Linus is still involved. Red Hat Software is still located in North Carolina; still trying to make Linux easier for people to use.

And Red Hat Linux is still package-based; always has been, always will be.

We make Red Hat Linux available by unrestricted FTP from our site and many mirror sites on the Internet. Red Hat Linux is also available on CD-ROM. For current information on our product offerings and links to other Linux resources please check Red Hat Software's web site at http://www.redhat.com.

On most systems, Red Hat Linux is easy to install; the installation program can walk you through the process in as little as 15 minutes. The system itself is very flexible. With RPM, you can install and uninstall individual software packages with minimal effort. Because of RPM, Red

Hat Linux is also easy to maintain – package installations can be verified and corrected, and packages can be installed and uninstalled simply and reliably. Furthermore, Red Hat Linux is easy to administer. Included are a rich set of administrative tools which reduce the hassle of everyday system administration. Complete source code is provided for the freely distributable components of the system.

An Overview of This Manual

This manual is organized to guide you through the process of installing Red Hat Linux quickly and easily. Toward that goal, let's take a quick look at each chapter to help you get acclimated:

Chapter 1, *New Features Of Red Hat Linux 5.1* contains information concerning new functionality that has been added to Red Hat Linux 5.1.

Chapter 2, *Before You Begin* contains information on tasks you should perform prior to starting the Red Hat Linux installation.

Chapter 3, *Starting the Installation* contains detailed instructions for starting the Red Hat Linux installation process.

Chapter 4, *Continuing the Installation* contains instructions on the main part of the installation process.

Chapter 5, *Finishing the Installation* contains instructions on the last steps required to complete the installation process.

Chapter 6, *What Do I Do Now?* contains information on logging in, performing system shutdowns, and configuring the more popular system components (such as X).

Chapters 7 – 11 explain how to find documentation on your system, and how to use the various system management and administration tools which accompany Red Hat Linux. They also include an explanation of what's special about your Red Hat Linux system, including where special files live and more.

Appendixes contain extra information about Red Hat Linux, including an explanation on Red Hat Software's support offerings, frequently asked questions, etc.

Quick Start Information

Those of you that have installed Red Hat Linux/Intel before and are in a hurry to get started need only boot from a boot diskette (or the Red Hat Linux/Intel CD-ROM, if your computer supports booting directly from CD-ROM). Next, select the desired installation method. If you are installing from an FTP site, a hard disk, or you'll be using a PCMCIA card during the installation, you'll be prompted to insert a supplemental diskette[1]. In either case, answer all questions as they are presented.

Upgrading from a Prior Version of Red Hat Linux

The installation process for Red Hat Linux 5.1 includes the ability to upgrade from prior versions of Red Hat Linux (2.0 through 5.0, inclusive) which are based on RPM technology. Upgrading your system installs the modular 2.0.x kernel as well as updated versions of the packages that are installed on your machine. The upgrade process preserves existing configuration files using a .rpmsave extension (e.g., sendmail.cf.rpmsave) and leaves a log telling what actions it took in /tmp/upgrade.log. As software evolves, configuration file formats can change, so you should carefully compare your original configuration files to the new files before integrating your changes.

A Word From the Developers

We would like to thank all our beta testers for entrusting their systems to early versions of Red Hat Linux and for taking the time to submit bug reports from the front, especially those of you who have been with Red Hat since the "Halloween" release and earlier. We would also like to thank Linus Torvalds and the hundreds of developers around the world for creating, truly, one of the wonders of distributed development.

And, again, we'd like to thank *you* for your interest in Red Hat Linux!

The Red Hat Development Team

Notes from the Editor

Our evolutionary process of expanding the scope of this Installation Guide continues. As before, we've updated the chapters related to the actual installation process. We've also updated the New Features chapter to reflect all the good stuff that's been added to Red Hat Linux 5.1. We consider this to be "business as usual".

We've also made some changes as a direct result of customer feedback. We've added an appendix containing a brief description of nearly every package included in Red Hat Linux. So now you'll be able to browse through the package descriptions before you start the installation, and decide what you're going to want on your system. You can even use it as a way of seeing what your newly-installed Red Hat Linux system can do. The Red Hat Linux Frequently

---

[1]If you need a supplemental diskette, you'll need to create one. Section 2.5 on page 19 describes how a supplemental diskette is created.

Asked Questions (Appendix E on page 241) is all-new, and covers many more subjects than the previous version.

Another change we've made is to include more information on post-installation issues. For all the people that sent mail to docs@redhat.com saying, "Everything installed just fine, and the system rebooted. What do I do now?", this chapter is for *you*. We'll be expanding this chapter in the future, so if you can think of something we should include, please let us know.

We Need Feedback!

If you spot a typo in the Installation Guide, or if you've thought of a way to make this manual better, we'd love to hear from you! Please send mail to:

docs@redhat.com

Be sure to mention the manual's identifier:

Inst-5.1-Print-MDP (5/98)

That way we'll know exactly which version of the guide you have. If you have a suggestion, try to be as specific as possible when describing it. If you've found an error, please include the section number and some of the surrounding text so we can find it easily. We may not be able to respond to every message sent to us, but you can be sure that we'll be reading them all!

I Couldn't Have Done it Without...

Thanks go out to the past authors of this manual. A great deal of their work is still here. A great, big "Thank You" is also owed to the Red Hat Linux 5.1 development team for putting up with the many questions, comments, and pleading requests for reviews of this manual. Without them, I wouldn't be here writing this, you wouldn't be there reading this, and things wouldn't be nearly as much fun. Thanks, guys!

Thanks are also due to the many readers of the 5.0 Installation Guide that took the time to send corrections, suggestions, and even the occasional "well done". I've tried to incorporate as much of your feedback as possible (pagecount and deadlines permitting). Keep the feedback coming – it's the only way I know whether you're getting what you need from our documentation!

Last but far from least is the support group at Red Hat Software. They have given many insightful suggestions regarding this manual, based on extensive experience with thousands of Red Hat Linux customers. So if you find yourself breezing through the installation chapters, it's due in no small part to their input. I thank them.

Edward C. Bailey

1

New Features Of Red Hat Linux 5.1

This chapter describes features that are new to Red Hat Linux 5.1.

1.1 Installation-Related Enhancements

There have been many changes made to make the Red Hat Linux installation process easier. Here's a list:

- Improved Installation Guide
- Network-related enhancements
- Installation simplified
- Boot diskette creation
- Internationalization
- Disk Druid-like "fstab editor" available
- SMB installation method returns

Let's take a look at each one in a bit more detail.

1.1.1   Improved Installation Guide

The Red Hat Linux 5.1 Installation Guide has been improved with:

- **Improved Installation Chapters** – The chapters covering the installation of Red Hat Linux have been expanded to include more detailed information in a more streamlined form.

- **A New Chapter** – There is now a chapter devoted to the single most-frequently-asked question – "What do I do now?".

- **All-New FAQ** – Appendix E contains a newly updated set of frequently asked questions. If you run into problems (before *or* after the installation), check it out...

- **Complete Package List** – Appendix C contains an entry for every package shipped with Red Hat Linux/Intel. Each entry includes the package name, version, size, and a description. The package list is a great way to see what Red Hat Linux is capable of. It also has its own index, making the search for a specific package easier.

1.1.2   Network-Related Enhancements

The installation program can now use both BOOTP and DHCP to obtain network information during the installation. Of course, it is still possible to manually enter this information manually.

1.1.3   Installation Simplified

Most dialog boxes displayed during the installation process now have a **Back** button, making it possible to fix many of those "Oops – I didn't want to do that" problems.

1.1.4   Boot Diskette Creation

The installation program now gives you the option of making a boot diskette (containing a copy of the installed kernel and all modules required to boot your system). The boot diskette can also be used to load a rescue diskette (described in Section 1.2.2 on page 5).

1.1.5 Internationalization

The installation program is now internationalized, and supports a variety of different languages. The first question asked by the installation program is for the desired language; all screens after that are presented in the language selected by the installer. In addition, information from RPM packages that have been internationalized will be displayed in the appropriate language.

1.1.6 Disk Druid-Like "fstab editor" Available

When partitioning drives using fdisk, a new method of specifying partition mount points is available. Similar to Disk Druid, it provides a concise view of all available partitions.

1.1.7 SMB Installation Method Returns

Red Hat Linux 5.1 once again supports installation from an SMB shared volume. This makes it possible to perform an installation on networks where there is no FTP or NFS server, but there is an SMB-capable system available.

1.2 System Administration-Related Enhancements

Red Hat Linux 5.1 has these features for system administrators:

- Linuxconf now included
- Improved rescue diskette
- Initscript documentation

1.2.1 Linuxconf Now Included

Red Hat Linux 5.1 now supports the use of linuxconf for many system configuration tasks. Linuxconf is an extremely full-featured configuration tool. Written by Jacques Gelinas, it can manage most aspects of system configuration through the following user interfaces:

- **Command line** – Linuxconf's command-line mode is handy for manipulating your system's configuration in scripts.

- **Character-Cell** – Using the same user interface style as the Red Hat Linux installation program, the character-cell interface makes it easy to navigate your way through linuxconf, even if you aren't running X.

- **X Window-Based** – Linuxconf can take advantage of X, and give you an easy-to-use "point and click" interface.

- **Web-Based** – A web-based interface makes remote system administration a breeze.

To launch linuxconf, simply type (as root) `linuxconf`. Linuxconf will then start in either character-cell or X mode, depending on the `DISPLAY` environment variable. The first time you run linuxconf, an introductory message will be displayed; although it is only displayed once, accessing help from the main screen will give you the same basic information.

Linuxconf has context-specific help available. For information on any specific aspect of linuxconf, please select **Help** from the screen you'd like help with. Note that not all help screens are complete at this time; they will included in subsequent versions of linuxconf.

Enabling Web-Based Linuxconf Access

Web-based access to linuxconf is disabled by default. Before attempting to access linuxconf with a web browser, you'll need to enable access. Here's how to do it from the text-mode interface:

- Start linuxconf by typing `linuxconf` while logged in as root.

- From the **Config** section, select **Networking**.

- Select **Misc**. Then select **Linuxconf network access**.

- In the "Linuxconf html access control" dialog box, enter the hostname of any computers that should be allowed access to linuxconf. This would also include your own system, if you wish to use the web-based interface locally. Web accesses related to linuxconf may be logged to your system's `htmlaccess.log` file by selecting the check box shown.

- Select the **Accept** button and press ⌷Space⌷. Then select the **Quit** buttons on each dialog box to back out of the menu hierarchy. When you come to a dialog box labelled "Status of the system", press ⌷Enter⌷ to take the default action, which is to apply the changes you've made.

At this point, web-based access has been enabled. To test it out, go to one of the systems that you added to the access control list. Launch your web browser, and enter the following URL:

```
http://<host>:98/
```

(Replacing `<host>` with your system's hostname, of course.) You should see the main linuxconf page. Note that you will need to enter your system's root password to gain access beyond the first page.

1.2.2   Improved rescue diskette

Going hand-in-hand with the new boot diskette available with Red Hat Linux 5.1, the new rescue diskette offers additional capabilities over the rescue mode available in prior versions of Red Hat Linux. Therefore, the rescue mode available with prior versions of the Red Hat Linux boot and supplementary diskettes has been discontinued. For more information on the new rescue mode, please read the file rescue.txt in the /doc directory of your Red Hat Linux CD-ROM.

1.2.3   Initscript documentation

Red Hat Linux uses files in /etc/sysconfig to control boot-time configuration. This information has been documented here for the first time. Please see Section 11.9 on page 155 for more information.

1.3   Miscellaneous New Features

These new features defy categorization:

- Window Manager-Related Enhancements
- New compiler technology available with egcs
- New utility replaces xv

1.3.1   Window Manager-Related Enhancements

Red Hat Linux 5.1 now includes the popular AfterStep window manager. The wmconfig utility has also been enhanced. See the wmconfig man page for more information.

1.3.2   New compiler technology available with egcs

The egcs compiler is now included with Red Hat Linux 5.1. This compiler is being actively developed, and is considered by many to be the next major step beyond the gcc compiler.

However, realizing that when it comes to compilers stability is a good thing, we have retained the gcc compiler as well. In Table 1.1 on the next page, you can see the circumstances under which the two compilers are invoked.

Please Note: The commands in Table 1.1 on the following page are symlinks to the appropriate compilers. If you would like to change this behavior, you may change the symlinks. The only

Command	Compiler
cc	gcc
egcs	egcs
c++	egcs
g++	egcs
g77	egcs

Table 1.1: Commands And the Compilers They Invoke

thing to keep in mind is that the version of gcc shipped with Red Hat Linux 5.1 was not built with C++ or Objective C support. This means that any makefiles that attempt to issue commands like "gcc foo.cc" should be changed to use g++.

1.3.3   New Utility Replaces xv

The new Electric Eyes utility replaces the shareware xv graphics display program. Electric Eyes (in conjunction with ImageMagick) should be able to handle everything that xv can do, and more.

2

Before You Begin

While installing Red Hat Linux is a straightforward process, taking some time prior to starting the installation can make things go much more smoothly. In this chapter, we'll discuss the steps that should be performed before you start the installation.

Please Note: If you are currently running a version 2.0 (or greater) Red Hat Linux system, you can perform an upgrade. Skim this chapter to review the basic issues relating to installation, and read the following chapters in order, following the directions as you go. The upgrade procedure starts out identically to the installation procedure; you will be directed to choose an installation or upgrade after booting the installation program and answering a few questions.

There are five things you should do prior to installing Red Hat Linux:

1. Make sure you have sufficient documentation to effectively use your Red Hat Linux system after the installation.

2. Make sure you have access to the Red Hat Linux components required for installation.

3. Make sure you know your computer's hardware configuration and networking information.

4. Decide, based on the first two tasks, what method you will use to install Red Hat Linux.

5. Determine where on your hard drive(s) Red Hat Linux will reside.

Let's start by making sure you have the documentation you'll need after you install Red Hat Linux.

2.1   Getting Documentation

Red Hat Linux is a powerful, full-featured operating system. Unless you're a Linux wizard, you're going to need documentation to make the most of your Red Hat Linux system. Everyone should review Chapter 7 on page 97 for more information on available Linux documentation. While many people find the resources described in chapter 7 to be very helpful, people who are just starting to use Linux will likely need additional information. The information that will be most helpful to you depends on your level of Linux expertise:

New To Linux – If this is your first time using Linux (or any Linux-like operating system, for that matter), you'll need solid introductory information on basic Unix concepts. For example, O'Reilly and Associates (http://www.ora.com/) produce a wide variety of Linux and Unix-related books. Give their more general titles a try.

Some Linux Experience – If you've used other Linux distributions (or a Linux-like operating system), you'll probably find what you're looking for in some of the more in-depth reference material available. Red Hat Software's *Linux Undercover* and *Linux Complete Command Reference* are great for overall documentation, while O'Reilly's more specialized titles are valuable when you need a lot of information on a particular subject.

Old Timer – If you're a long-time Red Hat Linux user, you probably don't need us telling you what documentation to read. Thanks for reading this far!

We also discuss the issue of additional documentation in Chapter 6 on page 79.

2.2   Getting the Right Red Hat Linux Components

If you've purchased the Red Hat Linux boxed set, you're ready to go! However, mistakes occasionally happen, so now is a good time to double-check the contents of your boxed set. If you haven't purchased a Red Hat Linux boxed set, skip to Section 2.2.3 on page 10.

2.2.1   Contents of the Red Hat Linux Boxed Set

The Red Hat Linux boxed set contains the following items:

- The Red Hat Linux Installation Guide.

- Red Hat Linux CDs 1 and 2.

- The Linux Applications CD.

- Boot diskette.

- License and Registration information.

Let's take a quick look at each item:

Installation Guide

The Red Hat Linux Installation Guide is what you're currently reading. It contains the information necessary to install Red Hat Linux. In addition, it contains information about aspects of the operating system that are unique to Red Hat Linux.

CDs 1 and 2

These two Compact Discs contain the entire Red Hat Linux distribution, including source code. CD 1 contains all the binary packages . CD 2 contains the source packages that were used to build the binary packages on CD 1.

Linux Applications CD

This Compact Disc contains demonstration versions of a number of commercial Linux software products. For more information, please refer to the README file on this CD.

Please Note: This CD and its contents are *completely unsupported* by Red Hat Software. All questions and issues concerning any software on this CD should be directed to the responsible company, and *not* Red Hat Software.

Boot Diskette

This diskette is used to start the installation process for Red Hat Linux/Intel. Depending on your computer's configuration and the type of installation you select, you may or may not need the boot diskette. In addition, you may require a *supplemental* diskette, again depending on your system's hardware configuration, and the installation method you choose. When we discuss the different installation methods later in this chapter, we'll explain which diskettes are needed for each type of installation, and give you instructions for producing any diskettes you require.

License and Registration Information

The CD-ROM case includes the the license terms for Red Hat Linux, in addition to the license terms for any commercial software that may be included on the Red Hat Linux CD. In addition, information about registering your copy of Red Hat Linux with Red Hat Software can be found here. Once registered, you can receive installation support. Red Hat Software's installation support program is discussed in Appendix A on page 169.

Please Note: There is an alphanumeric registration string printed on the CD-ROM case. It is used to register you for Red Hat Software's installation support. Please make sure you don't lose your registration string – you won't be able to get installation support without it!

2.2.2   Missing Something?

If you've purchased the Official Red Hat Linux boxed set from Red Hat Software, (or one of its distributors) and you're missing one or more of the items listed above, please let us know!

One thing to keep in mind is that Red Hat Software partners with companies (international and domestic) so that we can make Red Hat Linux available to you in the most convenient form. Because of this, you might find that your Red Hat Linux boxed set may not have been actually produced by Red Hat Software.

Not sure how to identify our official boxed set? Here's how: The bottom of our box has an ISBN number next to one of the bar codes. That ISBN number should be in the form:

$$1\text{-}888172\text{-}xx\text{-}y$$

(Where xx and y may vary.) If your box has an ISBN number in this form, and you're missing something, feel free to call us at 1-888-733-4281 (+1-919-547-0012 outside the USA), or to send mail to `sales@redhat.com`.

If your box has a different ISBN number (or none at all), you'll need to contact the company that produced your boxed set. Normally, third-party producers will include their logo and/or contact information on the outside of the box; an official Red Hat Linux boxed set has only our name and contact info on the outside...

If your Red Hat Linux boxed set is complete, please skip ahead to section 2.2.4 on the next page.

2.2.3   No Boxed Set? No Problem!

Of course, not everyone purchases a Red Hat Linux boxed set. It's entirely possible to install Red Hat Linux using a CD created by another company, or even via FTP. In these cases, you may need to create one or more diskettes to get started.

For people installing Red Hat Linux/Intel, you'll need a boot diskette and, optionally, a supplemental diskette. It may also be possible to start the installation directly from the CD, under certain conditions. We'll discuss this in more detail when we outline the various installation methods available.

2.2.4   Checking for Updated Diskette Images

From time to time, we find that the installation may fail, and that a revised diskette image is required in order for the installation to work properly. In these cases, we make special images available via the Red Hat Linux Errata.

Since this is a relatively rare occurrence, you will in general save time if you try to use the standard diskette images first, and then review the Errata only if you experience any problems completing the installation.

There are two ways to review the Errata:

1. **World Wide Web** – By pointing your web browser at
   http://www.redhat.com/errata, you can read the Errata on-line, and download diskette images easily.

2. **Electronic Mail** – By sending an empty mail message to
   errata@redhat.com, you will receive a mail message containing the complete Errata. Also included are URLs to each updated package and diskette image in the Errata. By using these URLs, you can then download any necessary diskette images. Remember to use binary mode when transferring a diskette image!

For now, concentrate only on the Errata entries that include new diskette images (the filenames always end in .img). If you find an entry that seems to apply to your problem, get a copy of the diskette images, and create them using the instructions in Appendix B on page 177.

2.3   Things You Should Know

In order to prevent any surprises during the installation, you should collect some information before attempting to install Red Hat Linux. You can find most of this information in the documentation that came with your system, or from the system's vendor or manufacturer.

Please Note: The most recent list of hardware supported by Red Hat Linux can be found at Red Hat Software's World Wide Web site at
http://www.redhat.com/hardware. It's a good idea to check your hardware against this list before proceeding.

2.3.1   Basic Hardware Configuration

You should have a basic understanding of the hardware installed in your computer, including:

- **hard drive(s)** – Specifically, the number, size, and type. If you have more than one, it's helpful to know which one is first, second, and so on. It is also good to know if your drives are IDE or SCSI. If you have IDE drives, you should check your computer's BIOS to see if you are accessing them in *LBA* mode.

- **memory** – The amount of RAM installed in your computer.

- **CD-ROM** – Most importantly, the unit's interface type (IDE, SCSI, or other interface) and, for non-IDE, non-SCSI CD-ROMs, the make and model number. IDE CD-ROMs (also known as ATAPI) are the most common type in recently manufactured, PC-compatible computers.

- **SCSI adapter (if one is present)** – The adapter's make and model number.

- **network card (if one is present)** – The card's make and model number.

- **mouse** – The mouse's type (serial, PS/2, or bus mouse), protocol (Microsoft, Logitech, MouseMan, etc.), and number of buttons; also, for serial mice, the serial port it is connected to.

On many newer systems, the installation program is able to automatically identify most hardware. However, it's a good idea to collect this information anyway, just to be sure.

Learning About Your Hardware With Windows® 95

If your computer is already running Windows 95, you can use the following procedure to get additional configuration information:

- With Windows 95 running, click on the "My Computer" icon using the secondary (normally the right) mouse button. A popup menu should appear.

- Select "Properties". The "System Properties" window should appear (See Figure 2.1 on the next page). Note the information listed under "Computer:" – in particular the amount of RAM listed.

- Click on the "Device Manager" tab. You will then see a graphical representation of your computer's hardware configuration. Make sure the "View devices by type" button is selected.

At this point, you can either double-click on the icons (or single-click on the plus sign ⊕) to look at each entry in more detail (See Figure 2.2 on page 14). Look under the following icons for more information:

- **Disk drives** – You will find the type (IDE or SCSI) of hard drive here. (IDE drives will normally include the word "IDE", while SCSI drives won't.)

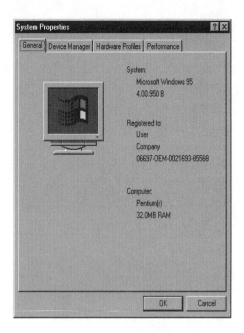

Figure 2.1: Windows 95 System Properties Window

- **Hard disk controllers** – You can get more information about your hard drive controller here.

- **CDROM** – Here is where you'll find out about any CD-ROM drives connected to your computer.

  Please Note: In some cases, there may be no CD-ROM icon, yet your computer has a functioning CD-ROM drive. This is normal, depending on how Windows was originally installed. In this case, you may be able to glean additional information by looking at the CD-ROM driver loaded in your computer's config.sys file.

- **Mouse** – The type of mouse present on your computer can be found here.

- **Display adapters** – If you're interested in running the X Window System, you should write down the information you find here.

- **Sound, video and game controllers** – If your computer has sound capabilities, you'll find more information about that here.

- **Network adapters** – Here you'll find additional info on your computer's network card (if you have one).

- **SCSI controllers** – If your computer uses SCSI peripherals, you'll find additional info on the SCSI controller here.

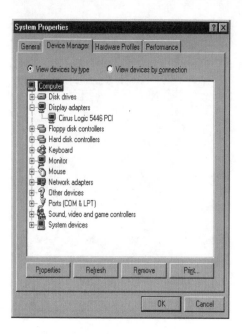

Figure 2.2: Device Manager Under Windows 95

While this method is not a complete substitute for opening your computer's case and physically examining each component, in many cases it can provide sufficient information to continue with the installation.

2.3.2 Video Configuration

If you will be installing the X Window System, you should also be familiar with the following:

- **your video card** – The card's make and model number (or the video chipset it uses), and the amount of video RAM it has. (Most PCI-based cards are auto-detected by the installation program.)

- **your monitor** – The unit's make and model number, along with allowable ranges for horizontal and vertical refresh rates.

2.3.3   Network-related Information

If you will be connected to a network, be sure you know your:

- **IP address** – Usually represented as a set of four numbers separated by dots, such as 10.0.2.15.

- **netmask** – Another set of four numbers separated by dots. An example netmask would be 255.255.248.0.

- **gateway IP address** – Yet another set of four dot-separated numbers. For instance, 10.0.2.254.

- **one or more name server IP addresses** – One or more sets of dot-separated numbers. 10.0.2.1 might be the address of a name server.

- **domain name** – The name given to your organization. For instance, Red Hat Software has a domain name of redhat.com.

- **hostname** – The name of your computer. A computer might be named pooh, for instance.

Please Note: The information given above is an example only! Do *not* use it when you install Red Hat Linux! If you don't know the proper values for your network, ask your network administrator.

2.4   Installation Methods

You can install or upgrade Red Hat Linux via any of several different methods. Each method works best in different situations, and has different requirements. But before we discuss each installation method, let's take a look at an issue that may affect some of you.

2.4.1   PCMCIA Support During the Installation

This section is specific to Intel-based computers only

Most Intel-based laptop computers support PCMCIA (also known as PC Card). Computers that support PCMCIA devices contain a controller having one or more slots in which a PCMCIA device can be installed. These devices may be modems, LAN adapters, SCSI adapters, and so on.

When installing Red Hat Linux/Intel on a PCMCIA-capable computer, it is important to note if a PCMCIA device will be used during installation. For example, if you want to install Red Hat Linux/Intel from a CD-ROM, and your CD-ROM drive is connected to a PCMCIA adapter, the installation program will require PCMCIA support. Likewise, if you are going to use one of the network-based installation methods, you will need PCMCIA support if your network adapter is PCMCIA-based.

Please Note: You don't need install-time PCMCIA support if you're installing Red Hat Linux on a laptop, and using the laptop's built-in CD-ROM drive.

PCMCIA support is dependent on two things:

1. The type of PCMCIA controller in your computer system.

2. The type of PCMCIA device that you wish to use during the installation.

While nearly every PCMCIA controller and most popular PCMCIA devices are supported, there are some exceptions. For more information, please consult the Red Hat Linux Hardware Compatibility List at
http://www.redhat.com/hardware.

The main thing to keep in mind is that if you require install-time PCMCIA support, you will need a supplemental diskette. We'll show you how to do this after you've determined which installation method is best for you.

2.4.2   Installing From a CD-ROM

If you have a Red Hat Linux CD-ROM, and your computer has a supported CD-ROM drive, you should consider this installation method. Installing directly from CD-ROM is the most straight-forward approach. When installing from CD-ROM, the packages you select are read from the CD-ROM, and are installed on your hard drive.

How To Do It

As the name implies, you'll need a Red Hat Linux CD-ROM, a supported CD-ROM drive, and a means of starting the installation program.

Intel systems will need to use the boot diskette (and the supplemental diskette if PCMCIA support is required). There is an alternate method of installing from CD-ROM that uses no diskettes, but requires that the system be running DOS. We'll discuss this approach (known as *autoboot*) in Chapter 3 on page 27. For now, note that PCMCIA support is not available when using *autoboot*.

Please Note: The Red Hat Linux/Intel CD-ROM can also be booted by newer computers that support bootable CD-ROMs. Not all computers support this feature, so if yours can't boot from CD-ROM, you'll have to use a boot diskette (or autoboot from DOS) to get things started. Note that you may need to change BIOS settings in your computer to enable this feature.

If you've determined that this installation method is most applicable to your situation, please skip ahead to Section 2.5 on page 19.

2.4.3 Installing From an FTP Site

If you don't have a Red Hat Linux CD-ROM or a CD-ROM drive, but you do have network access, then an FTP installation may be for you. When installing via FTP, the Red Hat Linux packages you select are downloaded (using FTP) across the network to your computer, and are installed on your hard drive.

How To Do It

When doing an FTP install, you'll need LAN-based access to a network; a dialup connection via modem won't cut it. If your Local Area Network has Internet access, you can use one of the many FTP sites that mirror Red Hat Linux. You can find a list of mirror sites at ftp://ftp.redhat.com/pub/MIRRORS.

If your LAN doesn't have Internet access, all is not lost. If there is a computer on your LAN that can accept anonymous FTP requests, simply put a copy of the Red Hat Linux distribution on that system, and you're ready to go.

Please Note: Your FTP server must be able to handle long filenames.

For an FTP installation, you must use both the boot and supplemental diskettes. You will need to have a valid nameserver configured or you must specify the IP address of the FTP server you will be using. You will also need the path to the Red Hat Linux directory on the FTP server.

If you've determined that this installation method is most applicable to your situation, please skip ahead to Section 2.5 on page 19.

2.4.4 Installing From an NFS Server

If your system doesn't have a CD-ROM drive, but you do have network access, then an NFS installation may be for you. When installing via NFS, the Red Hat Linux packages you select are NFS-served to your computer from an NFS server system. The packages are then installed on your hard drive.

How To Do It

If you wish to perform an NFS installation, you will need to mount the Red Hat Linux CD-ROM on a machine that supports ISO-9660 file systems with Rock Ridge extensions. The machine must also support NFS. Export the CD-ROM file system via NFS. You will need to have a nameserver configured, or know the NFS server's IP address, as well as the path to the exported CD-ROM.

Please Note: Your NFS server must be able to handle long filenames.

For an NFS installation, you'll need a boot diskette only.

If you've determined that this installation method is most applicable to your situation, please skip ahead to Section 2.5 on the facing page.

2.4.5   Installing From an SMB Shared Volume

If your system doesn't have a CD-ROM drive, but you do have network access, then installing Red Hat Linux using an SMB shared volume may be for you. When performing an SMB installation, your computer accesses the Red Hat Linux packages using a DOS-style network drive. The packages you select are then installed on your hard drive.

How To Do It

If you wish to install from an SMB shared volume, you will need to mount the Red Hat Linux CD-ROM on a Microsoft Windows NT or Windows 95 server that supports shared volumes. You will need to have nameservices configured; you will also need the name of the shared volume containing the Red Hat Linux CD-ROM and the account and password information required to access the volume.

Please Note: The Windows system's Microsoft Networking name must be identical to the system's DNS hostname. For example, given a Microsoft Networking name of `windows1`, the system's DNS hostname must be
`windows1.whatever.your.domain.is`.

For an SMB installation, you'll need boot and supplemental diskettes.

If you've determined that this installation method is most applicable to your situation, please skip ahead to Section 2.5 on the next page.

2.4.6   Installing From a Hard Drive

If none of the other installation methods will work for you, but you have some means of getting the Red Hat Linux package files written to your system's hard drive, you can install from your hard drive. In this installation method, the Red Hat Linux packages you select are read from one partition on a hard drive, and are installed on another partition (or set of partitions).

How To Do It

The hard drive installation method requires a bit of up-front effort on your part, as you must copy all the necessary files to a partition before starting the Red Hat Linux installation program. You must first create a `RedHat` directory at the top level of your directory tree. Everything you will install should be placed in that directory. First copy the `base` subdirectory and its contents.

Next, copy the packages you want to install to another subdirectory called RPMS. You can use available space on an existing DOS partition or a Linux partition that is not required in the install procedure (for example, a partition that would be used for data storage on the installed system).

If you are using a DOS filesystem, you will not be able to use the full Linux filenames for the RPM packages. The installation process does not care what the filenames look like, but it is a good idea that you keep track of them.

You'll need a boot and supplemental diskette when installing from a hard drive.

2.5   Need a Supplemental Diskette?

This section is specific to Intel-based computers only. If you are using an Alpha or SPARC computer, please skip ahead to 2.6.

Here's a checklist that you can use to see if you'll need to create a supplemental diskette:

- **Installing From a PCMCIA-Connected CD-ROM** – If you'll be installing Red Hat Linux from a CD-ROM, and your CD-ROM drive is attached to your computer through a PCMCIA card, you'll need a supplemental diskette.

- **Installing using a PCMCIA Network Card** – If you will be using a PCMCIA network adapter during the installation, you'll need a supplemental diskette.

- **FTP Install** – If you want to install Red Hat Linux via FTP, you'll need a supplemental diskette.

- **Hard Drive Install** – If you'll be performing an install from a hard drive, you'll need a supplemental diskette.

- **SMB Install** – If you want to install from an SMB shared drive, you'll need a supplemental diskette.

If you've determined you'll need a supplemental diskette, you'll have to make one. The supplemental diskette image file is supp.img, and is located in the images directory on your Red Hat Linux/Intel CD. Please turn to Appendix B on page 177 and follow the instructions there. Then, return here, and read on.

2.6   Disk Partitions

In order to install Red Hat Linux, you must make disk space available for it. This disk space needs to be separate from the disk space used by other operating systems you may have installed on your computer, such as Windows, OS/2, or even a different version of Linux.

A disk can be divided into different *partitions*. Each partition can be accessed as if it was a separate disk. Furthermore, each partition has a *type* that is used to indicate how information is stored in the partition. For example, there are different partition types used by DOS, OS/2, and Linux.

Please Note: You must install Red Hat Linux to one or more partitions having a partition type of "Linux native". Red Hat Linux also requires a *swap* partition, which has a partition type of "Linux swap". This means that an installation of Red Hat Linux requires at least two partitions:

- One or more partitions of type "Linux native"

- A partition of type "Linux swap"

We will discuss partitioning issues in more detail below. For now, keep in mind that Red Hat Linux requires at least two dedicated partitions, and that you *cannot* install Red Hat Linux to a DOS/Windows partition!

Even if you will be installing Red Hat Linux on its own hard disk, or on a computer which contains no other operating system, you'll still need to create partitions for Red Hat Linux to use. In this case it's pretty easy, as there are no other partitions on the hard disk to worry about.

On the other hand, you may wish to install Red Hat Linux on a disk which already contains software or data from a different operating system. Things can get a little trickier in this situation, since a mistake can destroy your existing partitions, not to mention the data they contain!

During the installation process, you'll be given the chance to create partitions for Red Hat Linux. At this point, your main concern is making sure you have sufficient disk space available to create those partitions. Let's review the different ways to free up space for Red Hat Linux partitions.

2.6.1   Partition Naming Scheme

Linux refers to disk partitions using a combination of letters and numbers which may be confusing, particularly if you're used to the "C drive" way of referring to hard disks and their partitions. Red Hat Linux uses a naming scheme that is more flexible and conveys more information than the approach used by other operating systems. Here is a summary:

First Two Letters – The first two letters of the partition name indicate the type of device on which the partition resides. You'll normally see either hd (for IDE disks), or sd (for SCSI disks).

The Next Letter – This letter indicates which device the partition is on. For example, /dev/hda (the first IDE hard disk) or /dev/sdb (the second SCSI disk).

The number denotes the partition. The first four (primary or extended) partitions are numbered 1 through 4. Logical partitions start at 5. E.g., /dev/hda3 is the third primary or extended partition on the first IDE hard disk; /dev/sdb6 is the second logical partition on the second SCSI hard disk.

Keep this information in mind; it will make things easier to understand when you're setting up the partitions Red Hat Linux requires.

2.6.2   Repartitioning Strategies

There are three possible scenarios you may face when attempting to repartition your hard disk:

- Unpartitioned free space is available.

- An unused partition is available.

- Free space in an actively used partition is available.

Let's look at each scenario in order.

Using Unpartitioned Free Space

In this situation, the partitions already defined do not span the entire hard disk, leaving unallocated space that is not part of any defined partition. If you think about it, an unused hard disk also falls into this category; the only difference is that *all* the space is not part of any defined partition.

In this case, you can simply create the necessary partitions from the unused space.

Using Space From An Unused Partition

Last year you replaced that tiny 105MB hard drive on your Windows system with a 1.2GB monster. You partitioned it into two equal parts, figuring that you'd use the C: "drive" (really the drive's first partition) for Windows, and the D: "drive" (really the drive's second partition) for your collection of freeware programs downloaded from the Internet. Well, you'd been so used to using C: that you never put anything of substance on D:.

If you find yourself in this situation, you can use the space allocated to the unused partition. In this case, you'll first need to delete the partition, and then create the appropriate Linux partitions in its place.

Using Free Space From An Active Partition

This is the most common situation. It is also, unfortunately, the hardest to deal with. The main problem is that you have enough free space, but it's presently allocated to a partition that is in use. If you purchased a computer with pre-installed software, the hard disk most likely has one massive partition holding the operating system and data.

Aside from adding a new hard drive to your system, you have two choices:

Destructive Repartitioning – Basically, you delete the single large partition, and create several smaller ones. As you might imagine, any data you had in that partition is destroyed. This means that making a complete backup is necessary. For your own sake, make two backups, use verification (if available in your backup software), and try to read data from your backup *before* you delete the partition. Note also that if there was an operating system of some type installed on that partition, it will need to be reinstalled as well.

After creating a smaller partition for your existing software, you can reinstall any software, restore your data, and continue with your Red Hat Linux installation.

Non-Destructive Repartitioning – Here, you run a program that does the seemingly impossible; it makes a big partition smaller without losing any of the files stored in that partition. Many people have found this method to be reliable and trouble-free. What software should you use to perform this feat? There are several disk management software products on the market; you'll have to do some research to find the one that is best for your situation.

As a convenience to our customers, we provide the fips utility. This is a freely available program that can resize FAT (File Allocation Table) partitions. It's included on the Red Hat Linux/Intel CD-ROM in the dosutils directory.

Please Note: Many people have successfully used fips to repartition their hard drives. However, because of the nature of the operations carried out by fips, and the wide variety of hardware and software configurations under which it must run, Red Hat Software cannot guarantee that fips will work properly on your system. Therefore, no installation support whatsoever is available for fips; use it at your own risk.

That said, if you decide to repartition your hard drive with fips, it is *vital* that you do two things:

- **Perform a Backup** – Make two copies of all the important data on your computer. These copies should be to removable media (such as tape or diskettes), and you should make sure they are readable before proceeding.

- **Read the Documentation** – Completely read the fips documentation, located in the /dosutils/fipsdocs subdirectory on Red Hat Linux/Intel CD 1.

2.6.3   Disk Partitions and Other Operating Systems

If your Red Hat Linux partitions will be sharing a hard disk with partitions used by other operating systems, most of the time you'll have no problems. However, there are certain combinations of Linux and other operating systems that require extra care. Information on creating disk partitions compatible with other operating systems is available in several HOWTOs and Mini-HOWTOs, available on the Red Hat Linux CD in the doc/HOWTO and doc/HOWTO/mini directories. In particular, the Mini-HOWTOs whose names start with Linux+ are quite helpful.

If Red Hat Linux/Intel will coexist on your machine with OS/2, you must create your disk partitions with the OS/2 partitioning software—otherwise, OS/2 may not recognize the disk partitions. During the installation, do not create any new partitions, but do set the proper partition types for your Linux partitions using the Linux fdisk.

2.6.4   One Last Wrinkle: Using LILO

LILO (the LInux LOader) is the most commonly used method to boot Red Hat Linux on Intel-based systems. Being an operating system loader, LILO operates "outside" of any operating system, using only the Basic I/O System (or BIOS) built into the computer hardware itself. This section describes LILO's interactions with PC BIOSes, and is specific to Intel-compatible computers.

BIOS-Related Limitations Impacting LILO

LILO is subject to some limitations imposed by the BIOS in most Intel-based computers. Specifically, most BIOSes can't access more than two hard drives and they can't access any data stored beyond cylinder 1023 (the 1024th cylinder) of any drive. Note that some recent BIOSes do not have these limitations, but this is by no means universal.

All the data LILO needs to access at boot time (including the Linux kernel) are located in the /boot directory, which is normally part of the root partition (known as /). Here are the guidelines you must follow if you are going to use LILO to boot your Red Hat Linux system:

On First Two IDE Drives – If you have 2 IDE (or EIDE) drives, /boot must be located on one of them. Note that this two-drive limit also includes any IDE CD-ROM drives on your primary IDE controller. So, if you have one IDE hard drive, and one IDE CD-ROM on your primary controller, /boot must be located on the first hard drive *only*, even if you have other hard drives on your secondary IDE controller.

On First IDE Or First SCSI Drive – If you have one IDE (or EIDE) drive and one or more SCSI drives, /boot must be located either on the IDE drive or the SCSI drive at ID 0. No other SCSI IDs will work.

On First Two SCSI Drives – If you have only SCSI hard drives, /boot must be located on a drive at ID 0 or ID 1. No other SCSI IDs will work.

Partition *Completely* Below Cylinder 1023 – No matter which of the above configurations apply, the partition that holds /boot must be located entirely below cylinder 1023. If the partition holding /boot straddles cylinder 1023, you may face a situation where LILO will work initially (because all the necessary information is below cylinder 1023), but will fail if a new kernel is to be loaded, and that kernel resides above cylinder 1023.

As mentioned earlier, it is possible that some of the newer BIOSes may permit LILO to work with configurations that don't meet our guidelines. Likewise, some of LILO's more esoteric features may be used to get a Linux system started, even if the configuration doesn't meet our guidelines. However, due to the number of variables involved, Red Hat Software cannot support such extraordinary efforts.

Please Note: Disk Druid is designed to take these BIOS-related limitations into account. However, if you decide to use `fdisk` instead, it is your responsibility to ensure that you keep these limitations in mind.

2.6.5   How Many Partitions?

Although you can install Red Hat Linux in a single large partition (subject to any of the partitioning considerations we've mentioned so far), it's a much better idea to split things up a bit. We recommend the following layout as a compromise between single-partition simplicity, and multi-partition flexibility:

Please Note: If you plan to install all the software packages that come with Red Hat Linux, you will need to use the larger partitions sizes shown here. In fact, you may want to increase the sizes above our recommendations, to allow for future growth without needing to repartition.

A swap partition – Swap partitions are used to support virtual memory. If your computer has 16 MB of RAM or less, you *must* create a swap partition. Even if you have more memory, a swap partition is still recommended. The minimum size of your swap partition should be equal to your computer's RAM, or 16 MB (whichever is larger). The largest useable swap partition is roughly 127 MB, so making a swap partition larger than that will result in wasted space. Note, however, that you can create and use more than one swap partition (although this is usually only necessary for large server installations).

A root partition – The root partition is where / (the root directory) resides. It only needs to contain things necessary to boot your system, as well as system configuration files. A root partition of 50 MB to 100 MB works well for most systems.

Don't forget the LILO constraints we mentioned in Section 2.6.4 on the preceding page!

A /usr partition – The /usr partition is where much of the software on a Red Hat Linux system resides. This partition should be between 300 MB and 700 MB, depending on how many packages you plan to install. If at all possible, try to be generous with the /usr partition. Any RPM-based packages you install later will (in general) use more space from /usr than from any other partition.

A /home partition – This is where users' home directories go; the size of /home depends on how many users you plan to have on your Red Hat Linux system and what they might store in their home directories.

Additionally, your circumstances may warrant creating one of more of the following partitions:

A /usr/local partition – Traditionally, /usr/local has been used to hold things you wish to keep separate from the rest of your Red Hat Linux system, such as software that is not available as an RPM package. The size depends on the amount of such software you anticipate putting on your system.

A /usr/src **partition** – There are two things that normally are stored in /usr/src on a Red Hat Linux system:

Linux Kernel Sources – The complete sources for the Linux kernel are stored here, and new kernels are built here. At present, the kernel sources are approximately 30MB in size. Keep in mind that you'll want to have additional free space for building kernels, and you may want to keep more than one version of the kernel available.

Sources For RPM-Based Packages – If a source package file (aka SRPM) is installed, the files are stored here. Note that, unless specified otherwise, any packages built will also use a build directory located here.

Again, the size of this partition would depend on the amount of software you anticipate building.

A /tmp **partition** – As the name implies, the /tmp partition is for temporary files. Creating a partition dedicated to /tmp is a good idea for larger, multiuser systems or network server machines. The reason is that many active users can fill the root partition (/), which is where /tmp is located. It's not necessary to dedicate a partition to /tmp on single-user workstations.

A /var **partition** – Your Red Hat Linux system will write to log files in /var/log. Files queued for printing will normally be written to /var/spool. These are just two examples of data that is written to /var. Unless otherwise configured, /var will be part of the root filesystem, and normally will not have much available free space. If you anticipate a lot of print, mail, or log activity on your system, you might want to consider creating a partition dedicated to /var. In general, only multiuser or server systems would make effective use of a separate /var filesystem.

A /boot **partition** – While many of the partitions mentioned here make sense only for very large, active systems, this partition might be very useful on a small system, where free space is tight. If you recall, back in Section 2.6.4 on page 23, we discussed the various limitatons imposed by the standard PC BIOS, and how these limitations impact the LILO bootloader. All the files LILO needs to access (at boot time) are in the /boot directory. Since the files (including the Linux kernel) in /boot only take up a megabyte or so, if you're having trouble finding space for a 100 MB root partition in a place where LILO can get at it, you might have better luck trying to squeeze in a 5-10 MB (generously oversized) partition for /boot. You'll still need to create a root partition, but it can now be located anywhere on your system – the BIOS restrictions only apply to the partition holding /boot.

2.7   A Note About Kernel Drivers

During installation of Red Hat Linux, there are some limits placed on the filesystems and other drivers supported by the kernel. However, after installation there is support for all file systems available under Linux. At install time the modularized kernel has support for (E)IDE devices, (including ATAPI CD-ROM drives), SCSI adapters, and network cards. Additionally, all mice, SLIP, CSLIP, PPP, PLIP, FPU emulation, console selection, ELF, SysV IPC, IP forwarding, firewalling and accounting, reverse ARP, QIC tape and parallel printers, are supported.

Please Note: Because Red Hat Linux supports installation on many different types of hardware, many drivers (including those for SCSI adapters, network cards, and many CD-ROMs) are not built into the Linux kernel used during installation; rather, they are available as *modules* and loaded as you need them during the installation process. If necessary, you will have the chance to specify options for these modules at the time they are loaded, and in fact these drivers will ignore any options you specify for them at the boot: prompt.

After the installation is complete you may want to rebuild a kernel that includes support for your specific hardware configuration. See Section 11.4 on page 149 for information on building a customized kernel. Note that, in most cases, a custom-built kernel is not necessary.

2.8   If You Have Problems...

If you have problems before, during, or after the installation, check the list of Red Hat Linux Frequently Asked Questions in Appendix E on page 241. In many cases, a quick check of the FAQ can quickly get you back in action.

2.9   One Last Note

Please read all of the installation instructions *before* starting; this will prepare you for any decisions you need to make and should eliminate potential surprises.

3

Starting the Installation

This chapter explains how to start the Red Hat Linux installation process. We'll cover the following areas in this chapter:

- Getting familiar with the installation program's user interface.
- Starting the installation program.
- Selecting an installation method.

By the end of this chapter, the installation program will be running on your system, and the appropriate installation method will have been selected.

3.1   The Installation Program User Interface

The Red Hat Linux installation program uses a screen-based interface that includes most of the on-screen "widgets" commonly found on graphical user interfaces. They may look a little different than their more graphical counterparts; Figures 3.1 on page 29 and 3.2 on page 30 are included here to make them easier to identify. Here's a list of the most important widgets:

- **Window** – Windows (also referred to as *dialog boxes* in this manual) will appear on your screen throughout the installation process. At times, one window may overlay another; in these cases, you may only interact with the window on top. When finished with that window, it will disappear, allowing you to continue with the window that was underneath.

- **Text Input** – Text input lines are regions where you can enter information required by the installation program. When the cursor rests on a text input line, you may enter and/or edit information on that line.

- **Check Box** – Check boxes allow you to select or deselect a particular feature offered to you by the installation program. When the cursor rests within a check box, pressing [Space] causes the check box to toggle between a selected and unselected state.

- **Text Widget** – Text widgets are regions of the screen that are devoted to the display of text. At times, text widgets may also contain other widgets, such as check boxes. It is possible that a text widget may contain more information than could be displayed at one time. In these cases, the text widget will have a scroll bar next to it; if you position the cursor within the text widget, you can then use the [↑] and [↓] keys to scroll through all the information available.

- **Scroll Bar** – Scroll bars provide a visual indication of your relative position in the information being displayed in a text widget. Your current position is shown by a # character, which will move up and down the scroll bar as you scroll back and forth.

- **Button Widget** – Button widgets are the primary method of interacting with the installation program. By "pressing" these buttons, you will progress through the series of windows that make up the installation process. Buttons may be pressed when they are highlighted by the cursor.

- **Cursor** – Although not a widget, the cursor is used to select (and interact) with a particular widget. As the cursor is moved from widget to widget, it may cause the widget to change color, or you may only see the cursor itself positioned in or next to the widget. In Figure 3.1 on the facing page, the cursor is positioned on the **Ok** button. Figure 3.2 on page 30 shows the cursor on the first line of the text widget at the stop of the window.

As you might have guessed by our description of these widgets, the installation program is character-based, and does not use a mouse. This is due to the fact that the installation program must run on a wide variety of computers, some of which may not even have a mouse. The following section describes the keystrokes necessary to interact with the installation program.

3.1.1   Using the Keyboard to Navigate

You can navigate around the installation dialogs using a simple set of keystrokes. You will need to move the cursor around by using various keys such as [←], [→], [↑], and [↓]. You can also use [Tab], and [Alt]-[Tab] to cycle forward or backward through each widget on the screen. In most cases, there is a summary of available function keys presented at the bottom of each screen.

To "press" a button, position the cursor over the button (using [Tab], for instance) and press [Space] (or [Enter]). To select an item from a list of items, move the cursor to the item you wish

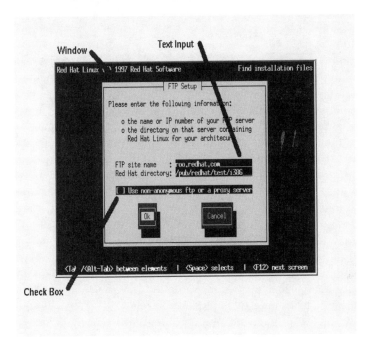

Figure 3.1: Installation Program Widgets

to select and press (Enter). To select an item with a *check box*, move the cursor to the check box and press (Space) to select an item. To deselect, press (Space) a second time.

Pressing (F12) accepts the current values and proceeds to the next dialog; it is usually equivalent to pressing the **OK** button.

Please Note: Unless a dialog box is waiting for your input, do not press any keys during the installation process – it may result in unpredictable behavior.

3.1.2 A Note About Virtual Consoles

There is more to the Red Hat Linux installation program than the dialog boxes it presents as it guides you through the installation process. In fact, the installation program makes several different kinds of diagnostic messages available to you, in addition to giving you a way to enter commands from a shell prompt. It presents this information on five *virtual consoles* which you can switch between using a single keystroke. These virtual consoles can be very helpful if you encounter a problem while installing Red Hat Linux. Messages displayed on the install or system

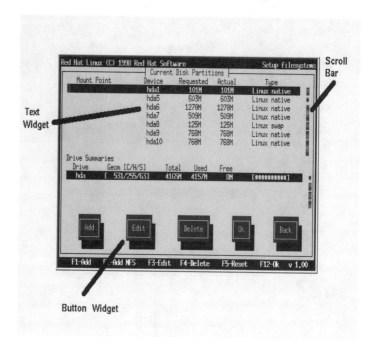

Figure 3.2: More Installation Program Widgets

consoles can help pinpoint the problem. Please see Figure 3.3 on the facing page for a listing of the virtual consoles, the keystrokes to switch to them, and their contents.

In general, there should be no reason to leave virtual console #1 unless you are attempting to diagnose installation problems. But if you are the curious type, feel free to look around.

3.2   Starting the Installation Program

Now it's time to start installing Red Hat Linux. To start the installation, it is first necessary to boot the installation program. Before we start, please make sure you have all the resources you'll need for the installation. If you've already read through Chapter 2 on page 7, and followed the instructions, you should be ready.

Console	Keystroke	Contents
1	(Alt)-(F1)	installation dialog
2	(Alt)-(F2)	shell prompt
3	(Alt)-(F3)	install log (messages from install program)
4	(Alt)-(F4)	system log (messages from kernel, etc.)
5	(Alt)-(F5)	other messages

Figure 3.3: Virtual Console Information

3.2.1 Booting the Installation Program

To start installing Red Hat Linux, insert your boot diskette into your computer's first diskette drive and reboot (or boot from the Red Hat Linux CD-ROM, if your computer supports it). After a short delay, a screen containing the boot: prompt should appear. The screen contains information on a variety of boot options. Each boot option also has one or more help screens associated with it. To access a given help screen, press the appropriate function key as listed in the line at the bottom of the screen. You should keep two things in mind:

- The initial screen will automatically start the installation program if you take no action within the first minute. To disable this feature, press one of the help screen function keys.

- If you press a help screen function key, there will be a slight delay as the help screen is read from diskette.

Normally, you'll only need to press (Enter) to boot. Watch the boot messages to see whether the Linux kernel detects your hardware. If it does not properly detect your hardware, you may need to restart the installation in "expert" mode. Expert mode disables most hardware probing, and gives you the option of entering options for the drivers loaded during the installation. Expert mode can be entered using the following boot command:

```
boot: expert
```

Please Note: The initial boot messages will not contain any references to SCSI or network cards. These devices are supported by modules that are loaded during the installation process.

Options can also be passed to the kernel. For example, to instruct the kernel to use all the RAM in a 128 MB system, enter:

```
boot: linux mem=128M
```

After entering any options, press (Enter) to boot using those options. If you do need to specify boot options to identify your hardware, please make note of them – they will be needed later.

Installing Without Using a Boot Diskette   The Red Hat Linux/Intel CD-ROM can also be booted by newer computers that support bootable CD-ROMs. Not all computers support this feature, so if yours can't boot from CD-ROM, there is one other way to start the installation without using a boot diskette. The following method is specific to Intel-based computers only.

If you have MS-DOS installed on your computer, you can boot the installation system directly from the CD without using any diskettes.

To do this, use the following commands (assuming your CD is drive d:):

```
C:\> d:
D:\> cd \dosutils
D:\dosutils> autoboot.bat
```

Note that this method will not work if run in a DOS window – the autoboot.bat file must be executed with DOS as the only operating system. In other words, Windows cannot be running.

If your computer can't boot directly from CD-ROM, and you can't use a DOS-based autoboot), you'll have to use a boot diskette to get things started.

3.3   Beginning the Installation

After booting, the installation program begins by displaying a welcome message. Press (Enter) to begin the installation. If you wish to abort the installation process at this time, simply eject the boot diskette now and reboot your machine.

3.3.1   Choosing a Language

After the welcome dialog, the installation program asks you to select the language to be used during the installation process (see Figure 3.4 on the facing page). Using the (↑) and (↓) keys, select the appropriate language. Note the scroll bar to the right of the languages – it indicates that there are more entries than can be displayed at one time. You'll be seeing scroll bars like this throughout the installation program.[1]

---

[1]The "Redneck" language entry represents a dialect of American English spoken by Red Hat Software's Donnie Barnes, and was used as a test case during the addition of internationalization support to the installation program. It is included solely for entertainment value (and to illustrate how difficult it is actually talking to Donnie).

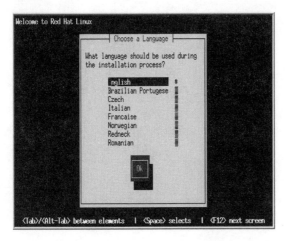

Figure 3.4: Selecting a Language

3.3.2 Selecting a Keyboard Type

Next, the installation program gives you an opportunity to select a keyboard type (see Figure 3.5 on the next page). You may navigate this dialog box the same way you did with the language selection dialog.

After selecting the appropriate keyboard type, press Enter; the keyboard type you select will be loaded automatically both for the remainder of the installation process and each time you boot your Red Hat Linux system. If you wish to change your keyboard type after you have booted your Red Hat Linux system, you may use the /usr/sbin/kbdconfig command.

3.3.3 PCMCIA Support

Next, the installation program will probe your system to determine if your system requires PCM-CIA (also known as PC Card) support. If a PCMCIA controller is found, you'll be asked if you require PCMCIA support during the installation. If you will be using a PCMCIA device during the installation (for example, you have a PCMCIA ethernet card and you'll be installing via NFS, or you have a PCMCIA SCSI card and will be installing from a SCSI CD), you should select **Yes**.

Please Note: This question applies *only* to PCMCIA support during the actual installation. Your installed Red Hat Linux system will still support PCMCIA, even if you say **No** here (assuming you installed the pcmcia-cs package).

If you require PCMCIA support, you will then be asked to insert the supplemental diskette – Select **OK** when you've done so.

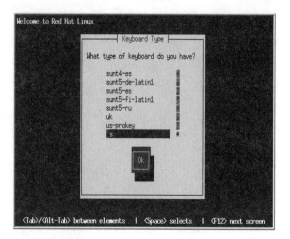

Figure 3.5: Selecting a Keyboard Type

The installation program will then display a progress bar as the supplemental diskette is loaded.

Please Note: If you are performing an installation in expert mode, you will be asked whether PCMCIA support is required. As you might imagine, you must answer **Yes** if the installation requires access to a PCMCIA device.

3.4   Selecting an Installation Method

Next, you are asked what type of installation method you wish to use (see Figure 3.6 on the facing page). Highlight the appropriate choice and select **OK**, or press (Enter). You can install Red Hat Linux via any of five basic methods (see Section 2.4 on page 15), some of which require the use of a supplemental diskette. To summarize, you can install Red Hat Linux from:

CD-ROM – If you have a CD-ROM drive and the Red Hat Linux CD-ROM. Does not require a supplemental diskette. Please refer to Section 3.4.1 on the facing page to select the CD-ROM installation method.

NFS – If you are installing from an NFS server which is exporting the Red Hat Linux CD-ROM or a mirror image of Red Hat Linux. Does not require a supplemental diskette. Please refer to Section 3.4.2 on page 36 to select the NFS installation method.

Hard Drive – If you copied the Red Hat Linux files to a local hard drive. Requires a supplemental diskette. Please refer to Section 3.4.6 on page 39 to select the hard drive installation method.

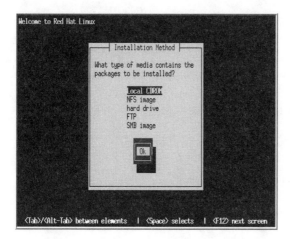

Figure 3.6: Selecting an Installation Method

FTP – If you are installing directly from an FTP server. Requires a supplemental diskette. Please refer to Section 3.4.7 on page 40 to select the FTP installation method.

SMB Image – If you are installing from a Windows "shared drive". Requires a supplemental diskette. Please refer to Section 3.4.8 on page 40 to select the SMB installation method.

3.4.1 Installing From CD-ROM

If you are going to install Red Hat Linux from CD-ROM, select "CD-ROM", and select **Ok**. The installation program will then probe your system, and attempt to identify your CD-ROM drive. It will start by looking for an IDE (also known as ATAPI) CD-ROM drive. If one is found, the installation will continue. If the installation program cannot automatically detect your CD-ROM drive, you will be asked what type of CD-ROM you have. You can choose from the following types:

SCSI Select this if your CD-ROM is attached to a supported SCSI adapter; the installation program will then ask you to choose a SCSI driver. Choose the driver that most closely resembles your adapter. You may specify options for the driver if necessary; however, most drivers will detect your SCSI adapter automatically.

Other If your CD-ROM is neither an IDE nor a SCSI CD-ROM, it's an "other". Sound cards with proprietary CD-ROM interfaces are good examples of this CD-ROM type. The installation program presents a list of drivers for supported CD-ROMs – choose a driver and, if necessary, specify any driver options.

Please Note:A partial list of optional parameters for CD-ROMs can be found in Appendix D on page 237. If you have an ATAPI CD-ROM, and the installation program fails to find it (in other words, it asks you what type of CD-ROM you have), you must restart the installation, and enter linux hd*X*=cdrom. Replace the *X* with one of the following letters, depending on the interface the unit is connected to, and whether it is configured as master or slave:

- **a** – First IDE controller, master

- **b** – First IDE controller, slave

- **c** – Second IDE controller, master

- **d** – Second IDE controller, slave

(If you have a third and/or fourth controller, simply continue assigning letters in alphabetical order, going from controller to controller, and master to slave.)

Once your CD-ROM drive has been identified, you will be asked to insert the Red Hat Linux CD-ROM into your CD-ROM drive. Select **Ok** when you have done so. After a short delay, the next dialog box will appear. Turn to Chapter 4 on page 41 to continue installing Red Hat Linux.

3.4.2   Installing via NFS

If you are going to install Red Hat Linux from an NFS-served filesystem, highlight "NFS image" and select **OK**.

3.4.3   Network Driver Configuration

Next, the installation program will probe your system and attempt to identify your network card. Most of the time, the driver can locate the card automatically. If it is not able to identify your network card, you'll be asked to choose the driver that supports your network card and to specify any options necessary for the driver to locate and recognize it.

3.4.4   Configuring TCP/IP Networking

After the installation program has configured your network card, it presents several dialogs for configuring your system's TCP/IP networking. The first screen (shown in Figure 3.7 on the next page) allows you to select from one of three approaches to network configuration:

- **Static IP address** – You must supply all the necessary network-related information manually.

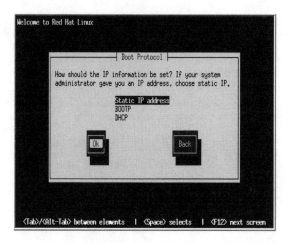

Figure 3.7: Selecting Method of Network Configuration

- **BOOTP** – The necessary network-related information is automatically provided using a `bootp` request.

- **DHCP** – The necessary network-related information is automatically provided using a `dhcp` request.

Please Note: The **BOOTP** and **DHCP** selections require an active, properly configured bootp (or dhcp) server running on your local area network.

If you choose **BOOTP** or **DHCP**, your network configuration will be set automatically, and you can skip the rest of this section.

If you've selected **Static IP address**, you'll need to specify all the networking information yourself. Figure 3.8 contains example networking information similar to what you'll be needing.

Field	Example Value
IP Address	10.0.2.15
Netmask	255.255.255.0
Default Gateway	10.0.2.254
Primary Nameserver	10.0.2.1
Domain Name	redhat.com
Hostname	pooh.redhat.com

Figure 3.8: Sample Networking Information

Please Note: The information in figure 3.8 on the page before is a sample only! You should obtain the proper information for your network from your network administrator.

The first dialog asks you for IP and other network addresses (see Figure 3.9). Enter the **IP address** you are using during installation and press [Enter]. The installation program attempts to guess your **Netmask** based on your IP address; you may change the netmask if it is incorrect. Press [Enter]. The installation program guesses the **Default gateway** and **Primary nameserver** addresses from your IP address and netmask; you may change them if they are incorrect.

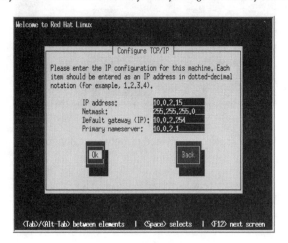

Figure 3.9: Configuring TCP/IP

In either case, choose **OK** to continue.

After the first dialog box, you may see a second one. It will prompt you for a domain name, a hostname, and other networking information (see Figure 3.10 on the next page). Enter the **Domain name** for your system and press [Enter]; the installation program carries the domain name down to the **Host name** field. Enter the hostname you are using in front of the domain name to form a fully qualified domain name (FQDN). If your network has more than one nameserver, you may enter IP addresses for additional nameservers in the **Secondary nameserver** and **Tertiary nameserver** fields. Choose **OK** to continue.

Please Note: If you're doing an FTP installation, head back to Section 4.5 on page 53, and pick up where you left off. If you're doing an SMB installation, head back to Section 4.6 on page 54, and continue from there. If you're doing an NFS installation, read on.

3.4.5 NFS Server Information

The next dialog requests information about the NFS server (see Figure 3.11 on page 40). Enter the name or IP address of your NFS server, and the name of the exported directory that contains

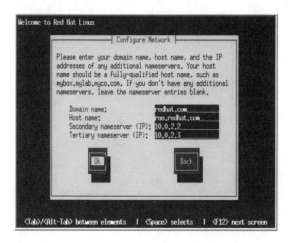

Figure 3.10: Configuring Networking

the Red Hat Linux CD. For example, if the NFS server has the Red Hat Linux CD mounted on
/mnt/cdrom, enter /mnt/cdrom in **Red Hat directory**. If the NFS server is exporting a mirror
of the Red Hat Linux installation tree instead of a CD, enter the directory which contains the
RedHat directory. For example, if your NFS server contains the directory
/mirrors/redhat/i386/RedHat, enter /mirrors/redhat/i386.

After a short delay, the next dialog box will appear. Turn to Chapter 4 on page 41 to continue
installing Red Hat Linux.

3.4.6   Installing From a Hard Drive

If you are going to install Red Hat Linux from a locally-attached hard drive, highlight "hard
drive" and select **OK**.

Before you started the installation program, you must first have copied all the necessary files
to a partition on a locally-attached hard drive. If you haven't done this yet, please refer to
Section 2.4.6 on page 18. Installing from a hard drive requires the supplemental diskette; when
you are directed to, please insert it in your computer's diskette drive, and select **OK**. A progress
bar will be displayed as the supplemental diskette is loaded.

Next, turn to Chapter 4 on page 41, and follow the directions there.

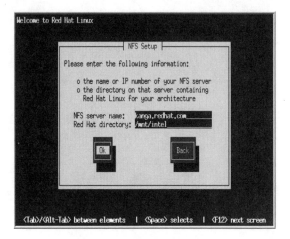

Figure 3.11: Installing via NFS

3.4.7   Installing via FTP

If you are going to install Red Hat Linux from an FTP site, highlight "FTP", and select **OK**. FTP installations require the supplemental diskette – when asked to insert it, do so, and select **OK**. The installation program will then display a progress bar as the supplemental diskette is loaded.

Next, turn to Chapter 4 on the facing page, and follow the directions there.

3.4.8   Installing via SMB

If you would like to install Red Hat Linux from a disk shared by a Windows system (or by a Linux system running the Samba SMB connectivity suite), select "SMB image", and select **Ok**. SMB installations require a supplemental diskette – when asked to insert it, do so, and select **Ok**. The installation program will then display a progress bar as the supplemental diskette is loaded.

Next, turn to Chapter 4 on the next page, and follow the directions there.

Continuing the Installation

4.1 Upgrading or Installing

After you choose an installation method, the installation program prompts you to either *install* or *upgrade* (see Figure 4.1 on the following page).

4.1.1 Installing

You usually install Red Hat Linux on a clean disk partition or set of partitions, or over another installation of Linux.

Please Note: Installing Red Hat Linux over another installation of Linux (including Red Hat Linux) does *not* preserve any information from the prior installation. Make sure you save any important files!

If you wish to perform a full install, choose **Install**, and skip to section 4.2 on the next page.

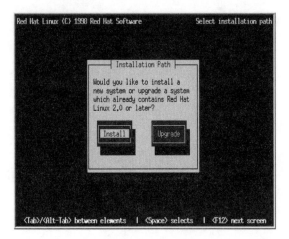

Figure 4.1: Upgrading or Installing

4.1.2 Upgrading

The installation process for Red Hat Linux 5.1 includes the ability to upgrade from prior versions of Red Hat Linux (version 2.0 and later) which are based on RPM technology. Upgrading your system installs the modular 2.0.*x* kernel as well as updated versions of the packages which are currently installed on your machine. The upgrade process preserves existing configuration files by renaming them using a .rpmsave extension (e.g., sendmail.cf.rpmsave) and leaves a log telling what actions it took in /tmp/upgrade.log. As software evolves, configuration file formats can change, so you should carefully compare your original configuration files to the new files before integrating your changes.

If you wish to upgrade your Red Hat Linux system, choose **Upgrade**.

Please Note: Some upgraded packages may require that other packages are also installed for proper operation. The upgrade procedure takes care of these *dependencies*, but it may need to install additional packages. You will be shown the names of the required packages, and you may then decide to install them or not. You should install all such packages; otherwise, some of the upgraded packages may not work properly (or at all).

4.2 SCSI Support

After you choose to perform an upgrade or a full install, the installation program will probe your system for SCSI adapters. In some cases, the installation program will ask you whether you have any SCSI adapters. If you choose **Yes**, the following dialog presents a list of SCSI drivers. Choose the driver that most closely resembles your SCSI adapter. The installation program then gives you an opportunity to specify options for the SCSI driver you selected; most SCSI drivers should detect your hardware automatically, however.

4.3 Creating Partitions for Red Hat Linux

At this point, it's necessary to let the installation program know where it should install Red Hat Linux. This is done by defining *mount points* for one or more disk partitions in which Red Hat Linux will be installed. You may also need to create and/or delete partitions at this time.

Please Note: If you have not yet planned how you will set up your partitions, please turn to Section 2.6 on page 19, and review everything up to Section 2.7 on page 25. As a bare minimum, you'll need an appropriately-sized root partition, and a swap partition of at least 16 MB.

The installation program then presents a dialog box that allows you to choose from two disk partitioning tools (see Figure 4.2). The two choices you have are:

- **Disk Druid** – This is Red Hat Linux's install-time disk management utility. It can create and delete disk partitions according to user-supplied requirements, in addition to managing mount points for each partition.

- **fdisk** – This is the traditional Linux disk partitioning tool. While it is somewhat more flexible than Disk Druid, the downside is that `fdisk` assumes you have some experience with disk partitioning, and are comfortable with its somewhat terse user interface.

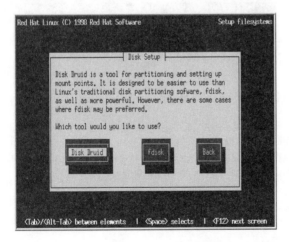

Figure 4.2: Selecting Disk Setup Method

With the exception of certain esoteric situations, Disk Druid can handle the partitioning requirements for a typical Red Hat Linux installation.

Select the disk partitioning tool you'd like to use, and press (Enter). If you choose Disk Druid, continue reading. If you'd rather use fdisk, please turn to Section 4.3.2 on page 49.

4.3.1   Using Disk Druid

If you selected Disk Druid, you will be presented with a screen that looks like figure 4.3. While it may look overwhelming at first, it really isn't. Let's go over each of Disk Druid's three sections.

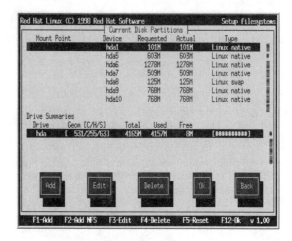

Figure 4.3: Disk Druid Main Screen

The "Current Disk Partitions" Section

Each line in the "Current Disk Partitions" section represents a disk partition. You'll note that this section has a scroll bar to the right, which means that there might be more partitions than can be displayed at one time. If you use the ⬆ and ⬇ keys, you can see if there are any additional partitions there. Each line in this section has five different fields:

Mount Point – This field indicates where the partition will be mounted when Red Hat Linux is installed and running.

Device – This field displays the partition's device name.

Requested – The "Requested" field shows the minimum size requested when the partition was defined.

Actual – The "Actual" field shows the space currently allocated to the partition.

Type – This field shows the partition's type.

Another Type of Partition   As you scroll through the "Current Disk Partitions" section, you might see an "Unallocated Requested Partitions" title bar, followed by one or more partitions. As the title implies, these are partitions that have been requested but, for one reason or another, have not been allocated. A common reason for having an unallocated partition is a lack of sufficient free space for the partition. In any case, the reason the partition remains unallocated will be displayed after the partition's mount point.

The "Drive Summaries" Section

Each line in the "Drive Summaries" section represents a hard disk on your system. Each line has the following fields:

Drive – This field shows the hard disk's device name.

Geom [C/H/S] – This field shows the hard disk's *geometry*. The geometry consists of three numbers representing the number of cylinders, heads, and sectors as reported by the hard disk.

Total – The "Total" field shows the total available space on the hard disk.

Used – This field shows how much of the hard disk's space is currently allocated to partitions.

Free – The "Free" field shows how much of the hard disk's space is still unallocated.

Bar Graph – This field presents a visual representation of the space currently used on the hard disk. The more pound signs there are between the square braces, the less free space there is. In Figure 4.3 on the preceding page, the bar graph shows no free space.

Please Note: The "Drive Summaries" section is displayed only to indicate your computer's disk configuration. It is not meant to be used as a means of specifying the target hard drive for a given partition. This is described more completely in Section 4.3.1 on the following page.

Disk Druid's Buttons

These buttons control Disk Druid's actions. They are used to add and delete partitions, and to change partition attributes. In addition, there are buttons that are used to accept the changes you've made, or to exit Disk Druid entirely. Let's take a look at each button in order.

Add – The "Add" button is used to request a new partition. When selected, a dialog box will appear containing fields that must be filled in.

Edit – The "Edit" button is used to modify attributes of the partition currently highlighted in the "Current Disk Partitions" section. Selecting this button will cause a dialog box to appear. Some or all of the fields in the "Edit Partition" dialog box may be changed, depending on whether the partition information has already been written to disk or not.

Delete – The "Delete" button is used to delete the partition currently highlighted in the "Current Disk Partitions" section. Selecting this button will cause a dialog box to appear asking you to confirm the deletion.

Ok – The "Ok" button causes any changes made to your system's partitions to be written to disk. You will be asked to confirm your changes before Disk Druid rewrites your hard disk partition table(s). In addition, any mount points you've defined are passed to the installation program, and will eventually be used by your Red Hat Linux system to define the filesystem layout.

Back – This button causes Disk Druid to abort without saving any changes you've made. When this button is selected, the installation program will take you back to the previous screen, so you can start over.

Handy Function Keys

While there is some overlap between Disk Druid's buttons and the available functions keys, there are two function keys that have no corresponding buttons:

- ⌨ F2 **(Add NFS)** – This function key is used to add a read-only NFS-served filesystem to the set of mount points on your Red Hat Linux system. When selected, a dialog box will appear containing fields that must be filled in.

- ⌨ F5 **(Reset)** – This function key is used to discard all changes you may have made while in Disk Druid, and return the list of partitions to those read from the partition table(s) on your hard disk(s). When selected, you'll be asked to confirm whether you want the changes discarded or not. Note that any mount points you've specified will be lost, and will need to be reentered.

Please Note: You will need to dedicate at least one partition to Red Hat Linux, and optionally more. This is discussed more completely in Section 2.6.5 on page 24.

Now let's see how Disk Druid is used to set up partitions for your Red Hat Linux system.

Adding a Partition

To Add a new partition, select the **Add** button, and press ⌨Space or ⌨Enter. A dialog box entitled "Edit New Partition" will appear (see Figure 4.4 on the facing page). It contains the following fields:

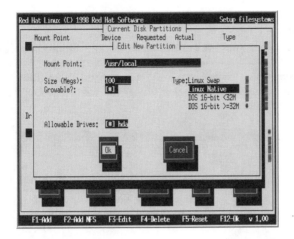

Figure 4.4: Creating a New Partition

- **Mount Point** – Highlight this field, and enter the partition's mount point. For example, if this partition should be the root partition, enter /, enter /usr for the usr partition, and so on.

- **Size (Megs)** – In this field, enter the size (in megabytes) of the partition. Note that this field starts with a "1" in it, meaning that unless you change it, you'll end up with a 1 MB partition. Delete it using the [Backspace] key, and enter the desired partition size.

- **Growable?** – This check box indicates whether the size you entered in the previous field is to be considered the partition's exact size, or its minimum size. Press [Space] to check and uncheck the box. When checked, the partition will grow to fill all available space on the hard disk. In this case, the partition's size will expand and contract as other partitions are modified.

- **Type** – This field contains a list of different partition types. Select the appropriate partition type by using the [↑] and [↓] keys.

- **Allowable Drives** – This field contains a list of the hard disks installed on your system, with a check box for each. If a hard disk's box is checked, then this partition may be created on that hard disk. If the box is *not* checked, then partition will *never* be created on that hard disk. By using different check box settings, you can direct Disk Druid to place partitions as you see fit, or let Disk Druid decide where partitions should go.

- **Ok** – Select this button and press [Space] when you are satisfied with the partition's settings, and wish to create it.

- **Cancel** – Select this button and press [Space] when you don't want to create the partition.

Problems When Adding a Partition If you attempt to add a partition and Disk Druid can't carry out your request, you'll see a dialog box like the one in Figure 4.5. In the box are listed any partitions that are currently unallocated, along with the reason they could not be allocated. Select the **Ok** button, and press [Space] to continue. Note that the unallocated partition(s) are also displayed on Disk Druid's main screen (though you may have to scroll the "Current Disk Partitions" section to see them).

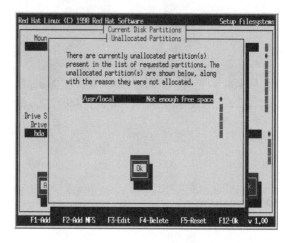

Figure 4.5: Unallocated Partition Warning

Deleting a Partition

To delete a partition, highlight the partition in the "Current Disk Partitions" section, select the **Delete** button, and press [Space]. You will be asked to confirm the deletion.

Editing a Partition

To change a partition's settings, highlight the partition in the "Current Disk Partitions" section, select the **Edit** button, and press [Space]. You will be presented with a dialog box very similar to the one shown in Figure 4.4 on the preceding page. Make the appropriate changes, select **Ok**, and press [Space].

Please Note: If the partition already existed on your hard disk, you will only be able to change the partition's mount point. If you want to make any other changes, you will need to delete the partition and recreate it.

Adding an NFS Mount

To add a read-only NFS-served filesystem, press F2. If you have not selected a network-related installation method, you will be presented with several dialog boxes concerning network config-uration (Turn back to Section 3.4.3 on page 36 for more information). Fill them in appropriately. You will then see a dialog box entitled, "Edit Network Mount Point" (similar to the one in Fig-ure 4.10 on page 53). In this dialog box you will need to enter the NFS server name, the path to the exported filesystem, and the mount point for the filesystem. Select the **Ok** or **Cancel** button as appropriate, and press Space.

Starting Over

If you'd like to abandon any changes you've made while in Disk Druid, and would rather use fdisk instead, you can select the **Back** button, and press Space. If you want to continue using Disk Druid, but would like to start over, press F5, and Disk Druid will be reset to its initial state.

When You're Finished...

Once you've finished configuring partitions and entering mount points, your screen should look something like the one in Figure 4.6 on the next page. Select **OK**, and press Space. Then turn to Section 4.4 on page 53.

4.3.2 Using fdisk

If you'd rather use fdisk to manage partitions, this is the section for you. Once you've selected fdisk, you'll be presented with a dialog box entitled "Partition Disks" (see Figure 4.7 on the next page). In this box is a list of every disk on your computer. Move the highlight to the disk you'd like to partition, select **Edit**, and press Space. You will then enter fdisk and can partition the disk you selected. Repeat this process for each disk you want to partition. When you're done, select "Done".

An Overview of fdisk

fdisk includes online help which is terse but useful. Here are a few tips:

- The command for help is m.

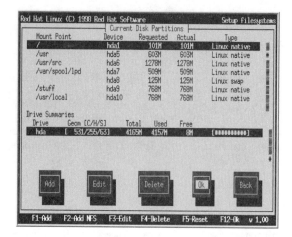

Figure 4.6: Partitions and Mount Points Defined

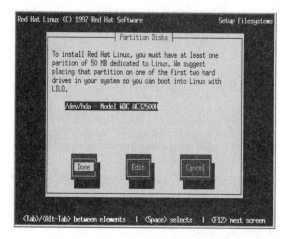

Figure 4.7: Selecting a Disk for Partitioning

- To list the current partition table, use the p command (see Figure 4.8).

- To add a new partition, use n.

- Linux fdisk creates partitions of type Linux native by default. When you create a swap partition, don't forget to change it to type Linux swap using the t command. The value for the Linux swap type is 82. For other partition types, use the l command to see a list of partition types and values.

- Linux allows up to four (4) partitions on one disk. If you wish to create more than that, one of the four may be an *extended* partition, which acts as a container for one or more *logical* partitions. Since it acts as a container, the extended partition must be at least as large as the total size of all the logical partitions it is to contain.

- It's a good idea to write down which partitions (e.g., /dev/hda2) are meant for which filesystems (e.g., /usr) as you create each one.

- **Please Note:** None of the changes you make take effect until you save them and exit fdisk using the w command. You may quit fdisk at any time without saving changes by using the q command.

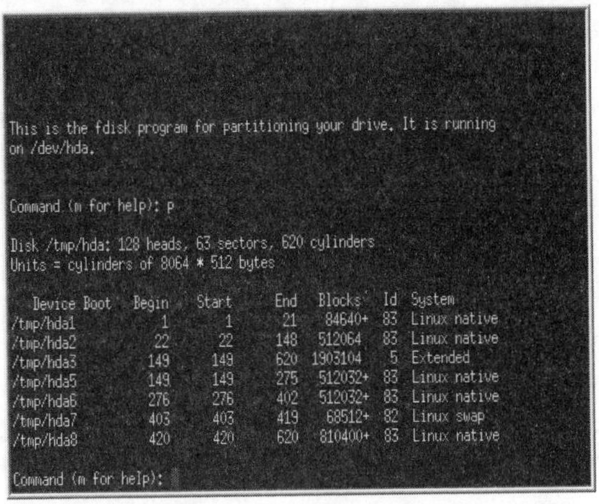

Figure 4.8: Sample Output From fdisk

Changing the Partition Table

When you are finished partitioning your disks, press **Done**; you may see a message indicating that the installation program needs to reboot. This is a normal occurrence after changing a disk's partition data; it usually happens if you created, changed, or deleted any extended partitions.

After you press **OK**, your machine will reboot. Follow the same installation steps you did up until **Partitioning Disks**; then simply choose **Done**.

4.3.3 Filesystem Configuration

The next dialog box contains a list of all disk partitions with filesystems readable by Red Hat Linux, including partitions for MS-DOS or Windows. This gives you the opportunity to assign these partitions to different parts of your Red Hat Linux filesystem. The partitions you assign will be automatically mounted when your Red Hat Linux system boots. Select the partition you wish to assign and press (Enter) (or choose **Edit**); then enter the *mount point* for that partition, e.g., /usr (see Figure 4.9).

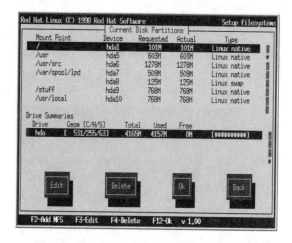

Figure 4.9: Filesystem Configuration

If you are performing an upgrade, the installation program tries to find your root partition automatically; if it does, it obtains all this information automatically, and goes on to the next step.

Adding an NFS Mount

Red Hat Linux also allows you to mount read-only NFS volumes when your system boots; this allows directory trees to be shared across a network. To do so, press (F2). If you have not selected a network-related installation method, you will be presented with several dialog boxes concerning network configuration (Turn back to Section 3.4.4 on page 36 for more information). Fill them in appropriately. You will then see a dialog box entitled "Edit Network Mount Point". Enter the NFS server's hostname, the path to the NFS volume, and the local mount point for that volume (see Figure 4.10 on the next page).

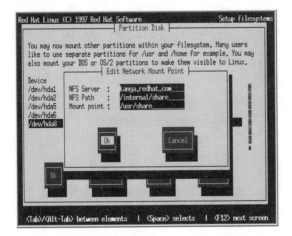

Figure 4.10: Adding an NFS Mount

4.4   Initializing Swap Space

After you've created partitions for Red Hat Linux, the installation program looks for swap partitions (see Figure 4.11 on the following page). If it finds any, it asks whether you want to initialize them. Select the partition(s) you wish to initialize as swap space using [Space]; if you wish to check the partitions for bad blocks, make sure the **Check for bad blocks during format** box is checked. Choose **OK**, and press [Space].

If the installation program can't find a swap partition and you're sure one exists, make sure you have set the partition type to Linux swap; see Section 4.3 on page 43 for information on how this is done with Disk Druid or fdisk.

4.5   For FTP Installations Only. . .

If you are *not* performing an FTP installation, please skip ahead to Section 4.6 on the following page.

If you *are* performing an FTP installation, please mark this place in the manual, because you'll be returning here later. Turn to Section 3.4.3 on page 36. This section will guide you through the necessary network configuration dialog boxes. When you get to the "FTP Setup" dialog box, come back here. . .

OK, you're back. You should have entered all the necessary network information, and should now be looking at the "FTP Setup" dialog box. Here's where you point the installation program

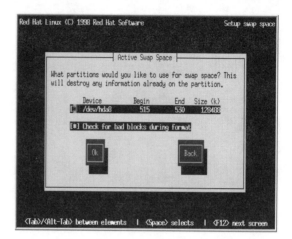

Figure 4.11: Initializing Swap Space

at the FTP site of your choice (see Figure 4.12 on the facing page). Enter the name or IP address
of the FTP site you are installing from, and the name of the directory there which contains the
RedHat directory for your architecture. For example, if the FTP site contains the directory
/pub/mirrors/redhat/i386/RedHat, enter /pub/mirrors/redhat/i386. If you are
not using anonymous FTP, or if you need to use a proxy FTP server (if you're behind a firewall, for example), check the check box, and another dialog box will request the FTP account
and proxy information.

If everything has been specified properly, you should see a message box indicating that
base/hdlist is being retrieved. Now turn to Section 4.8 on page 57 to continue installing Red
Hat Linux.

4.6   For SMB Installations Only...

If you are *not* performing an SMB installation, please skip ahead to Section 4.7 on page 56.

If you *are* performing an SMB installation, please mark this place in the manual, because you'll
be returning here later. Turn to Section 3.4.3 on page 36. This section will guide you through the
necessary network configuration dialog boxes. When you get to the "SMB Setup" dialog box,
come back here...

At this point, you should have entered all the necessary network information, and should now be
looking at the "SMB Setup" dialog box. This is where you'll specify which SMB server, share, and
account information the installation program should use (See Figure 4.13 on the facing page).

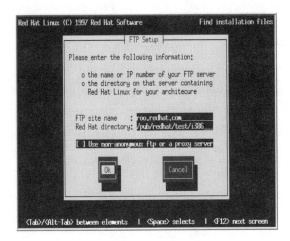

Figure 4.12: Installing via FTP

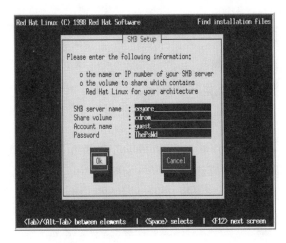

Figure 4.13: Installing via SMB

First, you'll need to enter the SMB server name. It's important to note that the name expected here is the server's Microsoft Networking name, and not a fully qualified domain name.

Next, enter the name of the shared volume. Since different implementations of the SMB protocol handle share names differently, you might find that the case of the share name is important. In most cases (no pun intended) entering the share name in lower case seems to work best.

Next, enter the account name and password. In general, the account name should be guest. A password (which *is* case-sensitive) *must* be present. If the share is made available *without* a password, it will most likely not work.

After entering all the required information, select **Ok**, and press (Space). If everything is working properly, there will be a slight delay as the list of available packages is read by the installation program. Skip ahead to Section 4.8 on the next page to continue the installation.

4.7 For Hard Drive Installations Only...

If you are *not* performing a hard drive installation, please skip ahead to Section 4.8 on the facing page. Otherwise, read on.

At this point, a dialog box entitled "Select Partition" is displayed (see Figure 4.14). Enter the device name of the partition holding the RedHat directory tree. There is also a field labelled "Directory". If the RedHat directory is not in the root directory of that partition (for example, /test/new/RedHat), enter the path to the RedHat directory (in our example, /test/new.

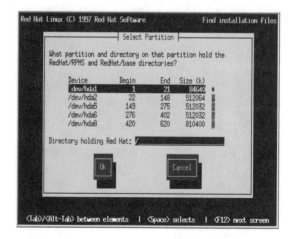

Figure 4.14: Selecting Partition for HD Install

If the installation program was unable to find the necessary files on the partition and directory you've specified, you'll be returned to the "Select Partition" dialog box to make the necessary corrections.

If everything has been specified properly, you should see a message box indicating that the packages are being scanned. Move on to the next section to continue installing Red Hat Linux.

4.8 Formatting Partitions

The next dialog box presents a list of partitions to format (see Figure 4.15). All newly created partitions should be formatted. In addition, any already-existing partitions that contain old data you no longer need should be formatted. However, partitions such as /home or /usr/local must not be formatted if they contain data you wish to keep. Select each partition to format and press Space. If you wish to check for bad blocks while formatting each filesystem, select **Check for bad blocks during format**. Select **OK**, and press Space.

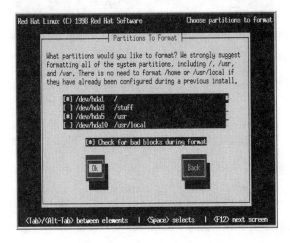

Figure 4.15: Formatting Partitions

4.9 Selecting and Installing Packages

After your partitions have been configured and selected for formatting, you are ready to select packages for installation. You can select *components*, which group packages together according to function, individual packages, or a combination of the two.

4.9.1 Selecting Components

Components group packages together according to the functionality they provide. For example, **C Development**, **Networked Workstation**, or **Web Server**. Select each component you wish to install and press Space. Selecting **Everything** (which can be found at the end of the component list) installs all packages included with Red Hat Linux (see Figure 4.16). Selecting every package will require over 700 MB of free disk space.

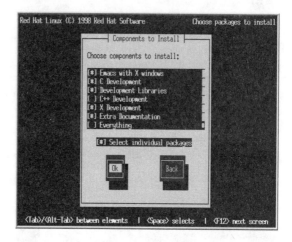

Figure 4.16: Selecting System Components

If you wish to select or deselect individual packages, check the **Select individual packages** check box.

4.9.2 Selecting Individual Packages

After selecting the components you wish to install, you may select or deselect individual packages. The installation program presents a list of the package groups available; select a group to examine and press Enter. The installation program presents a list of the packages in that group, which you may select or deselect by using the arrow keys to highlight a package, and pressing Space (see Figure 4.17 on the facing page).

Please Note: Some packages (such as the kernel and certain libraries) are required for every Red Hat Linux system and are not available to select or deselect.

When you are finished selecting individual packages, press **OK** in the **Select Group** dialog box.

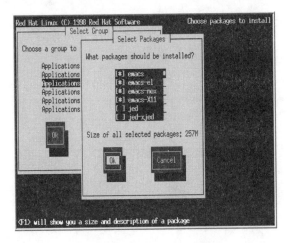

Figure 4.17: Selecting Packages

Getting Information About A Package

You may view a detailed description of the currently-highlighted package by pressing F1. A dialog box will appear containing a description of the package. You can use the arrow keys to scroll through the description if there is more than can fit on the screen. When you're done reading the description, press Ok, and the box will disappear. You can then continue selecting packages (and viewing their descriptions).

Please Note: If you'd rather read the package descriptions on paper, please turn to Appendix C on page 179.

4.9.3 Package Dependencies

Many software packages, in order to work correctly, depend on other software packages or libraries that must be installed on your system. For example, many of the graphical Red Hat system administration tools require the python and pythonlib packages. To make sure your system has all the packages it needs in order to be fully functional, Red Hat Linux checks package these *dependencies* each time you install or remove software packages.

After you have finished selecting packages to install, the installation program checks the list of selected packages for dependencies. If any package requires another package which you have not selected to install, the program presents a list of these *unresolved dependencies* and gives you the opportunity to resolve them (see Figure 4.18 on the following page). If you simply press OK, the program will resolve them automatically by adding all required packages to the list of selected packages.

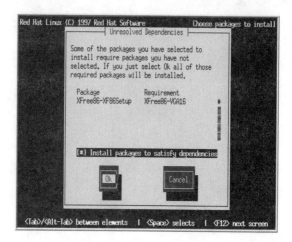

Figure 4.18: Unresolved Dependencies

4.9.4 Package Installation

After all package dependencies have been resolved, the installation program presents a dialog box telling you that a log file containing a list of all packages installed will be written to /tmp/install.log on your Red Hat Linux system. Select **Ok** and press [Space] to continue.

At this point, the installation program will format every partition you selected for formatting. This can take several minutes (and will take even longer if you directed the installation program to check for bad blocks).

Once all partitions have been formatted, the installation program starts to install packages. A window entitled "Install Status" is displayed with the following information:

Package – The name of the package currently being installed.

Size – The size of the package (in kilobytes).

Summary – A short description of the package.

Package Installation Progress Bar – A bar showing how complete the current package installation is.

Statistics Section – This section has three rows labeled "Total", "Completed", and "Remaining". As you might guess, these rows contain statistics on the total number of packages that will be installed, statistics on the number of packages that have been completely installed, and statistics on the packages that have not yet been installed. The information tracked on these three rows includes:

Packages – The number of packages.

Bytes – The size.

Time – The amount of time.

Overall Progress Bar – This bar changes color showing how close to completion the entire installation is.

If you're doing an FTP installation, a message box will pop up as each package is retrieved from the FTP site.

At this point there's nothing left for you to do until all the packages have been installed. How quickly this happens depends on the number of packages you've selected, and your computer's speed. Once all the packages have been installed, please turn to the next chapter to finish your installation of Red Hat Linux.

5

Finishing the Installation

5.1 Configuring a Mouse

Next, the installation program will probe your system and try to find a mouse. Some mice may be detected automatically; in this case, a dialog box is displayed showing the port on which the mouse was found. Press (Space) to continue. You may then be asked to give additional information, such as whether you have a two-button mouse, and would like it to emulate a three-button mouse. Make the appropriate selections, and continue to the next section.

If your mouse was not detected automatically, you will be asked to identify the type of mouse you have, and whether or not you have a two-button mouse and would like it to emulate a three-button model. Following this screen, you will be asked to identify the serial port to which your mouse is connected. Select the appropriate serial port, and press (Enter). You can then continue to the next section.

If you wish to change your mouse configuration after you have booted your Red Hat Linux system, you may use the /usr/sbin/mouseconfig command.

5.2   Configuring X Windows

After setting up your mouse, if you installed the X Windows packages, you will have the opportunity to configure your X server. If you did not choose to install the X Window System, you
may skip to Section 5.3 on the next page.

5.2.1   Configuring an XFree86 Server

If you wish to use XFree86, the installation program launches the Xconfigurator utility.

Xconfigurator first probes your system in an attempt to determine what type of video card
you have. Failing that, Xconfigurator will present a list of video cards. Select your video
card from the list and press [Enter]. If your video card does not appear on the list, XFree86 may
not support it. However, if you have technical knowledge about your card, you may choose
Unlisted Card and attempt to configure it by matching your card's video chipset with one of the
available X servers.

Once you have selected your video card, the installation program installs the appropriate XFree86
server, and Xconfigurator presents a list of monitors. If your monitor appears on the list, select it and press [Enter]. Otherwise, select **Custom**. If you do select **Custom**, Xconfigurator
prompts you to select the horizontal sync range and vertical sync range of your monitor (these
values are generally available in the documentation which accompanies your monitor, or from
your monitor's vendor or manufacturer).

Caution: It is not recommended to select a monitor "similar" to your monitor unless you are
certain that the monitor you are selecting does not exceed the capabilities of your monitor. If
you do so, it is possible you may overclock your monitor and damage or destroy it.

Next, Xconfigurator prompts you for the amount of video memory installed on your video
card. If you are not sure, please consult the documentation accompanying your video card. It
will not damage your video card by choosing more memory than is available, but the XFree86
server may not start correctly if you do.

If the video card you selected might have a video clockchip, Xconfigurator presents a list of
clockchips. The recommended choice is **No Clockchip Setting**, since XFree86 can automatically
detect the proper clockchip in most cases.

Finally, Xconfigurator prompts you to select the video modes you wish to use; select one or
more modes by pressing [Space]. Xconfigurator then writes a configuration file containing
all of your choices to /etc/X11/XF86Config.

5.3 Configuring Networking

Next, the installation program gives you an opportunity to configure (or reconfigure) network-ing. If you are installing from CD-ROM or from a local hard disk, the installation program asks if you want to configure networking. If you choose **No**, your Red Hat Linux system will be a standalone workstation. If you choose **Yes**, you may configure networking as described below.

If you are installing Red Hat Linux via NFS, FTP, or SMB, you have already entered temporary networking information that was used during the installation. The install program offers you three choices (see Figure 5.1):

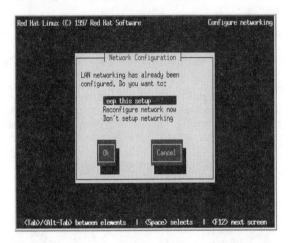

Figure 5.1: Network Configuration Options

- **Keep this setup** – Keeps the network configuration you used during the installation. All the networking information you entered previously becomes part of your system's permanent configuration.

- **Reconfigure network now** – The installation program presents the network configura-tion dialogs in Section 3.4.4 on page 36. The values you used during installation will be filled in as defaults. Choose this if your system will be installed on a network other than the one you used to install Red Hat Linux.

- **Don't setup networking** – Don't set up networking at all. Your system will not have networking configured. Choose this if you installed your system over a network, but it will be used as a standalone workstation.

5.3.1   Network Configuration Dialogs

If you elected to configure networking at this time, you will be presented with a series of dialog boxes. Please turn to Section 3.4.4 on page 36 for more information.

5.4   Configuring the Clock

Next, the installation program presents a dialog to help you configure your Red Hat Linux system's timezone (see Figure 5.2).

If you wish to set the hardware (CMOS) clock to GMT (Greenwich Mean Time, also known as UTC, or Coordinated Universal Time), select **Hardware clock set to GMT**. Setting your hardware clock to GMT means your Red Hat Linux system will properly handle daylight savings time, if your timezone uses it. Most networks use GMT.

Please Note: If your computer runs another operating system from time to time, setting the clock to GMT may cause the other operating system to display the incorrect time. Also keep in mind that if more than one operating system is allowed to automatically change the time to compensate for daylight savings time, it is likely that the time will be improperly set.

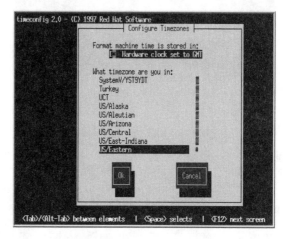

Figure 5.2: Configuring Timezones

Select the timezone your system will be operating in from the list, and press ⌐Enter⌐.

If you wish to change your timezone configuration after you have booted your Red Hat Linux system, you may use the /usr/sbin/timeconfig command.

5.5 Selecting Services for Start on Reboot

Next you'll see a dialog box entitled "Services" (see Figure 5.3). Displayed in this box is a list of services with a check box by each. Scroll through this list, and check every service that you would like automatically started every time your Red Hat Linux system boots. If you're not sure what a particular service is, move the highlight to it and press F1. You'll then get a brief description of the service.

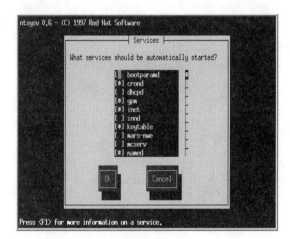

Figure 5.3: Selecting Services

Note that you can run /usr/sbin/ntsysv or /sbin/chkconfig after the installation to change which services automatically start on reboot.

5.6 Configuring a Printer

After you have set up networking, the installation program asks whether you would like to configure a printer. If you choose **Yes**, a dialog box will ask you to indicate how the printer is connected to your computer (see Figure 5.4 on the next page).

Here is a brief description of the three types of printer connections available:

Local – This printer is directly connected to your computer.

Remote lpd – This printer is connected to your local area network (either through another computer, or directly), and is capable of communicating via lpr/lpd.

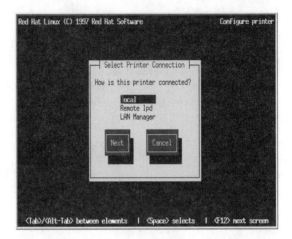

Figure 5.4: Selecting Printer Type

LAN Manager – This printer is connected to another computer which shares the printer via LAN Manager (or SMB) networking.

After selecting a printer type, you'll be presented with a dialog box entitled "Standard Printer Options" (see Figure 5.5 on the facing page). Enter the name of the queue and the spool directory you'd like to use, or accept the default information.

The dialog box you'll see next depends on the printer connection type you selected. Turn to the section that corresponds to your printer connection type:

Local – Section 5.6.1.

Remote lpd – Section 5.6.2 on page 70.

LAN Manager – Section 5.6.3 on page 70.

5.6.1   Locally Attached Printers

If you selected "Local" as your printer's connection type, you'll see a dialog box similar to the one in Figure 5.6 on the facing page.

Enter the printer device name in the field provided. As a convenience, the installation program attempts to determine which printer ports are available on your computer. Select **Next**, and press Space. Now turn to Section 5.6.4 on page 70 to continue.

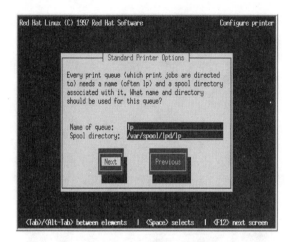

Figure 5.5: Standard Printer Options

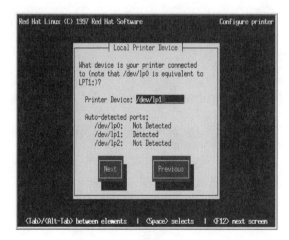

Figure 5.6: Local Printer Device

5.6.2   Remote lpd Printers

If you selected "Remote lpd" as your printer's connection type, you'll see a dialog box similar to the one in Figure 5.7.

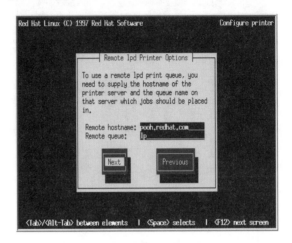

Figure 5.7: Remote lpd Printer Options

Enter the name of the computer to which the printer is directly connected in the "Remote host-name" field. The name of the queue *on the remote computer* that is associated with the remote printer goes in the "remote queue" field. Select **Next**, and press $\boxed{\text{Space}}$. Now turn to Section 5.6.4 to continue.

5.6.3   LAN Manager Printers

If you selected "LAN Manager" as your printer's connection type, you'll see a dialog box similar to the one in Figure 5.8 on the facing page.

Enter the necessary information in the fields provided. Select **Next**, and press $\boxed{\text{Space}}$.

5.6.4   Finalizing Printer Setup

Next, you'll see a dialog box entitled "Configure Printer" (see Figure 5.9 on the next page). Select the printer type that most closely matches your printer. Select **Next**, and press $\boxed{\text{Space}}$ to continue.

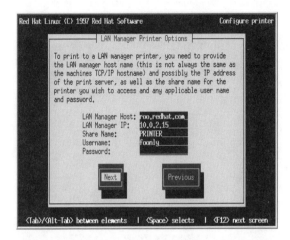

Figure 5.8: LAN Manager Printer Options

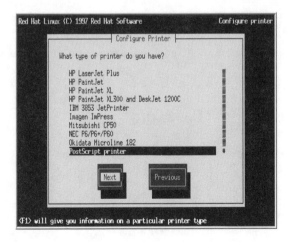

Figure 5.9: Configure Printer

After selecting the printer type, you will see a dialog box similar to the one in Figure 5.10. Set the paper size and resolution appropriately. The **Fix stair-stepping of text** check box should be checked if your printer does not automatically perform a carriage return after each line.

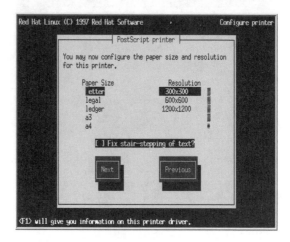

Figure 5.10: Printer Settings

Finally, you'll see a dialog box that contains all the information pertaining to your printer (see Figure 5.11 on the next page). Verify that the information is correct. If everything looks OK, select **Done**. If you need to make changes, select **Edit**. You can also select **Cancel** if you'd rather not configure a printer at this time.

If you select **Done,** you will be given the option to configure another printer, or you may continue with the installation.

5.7   Setting a Root Password

The installation program will next prompt you to set a *root password* for your system (see Figure 5.12 on page 74). You'll use the root password to log into your Red Hat Linux system for the first time.

The root password must be at least six characters long; the password you type is not echoed to the screen. You must enter the password twice; if the two passwords do not match, the installation program will ask you to enter them again.

You ought to make the root password something you can remember, but not something that is easy for someone else to guess. Your name, your phone number, `qwerty`, `password`, `root`, `123456,` and `anteater` are all examples of poor passwords. Good passwords mix numerals with upper and lower case letters and do not contain dictionary words: `Aard387vark` or

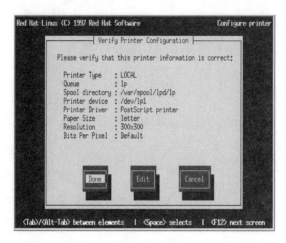

Figure 5.11: Verifying Printer Information

420BMttNT, for example. Remember that the password is case-sensitive. Write down this password and keep it in a secure place.

Please Note: The *root* user (also known as the *superuser*) has complete access to the entire system; for this reason, logging in as the root user is best done *only* to perform system maintenance or administration. Please see Section 9.1 on page 116 for instructions on how to add a user account for yourself after you reboot your system. A more basic method of creating a new user account can also be found in Section 6.2.3 on page 83.

5.8 Creating a Boot Diskette

Next, you'll be given the opportunity to create a customized boot diskette for your Red Hat Linux system (see Figure 5.13 on page 75).

A boot diskette can be handy for a number of reasons:

- **Use It Instead of LILO** – You can use a boot diskette instead of LILO. This is handy if you're trying Red Hat Linux for the first time, and you'd feel more comfortable if the boot process for your other operating system is left unchanged. With a boot diskette, going back to your other operating system is as easy as removing the boot diskette and rebooting.

- **Use It In Emergencies** – The boot diskette can also be used in conjunction with a rescue

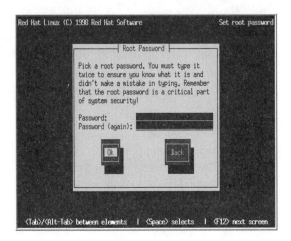

Figure 5.12: Root Password

disk, which will give you the tools necessary to get an ailing system back on its feet again[1].

- **Use It When Another Operating System Overwrites LILO** – Other operating systems may not be as flexible as Red Hat Linux when it comes to supported boot methods. Quite often, installing or updating another operating system can cause the master boot record (originally containing LILO) to be overwritten, making it impossible to boot your Red Hat Linux installation. The boot diskette can then be used to boot Red Hat Linux so you can reinstall LILO.

Given these reasons to create a boot diskette, you should seriously consider doing so. Select **Yes** and press (Space) to create a boot diskette. Next, you'll see a dialog box directing you to insert a blank diskette in your computer's diskette drive. Select **Ok**, and press (Space) when you've done so.

After a short delay, your boot diskette will be done. After removing it from your diskette drive, label it clearly. Note that if you would like to create a boot diskette after the installation, you'll be able to do so. If you boot your system with the boot diskette (instead of LILO), make sure you create a new boot diskette if you make any changes to your kernel. For more information, please see the mkbootdisk man page.

---

[1]To do this, you'll need to create a rescue diskette from the rescue.img image contained in the images directory of your Red Hat Linux CD-ROM. Appendix B on page 177 explains how to do this.

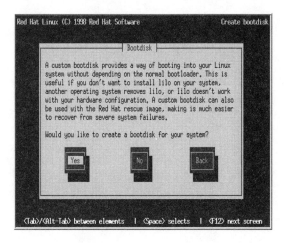

Figure 5.13: Creating a Boot Diskette

5.9   Installing LILO

In order to be able to boot your Red Hat Linux system, you usually need to install LILO (the LInux LOader). You may install LILO in one of two places:

The Master Boot Record (MBR) is the recommended place to install LILO, unless the MBR already starts another operating system loader, such System Commander or OS/2's Boot Manager. The master boot record is a special area on your hard drive that is automatically loaded by your computer's BIOS, and is the earliest point at which LILO can take control of the boot process. If you install LILO in the MBR, when your machine boots, LILO will present a boot: prompt; you can then boot Red Hat Linux or any other operating system you configure LILO to boot (see below).

The first sector of your root partition is recommended if you are already using another boot loader on your system (such as OS/2's Boot Manager). In this case, your other boot loader will take control first. You can then configure that boot loader to start LILO (which will then boot Red Hat Linux).

A dialog box will appear that will let you select the type of LILO installation you desire (see Figure 5.14 on the next page). Select the location you wish to install LILO and press **OK**. If you do not wish to install LILO, press **Skip**.

Please Note: If you choose **Skip**, you will not be able to boot your Red Hat Linux system directly, and will need to use another boot method (such as a boot diskette). Use this option only if you know you have another way of booting your Red Hat Linux system!

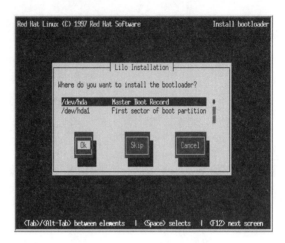

Figure 5.14: Installing LILO

5.9.1   Adding Options to the LILO Boot Command Line

Next, the installation program will ask if you wish to add default options to the LILO boot command (see Figure 5.15 on the facing page). Any options you enter will be passed to the Linux kernel every time it boots. When you reviewed your computer's BIOS settings in Section 2.3.1 on page 11, if you found your computer accesses a hard drive in LBA mode, check **Use linear mode**. Select **OK** and press Space when finished.

Finally, the installation program will display a screen similar to the one in Figure 5.16 on page 78. Every partition that may be bootable is listed, including partitions used by other operating systems. The "Boot label" column will be filled in with the word linux on the partition holding your Red Hat Linux system's root filesystem. Other partitions may also have boot labels. If you would like to add boot labels for other partitions (or change an existing boot label), use the arrow keys to highlight the desired partition. Then use the Tab key to select the **Edit** button, and press Space. You'll then see a small dialog box permitting you to enter/modify the partition's boot label. Press **Ok** when done.

There is also a column labeled "Default". Only one partition will contain an asterisk under that column. The partition marked as the default will be the partition LILO will boot if there is no user input during the boot process. Initially the root partition for your Red Hat Linux installation will be selected as the default. If you'd like to change this, use the arrow keys to highlight the partition you'd like to make the default, and press F2. The asterisk should move to the selected partition. When you've finished, select **Ok**, and press Space.

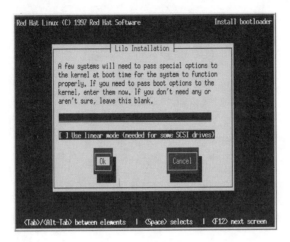

Figure 5.15: LILO options

5.9.2 Alternatives to LILO

If you do not wish to use LILO to boot your Red Hat Linux system, there are a few alternatives:

Boot Diskette You can use the boot diskette created by the installation program (if you elected to create one).

LOADLIN can load Linux from MS-DOS; unfortunately, it requires a copy of the Linux kernel (and an initial ram disk, if you have a SCSI adapter) to be available on an MS-DOS partition. The only way to accomplish this is to boot your Red Hat Linux system using some other method (e.g., from LILO on a diskette) and then copy the kernel to an MS-DOS partition. LOADLIN is available from
`ftp://sunsite.unc.edu/pub/Linux/system/boot/dualboot/`
and sunsite's various mirror sites.

SYSLINUX is an MS-DOS program very similar to LOADLIN; it is also available from
`ftp://sunsite.unc.edu/pub/Linux/system/boot/dualboot/` and sunsite's various mirror sites.

Some commercial bootloaders, such as System Commander, are able to boot Linux (but still require LILO to be installed in your Linux root partition).

5.10 Finishing Up...

After you have completed LILO installation, the installation program will reboot your system. Don't forget to remove any diskette that might be in the diskette drive (Unless you decided to

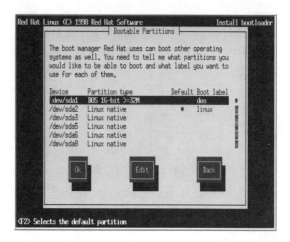

Figure 5.16: Selecting Bootable Partitions

skip the standard LILO installation, in which case you'll need to use the boot diskette created during the installation).

After your computer's normal power-up sequence has completed, you should see LILO's standard prompt, which is `boot:`. At the `boot:` prompt, you can do any of the following things:

- **Pressing** ⌈Enter⌉ – Causes LILO's default boot entry (as defined by the dialog box shown in Figure 5.16) to be booted.

- **Entering a Boot Label, followed by** ⌈Enter⌉ – Causes LILO to boot the operating system corresponding to the entered boot label.

- **Doing Nothing** – After LILO's timeout period, (which, by default, is five seconds) Lilo will automatically boot the default boot entry.

Do whatever is appropriate to boot Red Hat Linux. You should see one or more screens worth of messages scroll by. Eventually, you should see a `login:` prompt.

Congratulations! Your Red Hat Linux installation is complete! If you're not sure what to do next, turn to Chapter 6.

6

What Do I Do Now?

Now that your installation of Red Hat Linux is complete, you might be wondering, "What do I do now?" If so, this chapter is for you. We'll start with some basic things you should know in order to properly start and stop your Red Hat Linux system. Then we'll show you how to do some post-installation configuration so you can set things up just the way *you* want it. But before we do any of that, let's talk about documentation...

6.1 Getting the Documentation That's Right For You

As we mentioned in Section 2.1 on page 8, it is critical to make sure you have documentation that is appropriate to your level of Linux expertise. There is no more certain way to make your experience using Red Hat Linux a failure than to not have the documentation you need, when you need it.

As the name implies, the *Official Red Hat Linux 5.1 Installation Guide* is just that – a guide to installing Red Hat Linux on your system. While we make every effort to give you the information you need to get your Red Hat Linux system running, the Installation Guide can't do it all. For one, the Guide would baloon to more than a thousand pages. Besides, then we'd have to change the title, because it wouldn't be just an "Installation Guide" anymore!

Instead, let's take those categories we discussed back in Section 2.1 on page 8, and let's try to be more explicit in terms of the documentation you'll need. Let's start by figuring out your experience level. Here are the three basic categories:

New To Linux – Has never used any Linux (or Linux-like) operating system before, or has had only limited exposure to Linux. May or may not have experience using other operating systems (such as Windows). Is this you? If so, please turn to Section 6.1.1.

Some Linux Experience – Has installed and successfully used Linux (but not Red Hat Linux) before. Or, may have equivalent experience with other Linux-like operating systems. Does this describe you? If so, please turn to Section 6.1.2 on the next page.

Old Timer – Has installed and sucessfully used Red Hat Linux before. Are you an old-timer? If so, please turn to Section 6.1.3 on the facing page.

6.1.1   Documentation For First-Time Linux Users

"A journey of a thousand miles begins with a single step." This old saying can be applied to just about any endeavor; we're going to apply it to learning to use your Red Hat Linux system. Learning to use a Linux system effectively can be a long, rewarding journey, where you find that you can easily do things that that people with other operating systems can only dream of. But like all journeys, you've got to start somewhere, and take that first step.

And the first step you need to take is to get yourself some documentation! This cannot be stressed enough; without documentation you will only become frustrated at your inability to get your Red Hat Linux system working the way you want.

Here's what you should look for in terms of Linux documentation:

- **An brief history of Linux** – Many aspects of Linux are the way they are because of historical precedent. There is also a Linux culture that, again, is based to a great deal on past history. A bit of knowledge about the history of Linux will serve you well, particularly as you interact with more experienced Linux users on the Internet.

- **An explanation of how Linux works** – While it's not necessary to delve into the most arcane aspects of the Linux kernel, it's a good idea to know something about how Linux is put together. This is particularly important if you've been working with other operating systems; some of the assumptions you hold about how computers work may not transfer from that operating system to Linux. A few paragraphs that discuss how Linux works (and particularly how it differs from the operating system you're used to), can be invaluable in getting off to a good start with your Red Hat Linux system.

- **An introductory command overview (with examples)** – This is probably the most important thing to look for in Linux documentation. The design philosophy behind Linux is that it's better to use many small commands connected together in different ways than it is to have a few large (and complex) commands that do the whole job themselves. Without some examples that illustrate the Linux approach to doing things, you will find yourself intimidated by the sheer number of commands available on your Red Hat Linux system.

As you gain more experience using your Red Hat Linux system, you'll probably find that you'll need more in-depth information. Continue reading the next section to find out more about the kinds of documentation that will help you at that point.

6.1.2 Documentation For More Experienced Linux Users

If you've used other Linux distributions, you probably already have a basic grasp of the most frequently used commands. You may have installed your own Linux system, and maybe you've even downloaded and built software you found on the Internet. What sorts of information will you need?

- **An extensive list of available commands** – While you can find this sort of information on-line in the man pages, you might also want it in book form. While there are several such books on the market, Red Hat sells the *Linux Complete Command Reference*. This book contains the man page entries for hundreds of commands, system calls and file formats, all formatted for easy reading. Best of all, there is a comprehensive index, and a searchable version of the book on CD-ROM. A book like this is invaluable for:

  – Finding the right command for a particular task.

  – Learning how to use that command properly.

- **Task-oriented information** – Many times, you'll find that you'd like to configure your Red Hat Linux system in a certain way, but you're not sure where to begin. In this case, it's often a big help to see what others in similar circumstances have done. This is where the Linux Documentation Project (also known as the LDP) can come in handy. Each of their HOWTOs document a particular aspect of Linux, from low-level kernel esoterica, to using Linux in an amateur radio station.

  If you selected one of the various howto packages when you installed Red Hat Linux, you'll find the HOWTOs on your system in /usr/doc/HOWTO. If, on the other hand, you'd like a printed version of these documents, Red Hat Software sells *Linux Undercover*, which is a compendium of the most popular LDP documents.

6.1.3 Documentation For Linux Gurus

If you're a long-time Red Hat Linux user, you probably already know that the following pretty much says it all when it comes to documentation:

Use the Force – Read the source!

There are times when you'll just have to sit there and look at the sources to understand things. Fortunately, because of the freely available nature of Linux, it's easy to get the sources. Now if it were only that easy to understand them...

Now that we've covered documentation, let's look at some of the most commonly-performed system tasks.

6.2 Basic System Tasks

Remember when everyone upgraded from Windows 3.1 to Windows 95? For a while, people scrambled to figure out how to do the same things under '95 that they had done for a years under 3.x. It's no different here. If you have experience with other operating systems, but not with Linux, you'll need to adjust to different ways of doing things. Some tasks may be similar, some may be entirely different, and some may have no equivalent to anything you've ever done before.

Let's start by going through a few of the more common tasks.

6.2.1 Booting Your Red Hat Linux System

The process required to get your computer running Red Hat Linux may vary a bit from what you're used to. If you have no other operating system installed on your computer, just apply power, and wait. You'll see the computer pause for a moment while it says something about "LILO", but it should continue, displaying all sorts of strange messages.

However, if you are sharing your computer between Red Hat Linux and another operating system, you may have one of the following tasks to perform:

- **Selecting Red Hat Linux at the LILO prompt** – If you elected to install LILO, and you entered boot labels for other partitions containing other operating systems, your computer will be configured to *dual boot*. This means that you can enter the name of the operating system you want to boot at the LILO Boot: prompt. If you press the ⟨Tab⟩ key at the LILO prompt, you'll see a list of the operating systems LILO can boot for you. Select the entry for your Red Hat Linux installation, and you're off and running!

- **Booting from a diskette** – If you created a boot diskette when you installed Red Hat Linux, you can boot from that to get Linux running. Make sure the diskette is inserted in your computer's first diskette drive, and start the boot sequence by applying power, pressing the reset button, or typing the ⟨Ctrl⟩, ⟨Alt⟩, and ⟨Del⟩ keys simultaneously.

6.2.2 Logging In, Logging Out

After Red Hat Linux boots, you'll see something similar to this on your screen:

```
Red Hat Linux release 5.1 (Manhattan)
Kernel 2.0.34 on an i586
login:
```

As you might guess from the last line, it's time to log in...

Logging In

The first time you log into your Red Hat Linux system, you'll have to log in as "root". This is the name of the user account that has full access to everything on the system. Normally, the root account is only used when performing system administration tasks, such as creating new user accounts, shutting down the system, etc. That's because root's unrestricted access can wreak havoc if you enter the wrong command. So be careful when logged in as root, and use the root account only when needed!

To log in, enter root at the login: prompt. Press the [Enter] (or [Return]) key. A Password: prompt should appear. Type the same password you entered back in Section 5.7 on page 72, pressing [Enter] when done. You should then see something like this:

```
[root@bigdog /root]#
```

Congratulations! You've successfully logged in! Next, it's time to learn how to log out.

Logging Out

When you're done using your Red Hat Linux system, you should log out. Although many shells have a logout command, most people simply type [Ctrl]-[D]. This should return you to the login prompt you first saw when you booted your Red Hat Linux system.

Please Note: If you're using the X Window System, your log out procedure will be different, depending on how you've started X. We'll cover this in more detail later.

Now that you know how to log in and out, let's move on...

6.2.3   Accounts and Passwords

As we mentioned earlier, it's a bad idea to use the root account all the time. Inevitably, you'll end up making a mistake, and the access checks that normally protect you won't be there.

Well, if you're not supposed to log in as root, *who* exactly are you supposed to log in as?

Yourself, of course.

But to do that, you'll need to know how to add user accounts to your Red Hat Linux system.

Accounts

As it turns out, there are several different ways of creating new accounts. We'll use the most basic method; the useradd command. Basically, all you need to enter (as root, remember!) is:

```
[root@bigdog /root]# useradd blarg
[root@bigdog /root]#
```

That wasn't very exciting, was it? Well, let's try to login:

```
Red Hat Linux release 5.1 (Manhattan)
Kernel 2.0.34 on an i586
login: blarg
Password:
Login incorrect

login:
```

Not knowing what blarg's password was, we just pressed (Enter). Guess that wasn't the right password. Say, how *do* you specify a password for a new account?

Passwords

The passwd command can be used to:

- Specify passwords for newly-created user accounts.

- Change an already-existing account's password.

- Change the password of the account you're logged into.

The first two scenarios are really one and the same; there's really no difference (as far as passwd is concerned) between an account that's just be created, or one that has existed for the past five years. All you need to remember is that you must be logged in as root, and that you must specify the account name whose password you want to change. Using the account we just created as an example, let's give passwd a try:

```
[root@bigdog /root]# passwd blarg
New UNIX password:
Retype new UNIX password:
passwd: all authentication tokens updated successfully
[root@bigdog /root]#
```

As you might have guessed, the password is not displayed when you enter it. You also have to type the password twice, to make sure you didn't make a mistake while entering it. Let's try logging into the new account again:

```
Red Hat Linux release 5.1 (Manhattan)
Kernel 2.0.34 on an i586
login: blarg
Password:
[blarg@bigdog blarg]$
```

Once you're logged in to an account, you can change that account's password by using the passwd command without the account name. In this case, you will be asked for the account's current password, followed by the new password:

```
[blarg@bigdog blarg]$ passwd
Changing password for blarg
(current) UNIX password:
New UNIX password:
Retype new UNIX password:
passwd: all authentication tokens updated successfully
[blarg@bigdog blarg]$
```

It's as simple as that.

The su Command

There may be times when you'd like to issue a command or two as another user. Normally, system administrators need this capability – they (like all good sysadmins) use their personal, non-privileged account most of the time. But maybe a user's password needs to be changed, or the permissions on a system file need to be modified. Such things only take a minute, so it's a pain logging out, logging in as root, doing whatever it was they needed to do as root, logging out, and – finally – logging back into their personal accounts.

A much simpler approach is to use the su command. With su, your current login session can "become" a root (or other user's) login session. In the following example, user blarg decides they need to do something as root:

```
[blarg@bigdog blarg]$ su
Password:
[root@bigdog blarg]#
```

As you can see, after issuing the su command, the user is prompted for a password – the root password. After it's been entered correctly, the usual shell prompt is displayed. But if you look closely, you'll note that the shell prompt *is* different. For one, it starts with root, indicating that the current user has changed. The other difference is the prompt's ending character, which changed from a dollar sign ($) to a pound sign (#). This is a traditional way of indicating whether a shell is running as root or not.

It's also possible to use su to become another user. To do this, you must run su as root (whether you run su from a root login session, or from an su'ed shell prompt is immaterial), giving only the user's account name. So, for root to become user blarg, one need only issue the command su blarg. No password is required in this case – you're already root, so a password is somewhat redundant.

You'll find that su will come in handy, particularly if you, like most Linux users, act as your own system administrator.

6.2.4   Shutting Down Your Red Hat Linux System

When you're done using your Red Hat Linux system, you'll need to shut it down. However, this is a bit more involved than simply pressing the power switch. Here's why:

Even though *you* may not be running any programs when you're ready to shutdown, that doesn't mean there's nothing running on your Red Hat Linux system. To see what we mean, issue this command:

```
ps ax
```

Each one of the lines displayed by ps represents a *process*. You can think of each process as being a "running program". Each process may be working with files, and if you simply turn off your computer, these processes won't have a chance to close those files, and finish running in a clean manner. So when the time comes to shut your system down, you'll need some way of telling all these processes to finish up, and exit cleanly. And the way this is normally done is with the shutdown command.

The shutdown command can only be run by root, so you'll need to either be logged in as root, or you can use the su command to "become" root. The basic syntax for shutdown is:

```
shutdown <options> <time>
```

Please Note: The shutdown program resides in /sbin. If your PATH environment variable does not include /sbin, you will need to include the full path when you enter the command (i.e., /sbin/shutdown -h now).

In most cases, you should include one of the following options:

- -h – Halt the system when the shutdown is complete.

- -r – Reboot the system when the shutdown is complete.

If you don't include either option, shutdown will bring your system into "single user" mode. Unless you know why you want to be in single-user mode, you probably don't want to be in single-user mode. Simply enter the shutdown command (this time with -h or -r), and the shutdown will complete normally.

The shutdown command also gives you quite a bit of flexibility in terms of timing. If you want to the shutdown to proceed right away, just enter the word "now". If you want to shut the system down five minutes from now, you can enter "+5". Therefore, this command:

```
shutdown -r +15
```

means, "shut the system down starting fifteen minutes from now, and reboot after the shutdown has completed". While shutdown has more options available, we've only described the basics necessary to perform a clean shutdown. If you're interested in learning more, enter man shutdown to learn more about shutdown's capabilities.

6.3   The X Window System

While there are people that will use the character-cell interface present when you first log in, many people prefer a graphically-oriented user interface. For Linux systems, the graphical user interface of choice is the X Window System.

In order to run X, you need to have the necessary packages installed. If you selected the "X Window System" component to be installed when you originally installed Red Hat Linux, everything should be ready to go. In that case, please refer to section 6.3.2 on page 89.

6.3.1   If You Haven't Installed X

If you didn't select the "X Window System" component when you installed Red Hat Linux, your Red Hat Linux system won't have the necessary software installed. While it is possible to manually install the required packages, you'll probably find it easier to re-do the installation, particularly if you're new to Linux.

However, if you'd like to try, the Red Hat FAQ, Section E.8.1 on page 256 does discuss the packages required to manually install X.

XFree86 Configuration

There are three methods for configuring XFree86 on your machine:

- Xconfigurator
- xf86config

- by hand

Xconfigurator and xf86config are functional equivalents and should work equally well. If you are unsure of anything in this process, a good source of additional documentation is:

```
http://www.xfree86.org
```

Xconfigurator is a full-screen menu driven program that walks you through setting up your X server. xf86config is a line oriented program distributed with XFree86. It isn't as easy to use as Xconfigurator, but it is included for completeness. If these utilities fail to provide a working XF86Config file, you may have an unsupported card or you may need to write the config file by hand. Usually the former is the case, so check and make sure your card is supported before attempting to write the config file yourself.If your card is not supported by XFree86 you may wish to consider using a commercial X server. If you have questions about whether or not your video card is supported you can check out http://www.xfree86.org for information on XFree86.

The X Server Provided you selected the proper video card at install time, you should have the proper X server installed. When later running Xconfigurator or xf86config, you need to make sure you select the same video card or the autoprobe will fail.

If you think you installed the wrong X server for your video card, you will have to install the correct one before it can be configured. For instance, if the CD is mounted on /mnt/cdrom, and you need to install the S3 server, enter the following commands:

```
cd /mnt/cdrom/RedHat/RPMS
rpm -ivh XFree86-S3-3.1.2-1.i386.rpm
ln -sf ../../usr/X11R6/bin/XF86_S3 /etc/X11/X
```

This will install the S3 server and make the proper symbolic link.

Xconfigurator To configure X Windows you must first select your video card. Scroll down the list of supported cards until you locate the card in your machine. Figure 6.1 may help you determine the video server that matches your hardware. If your card is not listed it may not be supported by XFree86.In this case you can try the last card entry on the list (Unlisted Card) or a commercial X Windows server.

The next step is to select your monitor. If your monitor is not listed you can select one of the generic monitor entries or "Custom" and enter your own parameters. Custom monitor config-uration is recommended only for those who have a sound understanding of the inner workings of CRT displays. The average user should probably use one of the generic selections from the list. After selecting a monitor you need to tell Xconfigurator how much video memory you have. Move the highlight to the appropriate list entry and then press (Enter) or (F12) to continue. For the next step it is recommended that you select the default (No Clockchip Setting) entry, but experienced users may want to select a specific clockchip.

Selecting your Server   If you are unsure what chipset you have, the best way to find out is usually to look at the card. Figure 6.1 lists which chipsets and boards require which servers. Pick the one that best matches your hardware.

Server	Chipset
8514	IBM 8514/A Boards and true clones
AGX	All XGA graphics boards
I128	#9 Imagine 128 (including Series II) boards
Mach32	ATI boards using the Mach32 chipset
Mach64	ATI boards using the Mach64 chipset
Mach8	ATI boards using the Mach8 chipset
Mono	VGA boards in monochrome
P9000	Diamond Viper (but not the 9100) and Others
S3	#9 Boards, most Diamonds, some Orchids, Others
S3V	Boards using the S3 ViRGE (including DX, GX, VX) chipset
SVGA	Trident 8900 & 9400, Cirrus Logic, C & T, ET4000, S3 ViRGE, Others
VGA16	All VGA boards (16 color only)
W32	All ET4000/W32 cards, but not standard ET4000's

Figure 6.1: XFree86 X Servers

Finishing Up   If later you want to increase your refresh rate for your monitor, you can edit the config file by hand or you can run Xconfigurator again and pick a monitor from our list that more closely matches the specs of your monitor.

The final configuration step consists of selecting the video modes that you want to include in your XF86Config file. Use the arrow keys to move the cursor up and down the list under each color depth (8, 16 and 24 bit). Use the (Spacebar) to select individual resolutions and the (Tab) key to move between color depth fields. When you have selected the video modes you want to use move the cursor to the "OK" button and press (Enter), or use the (F12) shortcut. An information screen will give you the most current information on selecting video modes, starting and stopping the X server.

6.3.2   If You've Already Installed X

If you selected the "X Window System" component when you installed Red Hat Linux, you should be all set. All you'll need to do is to get X running. As it turns out, there are two ways to do this. You can:

- Start X manually after you log in.

- Start X automatically whenever the system boots.

Let's start with the manual procedure.

Starting X Manually

Red Hat Linux, as installed, will not start X automatically for you. Therefore, you'll see the same character-cell login prompt you saw when you first booted your Red Hat Linux system.

In order to get X started, you'll first need to log in. Do so (using your non-root account), and then enter the startx command. The screen should go blank, and (after a short delay) you should see a graphical desktop with one or more windows. The appearance of the desktop you'll see will vary, depending on the packages you installed and other variables.

When you're done, and you'd like to leave X, you can click on any part of the desktop (in other words, the part of the screen without any windows) using your mouse's primary button. Select the "Exit Fvwm", "Quit", or "logout" menu entry, and X will shut down, leaving you at your original character-cell shell prompt. You can then logout as usual.

Starting X Automatically

Please Note: Make sure you verify that your X configuration works properly before making X start automatically. Failure to do so can make it difficult to log into your Red Hat Linux system. If you haven't done so already, review the previous section before continuing.

It is possible to configure your Red Hat Linux system such that X will start automatically whenever the system is booted. When configured in this manner, xdm will run, which will present a graphically-oriented login screen. After logging in, you will have a regular X session running, just as if you had issued a startx command manually. Pretty neat, eh?

Here's a quick overview of how it's done:

- Test xdm using telinit.
- Edit /etc/inittab.
- Reboot.

Let's look at each step in more detail.

Testing xdm **Using** telinit – The telinit command is used to change your Red Hat Linux system's "run level". It is the run level that controls various aspects of system operation, including whether xdm should be started or not. Newly-installed Red Hat Linux systems use run level 3 as their default; this results in the character-cell login prompt you've seen. Since xdm is started at run level 5, you'll need to issue the command:

```
/sbin/telinit 5
```

Please Note: You will need to be logged in as root in order to use `telinit`. Also note that you should *not* be running anything else on your Red Hat Linux system when you change run levels, as any running programs may be killed by the run level change.

If everything is configured properly, after a short delay you should see an xdm login screen. Log in, verifying that an X desktop appears. Then log out to make sure that xdm reappears. If it does, your system is configured properly to automatically start X. If there are problems, you can go back to run level 3 using `telinit` (ie, "`/sbin/telinit 3`"), or by rebooting.

Editing `/etc/inittab` – The file `/etc/inittab` is used to, among other things, determine the system's default run level. We need to change the default run level from 3 to 5; therefore, we'll need to edit `/etc/inittab`. Using the text editor of your choice, change this line in `/etc/inittab`:

```
id:3:initdefault:
```

When you're done, it should look like this:

```
id:5:initdefault:
```

Please Note: Make sure you change *only* the number 3 to be 5! Do not change anything else, otherwise your Red Hat Linux system may not boot at all! When you've made the change, exit the editor, and use this command to review your handiwork:

```
less /etc/inittab
```

(Press the [Space] key to page through the file; [Q] will exit.) If everything looks OK, it's time to reboot.

Rebooting – Refer to Section 6.2.4 on page 86 to properly reboot your Red Hat Linux system. Congratulations! You're now fully graphical (well, your system is, at least)...

Changing Your Desktop

Thanks to wmconfig, it's easy to change the appearance of your desktop. Simply select the **Preferences** menu entry, and (under **WM Style**) you'll be able to pick from several different desktop (also known as window manager) styles. If you want to learn more about the nuts and bolts behind the scenes, read the wmconfig man page for more information.

Handy X-Based Tools

There are several tools that can make life easier for the new Red Hat Linux user. They perform tasks that either require root access, or can only be done by memorizing arcane commands. They all require X to run, so you'll need to get that set up first. These tools are:

- **User Information Tool** – Makes it easy to update your "gecos", or basic account information. Run /usr/bin/userinfo to start it.

- **User Password Tool** – Changing passwords is simple with this tool. It's started by running /usr/bin/userpasswd

- **Filesystem Mounting Tool** – Makes mounting and unmounting filesystems simple. Every user-mountable filesystem must have the user option present in /etc/fstab (see the mount man page for more information on the user option). Run /usr/bin/usermount to start it.

- **Network Device Tool** – Starting and stopping network interfaces becomes a point-and-click operation with this tool. Run /usr/bin/usernet to start this tool. Requires every user-controllable interface to be user-controllable.

6.4 Configuring Your Red Hat Linux System For Sound

By default, the only sound you'll hear out of your newly-installed Red Hat Linux system is the ordinary, boring, default beep. If your computer system has sound hardware, chances are you can make it work under Red Hat Linux. In some cases (particularly with non-Intel systems) sucessfully getting sound support to work requires a kernel rebuild. However, most of the time it's possible to use the modular sound drivers.

6.4.1 Modular Sound Drivers

Modular sound support is only supported for Intel-compatible systems.

In Red Hat Linux 5.1, the standard OSS/Free sound drivers have been modified to be completely modular. This allows for such things as loading and unloading of the various sound drivers without recompiling the kernel tree or rebooting. The work was performed by Alan Cox and was sponsored by Red Hat Software, Inc.

For additional information, please consult the README files in the rhsound documentation directory (/usr/doc/rhsound*). The latest information can always be found at ftp://ftp.redhat.com/pub/sound/.

If you have any issues concerning the modular sound drivers, please send mail to sound-bugs@redhat.com. There is also a mailing list associated with the modular sound drivers

(sound-list@redhat.com). To subscribe, send mail to
sound-list-request@redhat.com with "subscribe" as the subject line.

Supported Sound Cards

At present, only the following sound cards are recognized by the modular sound drivers:

- Sound Blaster 1.0

- Sound Blaster 2.0

- Sound Blaster Pro

- Sound Blaster 16

- Sound Blaster 16 PnP

- Sound Blaster AWE32/AWE64 (In SB-16 mode only)

6.4.2 Sound Card Configuration Tool

Also included in Red Hat Linux 5.1 is sndconfig, a screen-oriented utility that can properly configure modular sound card drivers.

There are a few things that you should know about sndconfig:

Plug and Play Aware – sndconfig is able to detect and configure Plug and Play sound cards such as the Sound Blaster 16 PnP. Please note, however, that the present version of sndconfig creates a new version of the file /etc/isapnp.conf with only the sound card's settings uncommented. Therefore, if you have other Plug and Play devices on your system, you must do one of two things:

- You can manually add your sound card's PnP information to your existing /etc/isapnp.conf, and run sndconfig using the --noprobe option.

- You can run sndconfig without the --noprobe option, and uncomment the configuration information for your other PnP cards in the /etc/isapnp.conf file created by sndconfig.

In any case, note that sndconfig saves your original /etc/isapnp.conf file as /etc/isapnp.conf.bak.

Modifies /etc/conf.modules – sndconfig modifies the module configuration file /etc/conf.modules by adding information about the module options required for your sound card. Note that sndconfig saves your original /etc/conf.modules file as /etc/conf.modules.bak.

To set up your sound card, run /usr/sbin/sndconfig. Note that you must be root in order to run sndconfig. After an initial screen, you'll be asked to select the type of sound card you have (See Figure 6.2).

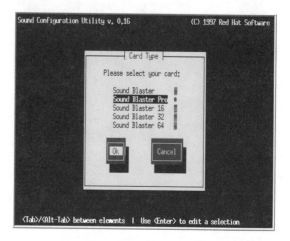

Figure 6.2: Selecting Sound Card Type

After selecting your sound card, you'll see a screen similar to the one in Figure 6.3 on the facing page. Here is where you can specify the settings for your sound card. Using the [Tab] key, select a field. Then use the arrow keys to select the desired setting for that field. When finished, select **Ok**, and press [Space].

After this screen, you may see an informational dialog box saying that /etc/conf.modules already exists. select **Ok** and press [Space] to continue.

Finally, sndconfig will attempt to play a sound sample to verify proper configuration of your sound card. If you can hear the sound sample (make sure the speaker volume is turned up), you're done!

6.5   Mouse configuration

To configure your mouse (or reconfigure your mouse after installation) enter the command /usr/sbin/mouseconfig. Scroll down the list with the arrow keys until your mouse type is highlighted. If you have *any* mouse connected to a PS/2 style port you should select **PS/2** as your mouse type. If you have a mouse connected to a mouse port on an ATI video card you should select **ATI Bus Mouse**. If you have a 2 button mouse and want to emulate the third (middle) mouse button with a simultaneous click of the left and right mouse buttons use [Tab] to

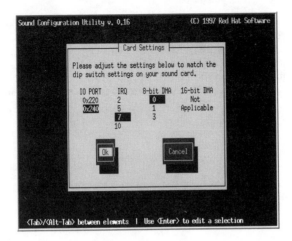

Figure 6.3: Configuring Sound Card

move the cursor to the **Emulate 3 Buttons** checkbox and press $\boxed{\text{Spacebar}}$ to toggle the selection.

6.6   World Wide Web

The World Wide Web is one of the hottest aspects of the Internet today. Red Hat Linux lets you get in on the action in two ways – as a web browser, and as a web server. Let's look at both.

6.6.1   World Wide Web Browsers

A variety of web browsers are available for Linux, including freely distributable browsers such as arena, lynx, and grail. The most popular commercial browsers are those from Netscape Communications Corporation. And now they're available with Red Hat Linux 5.1! If you selected the netscape-communicator or netscape-navigator packages, you're ready to surf. Enjoy!

6.6.2   World Wide Web Server

If you installed the Apache web server (from the apache package), then your Web service is already up and running! Just point your web browser at
http://localhost.

The default page shown is /home/httpd/html/index.html. You can edit this file (or completely replace it) to your liking. All the CGI programs, icons, and html pages are stored in /home/httpd, but this can be changed in the apache configuration files, all of which are stored in /etc/httpd/conf/. Logs of all httpd activity are kept in /var/log/httpd/. Setting up your web site is as easy as adding your own HTML pages and links to the /home/httpd/html/ directory. For more information on customizing your web server we recommend a reference such as *HTML: The Definitive Guide* by Chuck Musciano & Bill Kennedy, published by O'Reilly & Associates.

7

Finding Documentation

Red Hat Linux includes thousands of pages of online documentation to help you learn how to use the system. The man pages, info documents, and plain text files included provide information on almost every aspect of Linux. If you've installed it, Red Hat Linux also includes documentation produced by the Linux Documentation Project.

7.1   On Line Help

When you are looking for general help on commands and error messages, the best place to start is right on your system. There are several different sources of information at your fingertips:

- **Man Pages** – Authoritative reference material for commands, file formats, and system calls.

- **Package Documentation** – Many packages include additional documentation; RPM can help you find it.

- **HOWTOs and FAQs** – Helpful information from the Linux Documentation Project.

- **The** `locate` **Command** – A command that can help bridge the gap between a command and its documentation.

- `info` **Pages** – Hypertext documentation without the Web.

Let's take a look at each information source.

7.1.1   Man Pages

Almost every command on your system has an associated "man" page. This is documentation that you can get to instantly should you have questions or problems. For example, if you were having trouble with the ls command, you could use man to get more information by entering man ls. This will bring up the man page for ls.

The man page is viewed through the less program (which makes it easy to page forward and backward screen by screen), so all of the options to less will work while in a man page. The more important keystrokes for less are:

- q to quit

- Enter to page down line by line

- Space to page down page by page

- b to page back up by one page

- / followed by a string and Enter to search for a string

- n to find the next occurrence of the previous search

There are times when it's just a lot more convenient to read something from a sheet of paper. Providing you have a working printer, you can print man pages as well. If you don't have Postscript printing capability and just want to print ASCII, you can print man pages with:

```
man COMMAND | lpr
```

If you do have a postscript printer, you will probably want to print with:

```
man -t COMMAND | lpr
```

In both of those commands substitute "COMMAND" for the command you are trying to get help for.

Sometimes you'll find that certain system components have more than one man page. Here is a table showing the sections that are used to divide man pages:

Section	Contents
1	user commands
8	system commands
2	system calls
3	library calls
4	devices
5	file formats
6	games
7	miscellaneous
9	kernel internals
n	Tcl/Tk commands

This is also the order in which the sections are searched. This can be important; here's an example:

Let's say that you want to see the man page for the swapon system call. So, you type man swapon. You will actually get the man page for swapon(8), which is actually the command used to control swapping. Using the chart above, you can see that what you want is a "system call" and is located in section 2. You can then type man 2 swapon. All of this is because man searches the man directories in the order shown above, which means that the swapon(8) man page would be found before the swapon(2) man page.

You can also search the man pages for strings. You do this using man -k string_to_search_for. This won't work, however, unless the makewhatis database has been created. Under Red Hat Linux, this is done by a cron job overnight. If you don't leave your system running overnight the database won't get created. If that is the case, run the following command as the root user:

```
/etc/cron.weekly/makewhatis.cron
```

Once you've done that (note that it might take a while), you could enter man -k swapon. That command would return:

```
# man -k swapon
swapon, swapoff (2) - start/stop swapping to file/device
swapon, swapoff (8) - enable/disable devices and files for \
                      paging and swapping
```

So you can see that there are pages in section 2 and 8 both referring to swapon (and swapoff in this case).

How to Read a Man Page

Man pages provide a great deal of information in very little space. Because of this, they can be difficult to read. Here's a quick overview of the major sections in most man pages:

- **Name** – The name of the program or programs documented in the man page. There may be more than one name, if the programs are closely related.

- **Synopsis** – An overview of the program's command syntax, showing all options and arguments.

- **Description** – A short description of the program's function.

- **Options** – A list of all options, with a short description of each (often combined with the previous section).

- **See Also** – If present, lists the names of other programs that are related in some way to this program.

- **Files** – If present, contains a list of files that are used and/or modified by the program.

- **History** – If present, indicates important milestones in the program's development.

- **Authors** – The people that wrote the program.

If you are new to Linux, don't expect to be able to use man pages as tutorials; they are meant as concise reference material. Trying to learn about Linux using the man pages is similar to trying to learn how to speak English from reading a dictionary. But there are other sources of information that may be more useful to those people just starting out with Linux; let's continue our search for documentation. . .

7.1.2 Package Documentation

Many packages have README files and other documentation as part of the source package. Packages built for Red Hat Linux define a standard place to install those documents so that you don't have to search through the sources to find the documents. Every package containing documentation (other than man pages, and files that need to be in specific locations) places their documentation in a subdirectory of /usr/doc.

The name of the subdirectory depends on the package name and version number. For example, For example, the tin package might be at version 1.22. Therefore, the path to its documentation would be /usr/doc/tin-1.22.

For the most part, the documents in /usr/doc are in ASCII. You can view them with more filename or less filename.

Having this special documentation area can be handy, but what if you're looking for documentation on a specific command (or file), and you don't know what package that command came from? No problem! Take, for example, the file /usr/bin/rtin. You're not sure what package it's part of, but you'd like to learn a bit more about it. Simply enter:

```
rpm -qdf /usr/bin/rtin
```

This command will return a listing of all the documentation (including man pages) from the package containing the file /usr/bin/rtin. RPM is capable of a lot more than this simple example. For more information on RPM, turn to Chapter 8 on page 105.

Of course, maybe this kind of information is not exactly what you're looking for. Maybe you're more interested in task-oriented documentation. If so, read on...

7.1.3   HOWTOs and FAQs

If you elected to install it, most of the contents of the Linux Documentation Project (LDP) are available in /usr/doc on your system.

The directory /usr/doc/HOWTO contains the ASCII versions of all the available HOWTOs at the time your Red Hat Linux CD-ROM was mastered. They are compressed with gzip to save space, so you'll need to decompress them before reading. One way of reading compressed HOW-TOs without cluttering your disk with uncompressed versions is to use zless:

```
zless 3Dfx-HOWTO.gz
```

The zless command uses the same keystrokes as less, so you can easily move back and forth through a HOWTO.

/usr/doc/HOWTO/mini contains the ASCII versions of all the available mini-HOWTOs. They are not compressed and can be viewed with more or less.
/usr/doc/HOWTO/other-formats/html contains the HTML versions of all the HOWTOs and the *Linux Installation and Getting Started* guide. To view things here, just use the web browser of your choice.

/usr/doc/FAQ contains ASCII versions (and some HTML versions) of some popular FAQs, including the RedHat-FAQ. They can be viewed using more or less, or (in the case of HTML files) with the web browser of your choice.

7.1.4   The "locate" Command

When you don't know the full name of a command or file, but need to find it, you can usually find it with locate. locate uses a database to find all files on your system. Normally, this database gets built from a cron job every night. This won't happen, however, if your machine isn't booted into Linux all the time. So, if that is the case, you may occasionally want to run the following command:

```
/etc/cron.daily/updatedb.cron
```

You will need to be root on your system when doing that. That will allow locate to work properly.

So, if you know you need to find all the "finger" files, you could run:

```
locate finger
```

It should return something like:

```
/usr/bin/finger
/usr/lib/irc/script/finger
/usr/man/man1/finger.1
/usr/man/man8/in.fingerd.8
/usr/sbin/in.fingerd
```

One thing to note, however, is that locate not only returns hits based on file name, but also on path name. So if you have a /home/djb/finger/ directory on your system, it would get returned along with all files in the directory.

7.1.5 "info" Pages

While man is the most ubiquitous documentation format, info is much more powerful. It provides hypertext links to make reading large documents much easier and many features for the documentation writer. There are some very complete info documents on various aspects of Red Hat (especially the portions from the GNU project).

To read info documentation, use the info program without any arguments. It will present you with a list of available documentation. If it can't find something, it's probably because you don't have the package installed that includes that documentation. Install it with RPM and try again.

If you're comfortable using emacs, it has a built in browser for info documentation. Use the (Ctrl-h) (i) key sequence to see it.

The info system is a hypertext based system. Any highlighted text that appears is a link leading to more information. Use (Tab) to move the cursor to the link, and press (Enter) to follow the link. Pressing (p) returns you to the previous page, (n) moves you to the next page, and (u) goes up one level of documentation. To exit info, press (Ctrl-x) (Ctrl-c) (control-x followed by control-c).

The best way to learn how to use info is to read the info documentation on it. If you read the first screen that info presents you'll be able to get started.

7.2 Help from the Internet Community

7.2.1 Red Hat Mailing Lists

If you can't find help for your problem on line and you have WWW access, you should see
http://www.redhat.com/support/mailing-lists/. Here you can search the archives
of the redhat-list. Many questions have already been answered there.

The subscription addresses for our lists follow this format:

```
<list-name>-request@redhat.com
```

Simply replace <list-name> with one of the following:

```
applixware-list
axp-list
blinux-list
cde-list
gnome-announce
gtk-list
hurricane-list
linux-alert
linux-security
m68k-list
pam-list
redhat-announce-list
redhat-devel-list
redhat-install-list
redhat-list
redhat-ppp-list
rpm-list
sound-list
sparc-list
```

To subscribe, send mail to the address of the list you want to subscribe to with subscribe in
the Subject: line.

To unsubscribe, send mail to the address of the list you want to unsubscribe from with
unsubscribe in the Subject: line.

Then to send mail to the list, you just send it to the address above without the -request in the
name.

7.2.2 USENET Newsgroups

Another good source of help is the comp.os.linux hierarchy on USENET. If you are familiar
with news, you should check it out.

Red Hat-Specific Newsgroups

Red Hat Software currently hosts a number of newgroups specifically for users of our software. You can either read these groups directly from news.redhat.com, or ask your news admin to add the redhat.* hierarchy to their news server.

8

Package Management with RPM

The Red Hat Package Manager (RPM), is an open packaging system available for anyone to use, and works on both Red Hat Linux as well as other Linux and UNIX systems. Red Hat Software encourages other vendors to take the time to look at RPM and use it for their own products. RPM is distributable under the terms of the GPL.

For the end user, RPM provides many features that make maintaining a system far easier than it has ever been. Installing, uninstalling, and upgrading RPM packages are all one line commands, and all the messy details are taken care of for you. RPM maintains a database of installed packages and their files, which allows you to perform powerful queries and verification of your system. During upgrades RPM handles configuration files specially, so that you never lose your customizations – a feature that is impossible with straight .tar.gz files.

For the developer, RPM allows you to take source code for software and package it into source and binary packages for end users. This process is quite simple and is driven from a single file and optional patches that you create. This clear delineation of "pristine" sources and your patches and build instructions eases the maintenance of the package as new versions of the software are released.

8.1   RPM Design Goals

Before trying to understand how to use RPM, it helps to have an idea of what the design goals are.

Upgradability With RPM you can upgrade individual components of your system without completely reinstalling. When you get a new release of an operating system based on RPM (such as Red Hat Linux), you don't need to reinstall your machine (as you do with operating systems based on other packaging systems). RPM allows intelligent, fully-automated, in-place upgrades of your system. Configuration files in packages are preserved across upgrades, so you won't lose your customizations.

Powerful Querying RPM is also designed to have powerful querying options. You can do searches through your entire database for packages or just certain files. You can also easily find out what package a file belongs to and where it came from. The files an RPM package contains are in a compressed archive, with a custom binary header containing useful information about the package and its contents, allowing you to query individual packages quickly and easily.

System Verification Another powerful feature is the ability to verify packages. If you are worried that you deleted an important file for some package, simply verify the package. You will be notified of any anomalies. At that point, you can reinstall the package if necessary. Any configuration files that you modified are preserved during reinstallation.

Pristine Sources A crucial design goal was to allow the use of "pristine" software sources, as distributed by the original authors of the software. With RPM, you have the pristine sources along with any patches that were used, plus complete build instructions. This is a big advantage for several reasons. For instance, if a new version of a program comes out, you don't necessarily have to start from scratch to get it to compile. You can look at the patch to see what you *might* need to do. All the compiled-in defaults, and all of the changes that were made to get the software to build properly are easily visible this way.

This goal may only seem important for developers, but it results in higher quality software for end users too. We would like to thank the folks from the BOGUS distribution for originating the pristine source concept.

8.2   Using RPM

RPM has five basic modes of operation (not counting package building): installing, uninstalling, upgrading, querying, and verifying. This section contains an overview of each mode. For complete details and options try rpm --help, or turn to Section 8.4 on page 113 for more information on RPM.

8.2.1   Installing

RPM packages typically have file names like foo-1.0-1.i386.rpm, which includes the package name (foo), version (1.0), release (1), and architecture (i386). Installing a package is as simple as:

```
$ rpm -ivh foo-1.0-1.i386.rpm
foo                              ###################################
```

As you can see, RPM prints out the name of the package (which is not necessarily the same as the file name, which could have been 1.rpm), and then prints a succession of hash marks as the package is installed, as a sort of progress meter.

Installing packages is designed to be simple, but you can get a few errors:

Package Already Installed

If the package is already installed, you will see:

```
$ rpm -ivh foo-1.0-1.i386.rpm
foo                      package foo-1.0-1 is already installed
error: foo-1.0-1.i386.rpm cannot be installed
```

If you really want to install the package anyway, you can use --replacepkgs on the command line, which tells RPM to ignore the error.

Conflicting Files

If you attempt to install a package that contains a file that has already been installed by another packages, you'll see:

```
# rpm -ivh foo-1.0-1.i386.rpm
foo            /usr/bin/foo conflicts with file from bar-1.0-1
error: foo-1.0-1.i386.rpm cannot be installed
```

To cause RPM to ignore that error, use --replacefiles on the command line.

Unresolved Dependency

RPM packages can "depend" on other packages, which means that they require other packages to be installed in order to run properly. If you try to install a package for which there is such an unresolved dependency, you'll see:

```
$ rpm -ivh bar-1.0-1.i386.rpm
failed dependencies:
        foo is needed by bar-1.0-1
```

To handle this error you should install the requested packages. If you want to force the installation anyway (a bad idea since the package probably will not run correctly), use --nodeps on the command line.

8.2.2 Uninstalling

Uninstalling a package is just as simple as installing:

```
$ rpm -e foo
```

Notice that we used the package *name* "foo", not the name of the original package *file* "foo-1.0-1.i386.rpm".

You can encounter a dependency error when uninstalling a package if some other installed package depends on the one you are trying to remove. For example:

```
$ rpm -e foo
removing these packages would break dependencies:
        foo is needed by bar-1.0-1
```

To cause RPM to ignore that error and uninstall the package anyway (which is a bad idea since the package that depend on it will probably fail to work properly), use --nodeps on the command line.

8.2.3 Upgrading

Upgrading a package is almost just like installing.

```
$ rpm -Uvh foo-2.0-1.i386.rpm
foo                                 ##################################
```

What you don't see above is the fact that RPM automatically uninstalled any old versions of the foo package. In fact you may want to always use -U to install packages, since it works fine even when there are no previous versions of the package installed.

Since RPM performs intelligent upgrading of packages with configuration files, you may see a message like:

```
saving /etc/foo.conf as /etc/foo.conf.rpmsave
```

This means that your changes to the configuration file may not be "forward compatible" with the new configuration file in the package, so RPM saved your original file, and installed a new one. You should investigate and resolve the differences between the two files as soon as possible to ensure that your system continues to function properly.

Since upgrading is really a combination of uninstalling and installing, you can encounter any errors from those modes, plus one more: If RPM thinks you are trying to upgrade to a package with an *older* version number, you will see:

```
$ rpm -Uvh foo-1.0-1.i386.rpm
foo    package foo-2.0-1 (which is newer) is already installed
error: foo-1.0-1.i386.rpm cannot be installed
```

To cause RPM to "upgrade" anyway, use --oldpackage on the command line.

8.2.4 Querying

Querying the database of installed packages is accomplished with rpm -q. A simple use is rpm -q foo which will print the package name, version, and release number of the installed package foo:

```
$ rpm -q foo
foo-2.0-1
```

Instead of specifying the package name, you can use the following options with -q to specify what package(s) you want to query. These are called *Package Specification Options*.

- -a queries all currently installed packages.
- -f <file> will query the package owning <file>.
- -p <packagefile> queries the package <packagefile>.

There are a number of ways to specify what information to display about queried packages. The following options are used to select the information you are interested in. These are called *Information Selection Options*.

- -i displays package information such as name, description, release, size, build date, install date, vendor, and other miscellaneous information.

- -l displays the list of files that the package "owns".

- -s displays the state of all the files in the package.

- -d displays a list of files marked as documentation (man pages, info pages, README's, etc).

- -c displays a list of files marked as configuration files. These are the files you change after installation to adapt the package to your system (sendmail.cf, passwd, inittab, etc).

For those options that display file lists, you can add -v to your command line to get the lists in a familiar ls -1 format.

8.2.5 Verifying

Verifying a package compares information about files installed from a package with the same information from the original package. Among other things, verifying compares the size, MD5 sum, permissions, type, owner and group of each file.

rpm -V verifies a package. You can use any of the *Package Selection Options* listed for querying to specify the packages you wish to verify. A simple use is rpm -V foo which verifies that all the files in the foo package are as they were when they were originally installed. For example:

- To verify a package containing particular file:

  rpm -Vf /bin/vi

- To verify ALL installed packages:

  rpm -Va

- To verify an installed package against an RPM package file:

  rpm -Vp foo-1.0-1.i386.rpm

  This can be useful if you suspect that your RPM databases are corrupt.

If everything verified properly there will be no output. If there are any discrepancies they will be displayed. The format of the output is a string of 8 characters, a possible "c" denoting a config- uration file, and then the file name. Each of the 8 characters denotes the result of a comparison of one attribute of the file to the value of that attribute recorded in the RPM database. A single "." (period) means the test passed. The following characters denote failure of certain tests:

5 MD5 checksum

S File size

L Symbolic link

T File modification time

D Device

U User

G Group

M Mode (includes permissions and file type)

If you see any output, use your best judgment to determine if you should remove or reinstall the package, or somehow fix the problem.

8.3   Impressing Your Friends with RPM

RPM is a very useful tool for both managing your system and diagnosing and fixing problems. The best way to make sense of all the options is to look at some examples.

- Let's say you delete some files by accident, but you aren't sure what you deleted. If you want to verify your entire system and see what might be missing, you would enter:

```
rpm -Va
```

If some files are missing, or appear to have been corrupted, you should probably either re-install the package or uninstall, then re-install the package.

- Let's say you run across a file that you don't recognize. To find out which package owns it, you would enter:

```
rpm -qf /usr/X11R6/bin/xjewel
```

The output would look like:

```
xjewel-1.6-1
```

- We can combine the above two examples in the following scenario. Say you are having problems with /usr/bin/paste. You would like to verify the package that owns that program but you don't know which package that is. Simply enter:

```
rpm -Vf /usr/bin/paste
```

and the appropriate package will be verified.

- If you are using a program and want to find out more information about it, you can enter the following to find out what documentation came with the package that "owns" that program (in this case ispell):

```
rpm -qdf /usr/bin/ispell
```

The output would be:

```
/usr/man/man4/ispell.4
/usr/man/man4/english.4
/usr/man/man1/unsq.1
/usr/man/man1/tryaffix.1
/usr/man/man1/sq.1
/usr/man/man1/munchlist.1
/usr/man/man1/ispell.1
/usr/man/man1/findaffix.1
/usr/man/man1/buildhash.1
/usr/info/ispell.info.gz
/usr/doc/ispell-3.1.18-1/README
```

- You find a new koules RPM, but you don't know what it is. To find out some information on it, enter:

```
rpm -qip koules-1.2-2.i386.rpm
```

The output would be:

```
Name         : koules Distribution: Red Hat Linux Colgate
Version      : 1.2            Vendor: Red Hat Software
Release      : 2          Build Date: Mon Sep 02 11:59:12 1996
Install date: (none)      Build Host: porky.redhat.com
Group        : Games      Source RPM: koules-1.2-2.src.rpm
Size         : 614939
Summary      : SVGAlib action game; multiplayer, network
Description  :
This arcade-style game is novel in conception and
excellent in execution.  No shooting, no blood, no guts,
no gore.  The play is simple, but you still must develop
skill to play.  This version uses SVGAlib to run on a
graphics console.
```

- Now you want to see what files the koules RPM installs. You would enter:

```
rpm -qlp koules-1.2-2.i386.rpm
```

The output is:

```
/usr/man/man6/koules.6
/usr/lib/games/kouleslib/start.raw
/usr/lib/games/kouleslib/end.raw
/usr/lib/games/kouleslib/destroy2.raw
```

```
/usr/lib/games/kouleslib/destroy1.raw
/usr/lib/games/kouleslib/creator2.raw
/usr/lib/games/kouleslib/creator1.raw
/usr/lib/games/kouleslib/colize.raw
/usr/lib/games/kouleslib
/usr/games/koules
```

These are just several examples. As you use the system you will find many more uses for rpm.

8.4   Other RPM Resources

For more information on RPM, check out the man page, the help screen (rpm --help), and the RPM documents available at

```
http://www.rpm.org/
```

There is also an RPM book available. It's called Maximum RPM , and is available from Red Hat Software and your local bookstore. It contains a wealth of information about RPM for both the end-user and the package builder. An on-line version of the book is available at http://www.rpm.org/.

There is also a mailing list for discussion of RPM related issues, called rpm-list@redhat.com. The list is archived on http://www.redhat.com/support/mailing-lists/. To subscribe, send mail to rpm-list-request@redhat.com with the word subscribe in the subject line.

9

Control Panel

Please Note: The introduction of linuxconf with Red Hat Linux 5.1 gives our customers a more comprehensive system configuration utility. Most of what can be done with the control panel applications can also be done using linuxconf. In addition, linuxconf supports both character-cell *and* graphical user interfaces. Please refer to Section 1.2.1 on page 3 for an introduction to linuxconf.

The control panel is a launching pad for a number of different system administration tools (See Figure 9.1 on the following page). These tools make your life easier by letting you configure things without remembering configuration file formats and awkward command line options.

To start the control-panel, start the X Window System as root with startx and type control-panel in an xterm. You will need to be root to run the control-panel tools success-fully. You can do this as well if you already have X running as a normal user. Just type su -c control-panel and then type the root password when prompted. If you plan to do other tasks as root, you could type su followed by the root password when prompted.

Clicking on an icon starts up a tool. Please note that you are not prevented from starting two instances of any tool, but doing so is a very bad idea because you may try to edit the same files in two places and end up overwriting your own changes. If you do accidentally start a second copy of a tool, you should quit it immediately. Also, do not manually edit any files managed by the control-panel tools while the tools are running. Similarly, do not run any other programs that may change those files while the tools are running.

Figure 9.1: The Control Panel

9.1   User and Group Configuration

Please Note: User and group configuration can now be done using linuxconf; please turn to Section 1.2.1 on page 3 for information on linuxconf.

9.2   File System Configuration

The file system configuration tool shown in Figure 9.2 allows you to easily examine and manipulate file system mount points, types, options, etc. It is very useful for manipulating a large number of file systems. You probably don't want to do this unless you are an experienced system administrator. If you do know what you are doing, it should be fairly straightforward as to how to mount, unmount, and add devices.

The **Reload** entry in the **FSM** menu causes the file system configuration tool to re-load /etc/fstab from your hard drive. If you edit /etc/fstab by hand while the file system configuration tool is running (which you shouldn't do), you probably want to reload.

To use the buttons along the bottom of the window, select a filesystem in the main window, and click on one of the buttons. The buttons perform the following functions:

- **Info**: Displays information on the filesystem, including the device, partition type, filesystem type, mount point and options, comment, size, percent used, etc.

- **Check**: Performs a filesystem check (fsck) on the partition. You can do this only on *unmounted* partitions — if the partition is mounted, you will get an error and you will have to unmount it first.

- **Mount**: Mounts the selected filesystem.

- **Unmount**: Unmounts the selected filesystem.

- **Format**: Creates a new filesystem on the selected partition. This will erase all data on the selected partition! You can do this only on *unmounted* partitions — if the partition is mounted, you will get an error and you will have to unmount it first.

- **Edit**: Brings up a dialog box where you can edit the mount point, mount options, comment, etc.

9.2.1 Adding NFS Mounts

To mount a filesystem via NFS, select **Add Mount** from the **NFS** menu. A dialog box will appear and you will have to fill in the following values:

- **Device**: Enter the host name and path, separated by a colon. For example, `foo.bar.com:/usr/exported` indicates the `/usr/exported` directory on `foo.bar.com`.

- **Mount Point**: Enter the directory on your machine where you want to mount the NFS filesystem. For example, `/mnt/foo`.

- **Options**: Enter the mount options for this filesystem. The default is `soft,intr,rw`. The `rw` means the filesystem is read-write, and `soft,intr` are options that make your system a little more resilient when the remote server goes down. See the mount man page for a complete list of available options.

- **Comment**: This optional field can be used to store a small comment.

After filling everything out properly, click on **OK**. At this point the entry is made in your `/etc/fstab`, but the filesystem is not actually mounted. To mount it, select it in the main window and click on **Mount**.

9.3 Printer Configuration

The printer configuration tool (`printtool`) maintains `/etc/printcap`, print spool directories, and print filters. The filters allow you to print many different types of files, including:

- plain text (ASCII) files

- PostScript files

- TeX `.dvi` files

- GIF, JPEG, TIFF, and other graphics formats

Figure 9.2: File System Configuration Panel

- RPMs

Simply printing a GIF or RPM file using `lpr` does "the right thing".

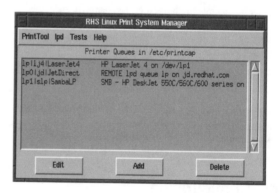

Figure 9.3: Print Tool

In order to create a new *print queue*, choose **Add**. Then, select what type of printer is being added. There are 3 types of print queues which can be configured with printtool:

- **Local**: print queues are for printers attached to a printer or serial port on your Red Hat Linux system.

- **Remote**: print queues are attached to a different system which you can access over a TCP/IP network.

- **SMB**: print queues are attached to a different system which uses LAN-Manager-type (SMB) networking.

Figure 9.4: Selecting a Printer Type

After you choosing the printer type, a dialog requests further information about the print queue. All types of print queues require the following information:

- **Queue Name**: What the queue will be called. Multiple names can be specifed with the | (pipe) character separating entries.

- **Spool Directory**: This is the directory on the local machine where files are stored before printing occurs. Be careful to not have more than one printer queue use a given spool directory.

- **File Limit**: Maximum size print job accepted, in kilobytes (1 kb = 1024 bytes). A size of 0 indicates no limit should be imposed.

- **Input Filter**: Filters convert printed files into a format the printer can handle. Press **Select** to choose the filter which best matches your printer.

  In addition to configuring print queue able to print graphical and PostScript output you can configure a *text-only* printer, which will only print plain ASCII text. Most printer drivers are also able to print ASCII text without converting it to PostScript first; simply choose **Fast text printing** when you configure the filter. **Please Note:** This only works for non-PostScript printers.

- **Suppress Headers**: Check this if you don't want a header page to be printed at the beginning of each print job.

For *local* printers, the following are also required:

- **Printer Device**: Usually /dev/lp1, the name of the port which the printer is attached to. Serial printers are usually on /dev/ttyS? ports. You will need to manually configure serial parameters.

For *remote* printers, fill in the following information:

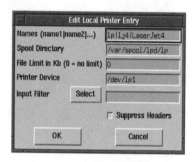

Figure 9.5: Adding a Local Printer

- **Remote Host**: Hostname of the remote machine hosting the printer.

- **Remote Queue**: Name of the queue to print to on the remote machine.

The remote machine must be configured to allow the local machine to print on the desired queue. Typically /etc/hosts.lpd controls this.

For *SMB* printers, fill in the following information:

- **Hostname of Printer Server**: Name of the machine to which the printer you want to use is attached.

- **IP number of Server**: The IP address of the machine to which the printer you want to use is attached; this is optional.

- **Printer Name**: Name of the printer on which you want to print.

- **User**: Name of user you must login as to access the printer (typically guest for Windows servers, or nobody for samba servers).

- **Password**: Password (if required) to use the printer (typically blank). Someone should be able to tell you this if you do not already know it.

Please Note: If you need to use a username and password for an SMB (LAN Manager) print queue, they are stored unencrypted in a local script and must be passed on the command line to the smbclient program. Thus, it is possible for another person to learn the username and password. It is therefore recommended that the username and password for use of the printer not to be the same as that for a user account on the local Red Hat Linux system, so that the only possible security compromise would be unauthorized use of the printer. If there are file shares from the SMB server, it is recommended that they also use a different password than the one for the print queue.

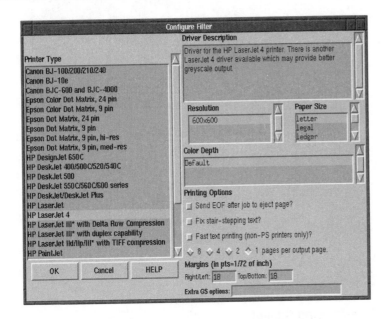

Figure 9.6: Configuring a Print Filter

After you have added your print queue, you may need to restart the printer daemon (lpd). To do so, choose **Restart lpd** from the **lpd** menu.

You may print a *test page* for any print queue you have configured. Select the type of test page you would like to print from the **Tests** menu.

9.4 Network Configuration

The network configuration tool (netcfg) shown in Figure 9.9 is designed to allow easy manipulation of parameters such as IP address, gateway address, and network address, as well as name servers and /etc/hosts.

Network devices can be added, removed, configured, activated, deactivated and aliased. Ethernet, arcnet, token ring, pocket (ATP), PPP, SLIP, PLIP and loopback devices are supported. PPP/SLIP/PLIP support works well on most hardware, but some hardware setups may exhibit unpredictable behavior. When using the Network Configuration Tool click **Save** to write your changes to disk, to quit without making any changes select **Quit**.

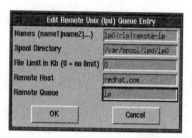

Figure 9.7: Adding a Remote Printer

Figure 9.8: Printing a Test Page

9.4.1 Managing Names

The **Names** panel of the Network Configuration tool serves two primary purposes: setting the hostname and domain of the computer, and determining which name server will be used to look up other hosts on the network. The Network tool is not capable of configuring a machine as a nameserver. To edit a field or add information to a field simply click on the field with the left mouse button and type the new information.

9.4.2 Managing Hosts

In the **Hosts** management panel you have the ability to add, edit, or remove hosts from the /etc/hosts file. Adding or editing an entry involves identical actions. An edit dialog box will appear, simply type the new information and click **Done** when you are finished. See Figure 9.10 for an example.

9.4.3 Adding a Networking Interface

If you have added a networking interface to your machine since installing Red Hat Linux, or you didn't configure your ethernet card at install time, you can configure it with a few clicks of a mouse.

Please Note: You may need to configure kerneld to load a driver for the network interface you are adding (e.g., eth0); see Section 9.6 for more information.

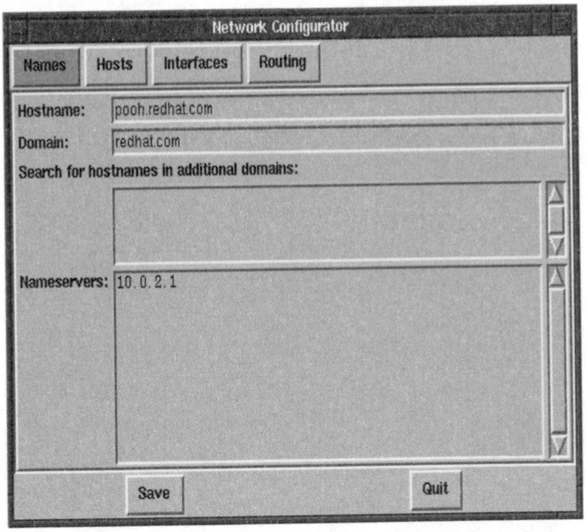

Figure 9.9: Network Configuration Panel

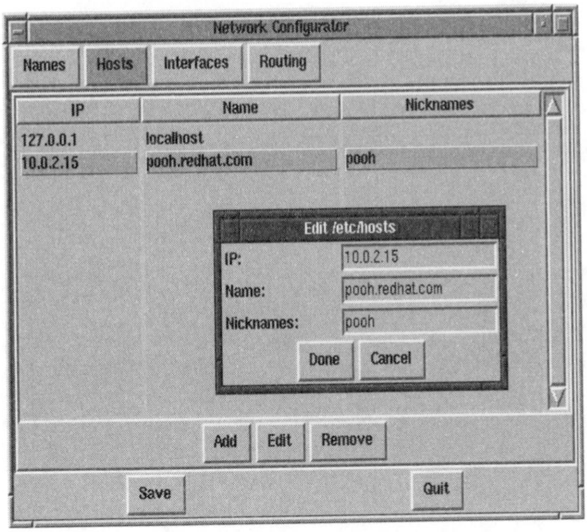

Figure 9.10: Adding/Editing Hosts

Begin adding an interface by clicking on **Interfaces** in the main panel. This will bring up a
window of configured devices with a row of available options, see figure 9.11.

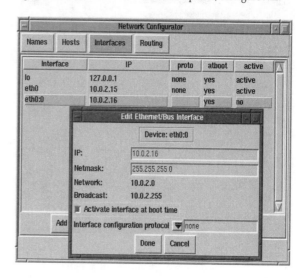

Figure 9.11: Configured Interfaces

To add a device, first click the **Add** button then select the type of interface you want to configure
from the box that appears (See Figure 9.12).

Please Note: There is now a **clone** button available in `netcfg`. This button can be used to create
a "clone" of an already-existing interface. By using clone interfaces, it is possible for a laptop to
have one Ethernet interface defined for a work LAN, and a clone Ethernet device defined for a
home LAN.

PPP Interface

Adding a PPP interface can be as simple as supplying the phone number, login name and password in the **Create PPP Interface** dialog shown in Figure 9.13. If you need to use PAP authentication for your PPP connection, choose **Use PAP authentication**. In many cases some degree
of customization will be needed to establish a PPP connection. Choosing the **Customize** button
will allow you to make changes to the hardware, communication, and networking settings for
the PPP interface.

Figure 9.12: Choose Interface Type

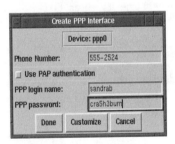

Figure 9.13: Create PPP Interface

SLIP Interface

In order to configure a SLIP interface you must first supply a phone number, login name, and password. This will supply the initial parameters for the chat script needed to establish a SLIP connection. When you choose **Done**, a dialog titled **Edit SLIP Interface** appears that enables you to further customize the hardware, communication and networking parameters for your SLIP interface.

PLIP Interface

To add a PLIP interface to your system you only have to supply the IP address, the remote IP address, and the Netmask. You can also select if you want to activate the interface at boot time.

Ethernet, Arcnet, Token Ring and Pocket Adaptor Interfaces

If you are adding an ethernet, arcnet, token ring or pocket adapter to your computer you will need to supply the following information:

- **Device**: This is determined by netconfig based on the devices already configured.

- **IP Address**: Enter an IP address for your network device.

- **Netmask**: Enter the network mask for your network device.

  The network and broadcast addresses are calculated automatically based on the IP address and netmask you enter.

- **Activate interface at boot time**: If you want the device to be configured automatically when your machine boots select this by clicking on the box.

- **Allow any user to (de)activate interface**: Check this if you want any user to be able to activate or deactivate the interface.

- **Interface configuration protocol**: If you have a BOOTP or DHCP server on your network and would like to use it to configure the interface, choose the appropriate option; otherwise, choose **none**.

After providing the configuration information for your new device, click **Done**. The device should appear in your **Interfaces** list as an inactive device. (The active column should have a label of **no**). To activate the new device, first select it with a mouse click and then choose on the **Activate** button. If it does not come up properly, you may need to reconfigure it by choosing on **Edit**.

9.4.4 Managing Routes

In the Routes management screen you have the ability to add, edit, or remove static networking routes. Adding or editing an entry involves identical actions, just like the Hosts panel. An edit dialog box will appear, simply type the new information and click **Done** when you are finished. See figure 9.14 for an example.

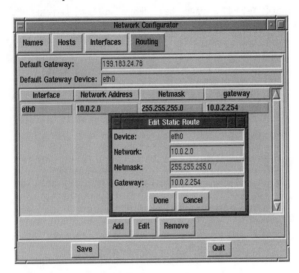

Figure 9.14: Adding/Editing Routes

9.5 Time and Date

The time machine allows you to change the time and date by clicking on the appropriate part of the time and date display and clicking on the arrows to change the value.

The system clock is not changed until you click on the **Set System Clock** button.

Click on **Reset Time** to set the time machine time back to that of the system.

Please Note: Changing the time can seriously confuse programs that depend on the normal progression of time, and could possibly cause problems. Try to quit as many applications and processes as possible before changing the time or date.

9.6   Kernel Daemon Configuration

Red Hat Linux includes kerneld, the Kernel Daemon, which automatically loads some software and hardware support into memory as it is needed, and unloads it when it is no longer being used.

The tool shown in Figure 9.15 manages the configuration file for kerneld. While kerneld can load some things, such as filesystems, without explicit configuration, it needs to be told what hardware support to load when it is presented with a generic hardware request.

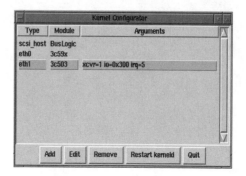

Figure 9.15: Kernel Module Management

For instance, when the kernel wants to load support for ethernet, kerneld needs to know which ethernet card you have, and if your ethernet card requires special configuration, it needs to know about that, too.

9.6.1   Changing Module Options

To change the options being given to a module when it is loaded, click on the line to select it, then click the **Edit** button. kernelcfg will bring up a window which looks like Figure 9.16. The options kernelcfg knows about (normally all available options) will each have their own field. Normally, you will want to ignore the **Other arguments** field. Some modules normally take no arguments; just in case, they have an **Arguments** field which allows you to enter configuration information.

9.6.2   Changing Modules

To change which module gets invoked to provide a generic service, such as an ethernet card or SCSI host adapter module, you need to delete the old one and add a new one. To delete

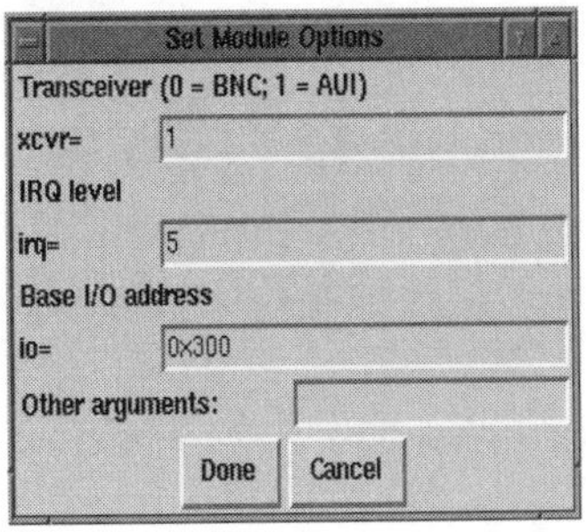

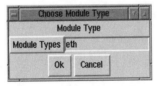

Figure 9.16: Editing Module Options

a module, select it by clicking on it, then click on **Delete**. Then click on **Add** to add the new module, as explained in the following section.

If you have changed your SCSI controller (scsi_hostadapter), remember to make a new initial ramdisk with the /sbin/mkinitrd command as documented in section 11.4.2.

9.6.3   Adding Modules

To add a module of any type, click on the **Add** button. You will be presented with a dialog box (Figure 9.17) asking you to choose a module type. Ethernet is eth, Token Ring is tr, SCSI controllers are scsi_hostadapter, and so on. Click **OK** to continue to

Figure 9.17: Adding a module

the next dialog box. If there is more than one module which can be used for the module type you have chosen, you will be presented with a dialog box (Figure 9.18) which asks which module you want to use, and may also ask for specifics about the type of module; for ethernet, for example, you need to choose from eth0, eth1, etc. When you are done, click **OK** again to continue to specify any module options in the next dialog box (Figure 9.18), which is the same as the dialog for editing a module.

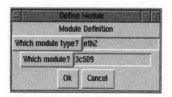

Figure 9.18: Selecting from available modules

9.6.4   Restarting Kerneld

The changes that you make with the Kernel Daemon Configuration tool will be made in the
/etc/conf.modules file, which kerneld reads whenever it is started. Once you have made
changes, you can restart kerneld by clicking on the **Restart kerneld** button. This will **not** cause
any modules which are currently in use to be reloaded, it will only notify kerneld to use the
configuration when it loads more modules in the future.

10

Glint

Red Hat provides a graphical tool to aid in package installation and removal. It's called glint (Graphical Linux INstallation Tool) and runs under the X Window System. It allows easy installation, uninstallation, upgrading, querying, and verification of packages. The interface is similar to the one found in many popular file managers and is simple to use.

Operations are performed in glint by selecting the packages to operate on and then selecting the operation to perform via pushbuttons. Installing a package places all of the components of that package on your system. Uninstalling one removes all traces of the package except for configuration files you have modified. Upgrading a package installs the newly available version and uninstalls all other versions that were previously installed. This allows quick upgrading to the latest releases of packages.

The query operation lets you examine the details of both installed or available packages. You can view the description of the package, where and when it was built, the files in the package, and other attributes. All of the configuration and documentation components of each package are clearly marked as such to reduce the time you spend looking for them.

Using glint to perform all of these operations is the same as using rpm to do them from the command line. However, the graphical nature of glint often makes these operations easier to perform.

The normal way to handle glint is to display the available packages and files, select the ones you want to operate on, and then press a button or choose a menu item that performs the operation. For instance, you can install several packages with a few button clicks.

10.1   Starting glint

To start glint, simply run `glint &` from any X terminal window. That will bring up a window
that looks like the one in figure 10.1. Any user can use glint to query and verify packages, but if
you need to install, uninstall, or upgrade packages be sure to run glint as root.

There are two main parts to the glint interface. The first, on the left, allows you to browse and
select the packages installed on your system. The right side contains buttons that manipulate
the selected packages.

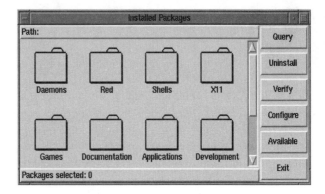

Figure 10.1: Main Glint Window

10.2   The Package Display

Each folder icon in glint represents a group of packages. Each group can contain other groups,
which allows for flexible locations of packages. Groups are used to place packages that perform
similar functions in similar locations. For example, Red Hat includes many application programs such as editors and spreadsheets. All of the text based ones appear in the "Applications"
group. Inside of that group, there is another grouping for all of the editors that are shipped.

By convention, groups are written in the same way as UNIX paths. The top most group is written
first, and subsequent groups follow with a slash separating the group names. This means that
an X-based drawing program appears in the
X11/Applications/Graphics group.

To view the packages and subgroups within a group, double click the left mouse button on a
group's folder icon. The window then changes to show what that package contains. The top line
of the package display shows which group you're currently looking in, as well as the groups
leading to the current one. To return to the previous group you were looking at, double click

on the "Back" folder, which is always in the upper left hand corner of the folder area (though it often gets scrolled away).

If you'd like to examine a subgroup in a new window, double click the middle mouse button on its folder. If your mouse has only two buttons, click both. This will create a new window with that group in it.

10.2.1 Context Sensitive Menus

Pressing the right mouse button on any icon in the package window brings up a small, *context sensitive* menu. The exact items it contains depends on exactly where you press it. They all contain options to select or deselect the item, and many let you install, uninstall, query, upgrade, or verify the item you clicked on. There's more information on how to do these things later.

To choose an item from a context sensitive menu, press and hold the right mouse button on a icon. While still holding the right button down, move the mouse pointer over the item you'd like to select (which will then become highlighted). Release the right mouse button to select that item and make the menu disappear.

10.2.2 Selecting Packages

To select a single package, click the left mouse button on it. You'll notice a thin border appear around the package's icon (as shown in figure 10.2) which shows that it's currently selected. To unselect it, click the left mouse button on it and the border will disappear. The number of packages currently selected is always displayed at the bottom of the window. A group's folder icon displays the number of packages within that group that have been selected, or All if all have been selected.

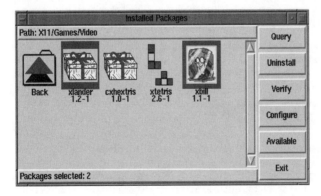

Figure 10.2: Selecting Packages in Glint

The context sensitive menu for a package also allows easy selection and unselection. Using the select and unselect options on a package's icon selects or unselects that package, while those options on a group's folder icon select and unselect all of the packages in that group. Using these menu options makes selecting groups of packages much quicker than selecting each package individually.

10.2.3 Viewing Available Packages

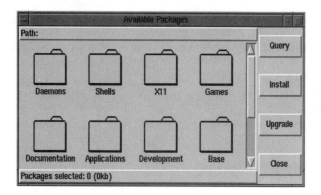

Figure 10.3: Available Window

To see what packages are available for you to install, choose the Available pushbutton from any glint window. After a few moments, a new window, like the one shown in figure 10.3, will appear. The differences in the title and buttons indicate that this window is listing packages you may install. Navigating through these packages and selecting them is the same as in the other glint windows.

If you get an error message from glint saying that it can't find any RPMs, see the section below on Configuration.

10.3 Configuration

The only configuration information glint needs is the path to new RPMs. When you're using your Red Hat Linux CD-ROM, this will probably be
/mnt/cdrom/RedHat/RPMS, which is the default path for glint. If you download new RPMs from the Internet or want to install RPMs via a NFS mounted CD-ROM this path will probably be different for you.

To change this path, first be sure to close all of the windows listing available packages you may have open. Then choose the Configuration option from one of the remaining windows. This

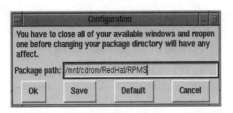

Figure 10.4: Configuration Window

will open a dialog box like the one shown in figure 10.4. Here you can type the full path to the RPMs you'd like to look at. Choosing the Save button will save this path, making it the default for future glint sessions. The Default button restores the path to the one that glint used when it started.

After changing this path and closing the dialog box, you can use the Available button to view the packages available in the new location.

10.4   Package Manipulation

10.4.1   Querying Packages

The easiest way to query a single package or group is to use the query option from the icon's context sensitive menu. If you want to query a more diverse set of packages, select them all and use the Query button in one of the windows.

Using either of these methods creates a window like the one shown in figure 10.5. If you choose only one package, it will look a bit different however, so some of this won't apply.

On the very left of the window is a list of the packages that have been queried. Selecting one of them will change the information in the rest of the window. You may step through them in order by using the Next and Previous buttons on the right side of the window.

The name, version, and release of the current package are in the top middle of the query window. Immediately below this is the description of the package, which can be quite large. A scroll bar is there to let you read the whole thing.

Below the description is a list of the files contained in the package. Along with the full path to the file, the file list tells you a couple of other things. If a D appears to the left of the path, that file is a documentation file and would be a good thing to read. If a C appears there, then the file is a configuration file. A * means that the correct version of that file is not installed on your system. This can occur because a more recent version of a package was installed or because two packages contain different versions of the same file.

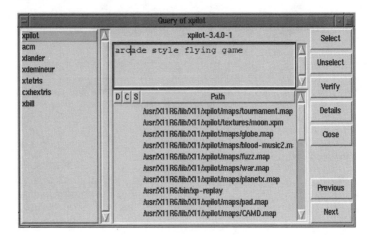

Figure 10.5: Query Window

More information on a package can be seen by clicking on the Details pushbutton. A window like the one in figure 10.6 will then appear. This lists more information about the package being displayed in the main query window. When you select a new package in the query window, the information in the details window will change to reflect your new choice.

You may also select, unselect, or verify a package while querying it by using the buttons provided. Click on the Close button when you are finished looking at the packages.

10.4.2   Verifying Packages

Verifying a package checks all of the files in the package to insure they match the ones present on your system. The checksum, file size, permissions, and owner attributes are all checked against the database. This check can be used when you suspect that one of programs files has become corrupted due to the installation of new programs.

Choosing the packages to verify is the same as choosing the packages to query. Select the packages and use the Verify button or choose the Verify entry from a context sensitive menu. A window opens like the one in figure 10.7.

The three columns in this window describe the package with a problem in it, the file that has the problem, and a brief description of the discrepancies that were found. While the check is running, the current file being checked appears as the last element in the list, and the problem is listed as (checking). A full list of the problems that can be found through verification appears in figure 10.8.

To get more information on the problems found with a file, double click on the file's path. A

Figure 10.6: Query Details

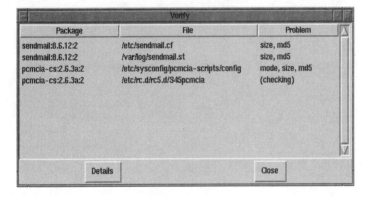

Figure 10.7: Verify Window

window like the one shown in figure 10.9 lists the expected and current values of the attributes that are amiss.

10.4.3   Installing New Packages

Installing new packages from glint is very simple. First look at the packages available for instal-lation (see the section 10.2.3 for how to do this). You may select any number of these (and query them if you're not sure what they are) for installation (in the same manner you select packages for verification.) If you want to install a single package or group, the context sensitive menus provide a shortcut for doing so. Figure 10.10 shows a window with some packages selected for installation.

Problem	Description
missing	The file is no longer on your system
mode	permission bits have changed
size	file's size has changed
uid	owner's uid has changed
gid	owner's gid has changed
md5	the md5 checksum has changed
link	the file is a symlink to the wrong place

Figure 10.8: Possible Problems found by Verification

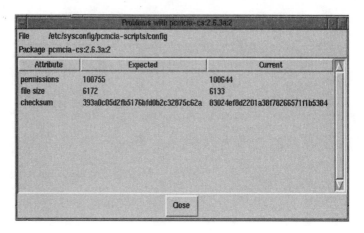

Figure 10.9: Verification Details

After you've begun the installation, a window appears like the one in figure 10.11. It tracks the progress of the installation so you'll know something is happening. The top bar shows how much of the current package (whose name is listed inside of it) has been installed while the bottom graph shows how much of the total installation has been finished. The number of packages, package sizes, and time estimates are continually updated.

If a problem occurs during the installation, a window will appear listing any errors that occurred. If this happens, you should correct the problems and then try again.

After the installation has completed, the package and groups that have been installed are moved from the available window to the main glint window to show you that they have been successfully installed.

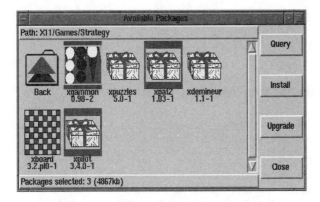

Figure 10.10: Packages Selected for Installation

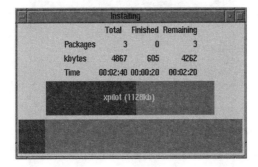

Figure 10.11: Installation Progress

Upgrading Packages

When a new version of a package has been released, it is easy to install it on your system. Select the packages from the window of available packages in the same way you select packages for installation. Both the Upgrade button and the context sensitive menus will begin the upgrade.

During the upgrade, you'll see a progress indicator like the one for installing packages. When it's finished, the installed packages will appear in the the main glint windows and any old versions of the packages will be removed.

It is much better to use the upgrade option than to uninstall the old versions of a package and then install the new one. Using upgrade ensures that any changes you made to package configuration files get preserved properly, while doing it manually could cause those changes to be lost.

If you run out of disk space during an installation, the install will fail. However, the package which was being installed when the error occurred may leave some files around. To clean this up, reinstall the package after you've made more disk space available.

10.4.4 Uninstalling Packages

Uninstalling a package is not the same as upgrading one. When a package is uninstalled, any files it uses that are not needed by other packages on your system are removed. Changed configuration files are copied to <filename>.rpmsave so you can reuse them later.

Like verifying and querying packages, you can remove a package through the buttons on the right of the glint window or through a context sensitive menu. Remember that when you make a choice from a group's menu, the operation is performed on all of the packages in that group, so be careful!

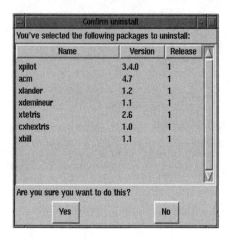

Figure 10.12: Uninstall Window

Once you've begun the uninstall, glint asks for confirmation, showing a window like the one in figure 10.12. All of the packages that are about to be uninstalled are listed. You should look at them all to ensure you're not about to remove something you want to keep. Clicking the Yes button will start the uninstallation process. After it completes, the packages and groups that have been removed will disappear from any windows they were in.

11

System Administration

This chapter is an overview of the Red Hat Linux system. It will illustrate things that you may not know about the system and things that are somewhat different from other UNIX systems.

11.1 Users, Groups and User-Private Groups

Managing users and groups has traditionally been tedious. Red Hat Linux has a few tools and conventions that make user and groups easier to manage, and more useful.

The easiest way to manage users and groups is through the Users and Groups module of the control-panel (see section 9 for details on the control-panel and section 9.1 for details on the Users and Groups module).

You can also use adduser to create a new user from the command line.

11.1.1 Standard Users

Table 11.1.1 lists the standard users set up by the installation process (this is essentially the /etc/passwd file). The group id (GID) in this table is the *primary group* for the user. See section 11.1.3 for details on how groups are used.

User	UID	GID	Home Directory	Shell
root	0	0	/root	/bin/bash
bin	1	1	/bin	
daemon	2	2	/sbin	
adm	3	4	/var/adm	
lp	4	7	/var/spool/lpd	
sync	5	0	/sbin	/bin/sync
shutdown	6	0	/sbin	/sbin/shutdown
halt	7	0	/sbin	/sbin/halt
mail	8	12	/var/spool/mail	
news	9	13	/var/spool/news	
uucp	10	14	/var/spool/uucp	
operator	11	0	/root	
games	12	100	/usr/games	
gopher	13	30	/usr/lib/gopher-data	
ftp	14	50	/home/ftp	
nobody	99	99	/	

Figure 11.1: Standard Users

11.1.2   Standard Groups

Table 11.1.2 lists the standard groups as set up by the installation process (this is essentially the /etc/group file).

11.1.3   User Private Groups

Red Hat Linux uses a user private group (UPG) scheme, which makes UNIX groups much easier to use. The UPG scheme does not add or change anything in the standard UNIX way of handling groups. It simply offers a new convention for handling groups. Whenever you create a new user, by default, he or she has a unique group. The scheme works as follows:

User Private Group   Each user has its own primary group, to which only it is a member.

umask = 002   The traditional UNIX umask is 022, which prevents other users *and other members of a user's primary group* from modifying a user's files. Since every user has their own private group in the UPG scheme, this "group protection" is not needed. A umask of 002 will prevent users from modifying other users' private files. The umask is set in /etc/profile.

Group	GID	Members
root	0	root
bin	1	root,bin,daemon
daemon	2	root,bin,daemon
sys	3	root,bin,adm
adm	4	root,adm,daemon
tty	5	
disk	6	root
lp	7	daemon,lp
mem	8	
kmem	9	
wheel	10	root
mail	12	mail
news	13	news
uucp	14	uucp
man	15	
games	20	
gopher	30	
dip	40	
ftp	50	
nobody	99	
users	100	
floppy	19	

Figure 11.2: Standard Groups

SGID bit on Directories If you set the SGID bit on a directory (with chmod g+s *directory*), files
created in that directory will have their group set to the directory's group.

Most computing sites like to create a group for each major project and assign people to the
groups they need to be in. Managing files traditionally has been difficult, though, because when
someone creates a file it is owned by the primary group he or she belongs to. When a single
person works on multiple projects, it becomes hard to make the files owned by the group that is
associated with that project. In the UPG scheme, groups are automatically assigned to files on a
project-by-project basis, which makes managing group projects very simple.

Let's say you have a big project called *devel*, with many people editing the devel files in a devel
directory. Make a group called devel, chgrp the devel directory to devel, and add the all
the devel users to the devel group. Now, all the devel users will be able to edit the devel files
and create new files in the devel directory, and these files will always retain their devel group.
Thus, they will always be edit-able by other devel users.

If you have multiple projects like *devel*, and users who are working on multiple projects, these
users will never have to change their umask or group when they move from project to project.
The SGID bit on each project's main directory "selects" the proper group.

Since each user's HOME directory is owned by the user and their private group, it is safe to set
the SGID bit on the HOME directory. However, by default, files are created with the primary
group of the user, so the SGID bit would be redundant.

User Private Group Rationale

Since the UPG scheme is new, many people have questions about it, and they wonder why it is
necessary. The following is the rationale for the scheme.

- You'd like to have a group of people work on a set of files in say, the
  /usr/lib/emacs/site-lisp directory. You trust a few people to mess around in there,
  but certainly not everyone.
- So you enter:

      chown -R root.emacs /usr/lib/emacs/site-lisp

  and you add the proper users to the group.
- To allow the users to actually create files in the directory you enter:

      chmod 775 /usr/lib/emacs/site-lisp

- But when a user creates a new file it is assigned the group of the users default group
  (usually users). To prevent this you enter

      chmod 2775 /usr/lib/emacs/site-lisp

which causes everything in the directory to be created with the "emacs" group.

- But the new file needs to be mode 664 for another user in the emacs group to be able to edit it. To do this you make the default umask 002.

- Well, this all works fine, except that if your default group is "users", every file you create in your home directory will be writable by everybody in "users" (usually everyone).

- To fix this, you make each user have a "private group" as their default group.

At this point, by making the default umask 002 and giving everyone a private default group, you can easily set up groups that users can take advantage of without doing any magic. Just create the group, add the users, and do the above chown and chmod on the group's directories.

11.2   User Authentication with PAM

Programs which give users access to privileges of any sort need to be able to authenticate the users. When you log into a system, you provide your name and password, and the login process uses those to authenticate the login—to verify that you are who you say you are. Other forms of authentication than passwords are possible, and it is possible for the passwords to be stored in different ways.

PAM, which stands for "Pluggable Authentication Modules", is a way of allowing the system administrator to set authentication policy without having to recompile programs which do authentication. With PAM, you control how the modules are plugged into the programs by editing a configuration file.

Most Red Hat Linux users will never need to touch this configuration file. When you use RPM to install programs that need to do authentication, they automatically make the changes that are needed to do normal password authentication. However, you may want to customize your configuration, in which case you need to understand the configuration file.

11.2.1   PAM Modules

There are four types of modules defined by the PAM standard. `auth` modules provide the actual authentication, perhaps asking for and checking a password, and set "credentials" such as group membership or kerberos "tickets". `account` modules check to make sure that the authentication is allowed (the account has not expired, the user is allowed to log in at this time of day, etc.). `password` modules are used to set passwords. `session` modules are used once a user has been authenticated to make it possible for them to use their account, perhaps mounting the user's home directory or making their mailbox available.

These modules may be *stacked*, so that multiple modules are used. For instance, rlogin normally makes use of at least two authentication methods: if "rhosts" authentication succeeds, it is sufficient to allow the connection; if it fails, then standard password authentication is done.

New modules can be added at any time, and PAM-aware applications can then be made to use them. For instance, if you have a one-time-password calculator system, and you can write a module to support it (documentation on writing modules is included with the system), PAM-aware programs can use the new module and work with the new one-time-password calculators without being recompiled or otherwise modified in any way.

11.2.2   Services

Each program which uses PAM defines its own "service" name. The login program defines the service type login, ftpd defines the service type ftp, etc. In general, the service type is the name of the program used to **access** the service, not (if there is a difference) the program used to **provide** the service.

11.2.3   The Configuration Files

The directory /etc/pam.d is used to configure all PAM applications. (This used to be /etc/pam.conf in earlier PAM versions; while the pam.conf file is still read if no /etc/pam.d/ entry is found, its use is deprecated.) Each application (really, each **service**) has its own file. A file looks like this:

```
#%PAM-1.0
auth      required   /lib/security/pam_securetty.so
auth'     required   /lib/security/pam_pwdb.so shadow nullok
auth      required   /lib/security/pam_nologin.so
account   required   /lib/security/pam_pwdb.so
password  required   /lib/security/pam_cracklib.so
password  required   /lib/security/pam_pwdb.so shadow
                                       nullok use_authtok
session   required   /lib/security/pam_pwdb.so
```

The first line is a comment. Any line that starts with a # character is a comment. The next three lines stack up three modules to use for login authorization. The first line makes sure that *if* the user is trying to log in as root, the tty on which they are logging in is listed in the /etc/securetty file *if* that file exists. The second line causes the user to be asked for a password and the password checked. The third line checks to see if the file /etc/nologin exists, and if it does, displays the contents of the file, and if the user is not root, does not let him or her log in.

Note that all three modules are checked, *even if the first module fails*. This is a security decision—it is designed to not let the user know why their authentication was disallowed, because knowing why it was disallowed might allow them to break the authentication more easily. You can change this behavior by changing required to requisite; if any requisite module returns failure, PAM fails immediately without calling any other modules.

The fifth line causes any necessary accounting to be done. For example, if shadow passwords have been enabled, the pam_pwdb.so module will check to see if the account has expired, or if the user has not changed his or her password and the grace period for changing the password has expired.

The sixth line (which we've had to wrap) specifies that if the login program changes the user's password, it should use the pam_pwdb.so module to do so. (It will do so only if an auth module has determined that the password needs to be changed—for example, if a shadow password has expired.)

The final line specifies that the pam_pwdb.so module should be used to manage the session. Currently, that module doesn't do anything; it could be replaced (or supplemented by stacking) by any necessary module.

Note that the order of the lines within each file matters. While it doesn't really matter much in which order required modules are called, there are other *control flags* available. While optional is rarely used, and never used by default on a Red Hat Linux system, sufficient and requisite cause order to become important.

Let's look at the auth configuration for rlogin:

```
auth    required     /lib/security/pam_securetty.so
auth    sufficient   /lib/security/pam_rhosts_auth.so
auth    required     /lib/security/pam_pwdb.so shadow nullok
auth    required     /lib/security/pam_nologin.so
```

That looks *almost* like the login entry, but there's an extra line specifying an extra module, and the modules are specified in a different order.

First, pam_securetty.so keeps root logins from happening on insecure terminals. This effectively disallows all root rlogin attempts. If you wish to allow them (in which case we recommend that you either not be internet-connected or be behind a good firewall), you can simply remove that line.

Second, pam_nologin.so checks /etc/nologin, as specified above.

Third, if pam_rhosts_auth.so authenticates the user, PAM immediately returns success to rlogin without any password checking being done. If pam_rhosts_auth.so fails to authenticate the user, that failed authentication is ignored.

Finally (if pam_rhosts_auth.so has failed to authenticate the user), the pam_pwdb.so module performs normal password authentication.

Note that if you do not want to prompt for a password if the securetty check fails, you can change the pam_securetty.so module from required to requisite

11.2.4 Shadow Passwords

The pam_pwdb.so module will automatically detect that you are using shadow passwords and make all necessary adjustments. Please refer to Section 11.3 for more information on the utilities that support shadow passwords.

11.2.5 More Information

This is just an introduction to PAM. More information is included with the system in /usr/doc/pam*, including a *System Administrators' Guide*, a *Module Writers' Manual*, an *Application Developers' Manual*, and the PAM standard, DCE-RFC 86.0. In addition, documentation is available from the Red Hat web site, at http://www.redhat.com/linux-info/pam/.

11.3 Shadow Utilities

Support for shadow passwords has been enhanced significantly for Red Hat Linux 5.1. The shadow-utils package contains a number of utilities that support:

- Conversion from normal to shadowed passwords and back (pwconv, pwunconv).

- Verification of the password, group, and associated shadow files (pwck, grpck).

- Industry-standard methods of adding, deleting and modifying user accounts (useradd, usermod, and userdel).

- Industry-standard methods of adding, deleting, and modifying user groups (groupadd, groupmod, and groupdel).

- Industry-standard method of administering the /etc/group file (gpasswd).

Please Note: There are a few additional points of interest concerning these utilities:

- The utilities will work properly whether shadowing is enabled or not.

- The utilities have been slightly modified to support Red Hat Software's user private group scheme. For a description of the modifications, please see the useradd man page. For more information on user private groups, please turn to Section 11.1.3 on page 142.

- The adduser script has been replaced with a symlink to /usr/sbin/useradd.

11.4 Building a Custom Kernel

With the introduction of modularization in the Linux 2.0.x kernel there have been some significant changes in building customized kernels. In the past you were required to compile support into your kernel if you wanted to access a particular hardware or filesystem component. For some hardware configurations the size of the kernel could quickly reach a critical level. To require ready support for items that were only occasionally used was an inefficient use of system resources. With the capabilities of the 2.0.x kernel, if there are certain hardware components or filesystems that are used infrequently, driver modules for them can be loaded on demand. For information on handling kernel modules see Chapter 9, Section 9.6.

11.4.1 Building a modularized kernel

These instructions provide you with the knowledge required to take advantage of the power and flexibility available through kernel modularization. If you do not wish to take advantage of modularization, please see Section 11.4.3 for an explanation of the different aspects of building and installing a monolithic kernel. It is assumed that you have already installed the kernel-headers and kernel-source packages and that you issue all commands from the /usr/src/linux directory.

It is important to begin a kernel build with the source tree in a known condition. Therefore, it is recommended that you begin with the command make mrproper. This will remove any configuration files along with the remains of any previous builds that may be scattered around the source tree. Now you must create a configuration file that will determine which components to include in your new kernel. Depending upon your hardware and personal preferences there are three methods available to configure the kernel.

- make config An interactive text program. Components are presented and you answer with Y (yes), N (no), or M (module).

- make menuconfig A graphic, menu driven program. Components are presented in a menu of categories, you select the desired components in the same manner used in the Red Hat Linux installation program. Toggle the tag corresponding to the item you want included; **Y** (yes), **N** (no), or **M** (module).

- make xconfig An X Windows program. Components are listed in different levels of menus, components are selected using a mouse. Again, select **Y** (yes), **N** (no), or **M** (module).

Please Note: In order to use kerneld (see Section 9.6 for details) and kernel modules you must answer **Yes** to **kerneld support** and **module version (CONFIG_MODVERSIONS) support** in the configuration.

Please Note: If you are building a Linux/Intel kernel on (or for) a machine that uses a "clone" processor (for example, one made by Cyrix or AMD), it is recommended to choose a **Processor type** of **386**.

If you wish to build a kernel with a configuration file (`/usr/src/linux/.config`) that you have already created with one of the above methods, you can omit the `make mrproper` and `make config` commands and use the command `make dep` followed by `make clean` to prepare the source tree for the build.

The next step consists of the actual compilation of the source code components into a working program that your machine can use to boot. The method described here is the easiest to recover from in the event of a mishap. If you are interested in other possibilities details can be found in the Kernel-HOWTO or in the `Makefile` in `/usr/src/linux` on your Linux system.

- Build the kernel with `make boot`.

- Build any modules you configured with `make modules`.

- Move the old set of modules out of the way with:

  ```
  rm -rf /lib/modules/2.0.29-old
  mv /lib/modules/2.0.29 /lib/modules/2.0.29-old
  ```

  Of course, if you have upgraded your kernel, replace `2.0.29` with the version you are using.

- Install the new modules (even if you didn't build any) with `make modules_install`.

If you have a SCSI adapter and made your SCSI driver modular, build a new `initrd` image (see Section 11.4.2; note that there are few practical reasons to make the SCSI driver modular in a custom kernel).

In order to provide a redundant boot source to protect from a possible error in a new kernel you should keep the original kernel available. Adding a kernel to the LILO menu is as simple as renaming the original kernel in `/boot`, copying the new kernel to `/boot`, adding a few lines in `/etc/lilo.conf` and running `/sbin/lilo`. Here is an example of the default `/etc/lilo.conf` file shipped with Red Hat Linux:

```
boot=/dev/hda
map=/boot/map
install=/boot/boot.b
prompt
timeout=100
image=/boot/vmlinuz
        label=linux
        root=/dev/hda1
        read-only
```

Now you must update `/etc/lilo.conf`. If you built a new initrd image you must tell LILO to use it. In this example of `/etc/lilo.conf` we have added four lines at the bottom of the file

to indicate another kernel to boot from. We have renamed /boot/vmlinuz to
/boot/vmlinuz.old and changed its label to old. We have also added an initrd line for
the new kernel:

```
boot=/dev/hda
map=/boot/map
install=/boot/boot.b
prompt
timeout=100
image=/boot/vmlinuz
        label=linux
        initrd=/boot/initrd
        root=/dev/hda1
        read-only
image=/boot/vmlinuz.old
        label=old
        root=/dev/hda1
        read-only
```

Now when the system boots and you press Tab at the LILO boot: prompt two choices will be
shown;

```
LILO boot:
linux    old
```

To boot the new kernel (linux) simply press Enter, or wait for LILO to time out. If you want
to boot the old kernel (old), simply enter old and press Enter.

Here is a summary of the steps;

- mv /boot/vmlinuz /boot/vmlinuz.old
- cp /usr/src/linux/arch/i386/boot/zImage /boot/vmlinuz
- edit /etc/lilo.conf
- run /sbin/lilo

You can begin testing your new kernel by rebooting your computer and watching the messages
to ensure your hardware is detected properly.

11.4.2 Making an initrd image

An initrd image is needed for loading your SCSI module at boot time. The shell script
/sbin/mkinitrd can build a proper initrd image for your machine if the following conditions are met:

- The loopback block device is available.

- The /etc/conf.modules file has a line for your SCSI adapter; for example:

```
alias scsi_hostadapter BusLogic
```

To build the new initrd image, run /sbin/mkinitrd with parameters such as this:

```
/sbin/mkinitrd /boot/newinitrd-image 2.0.12
```

where /boot/newinitrd-image is the file to use for your new image, and 2.0.12 is the kernel whose modules (from /lib/modules) should be used in the initrd image (not necessarily the same as the version number of the currently running kernel).

11.4.3   Building a monolithic kernel

To build a monolithic kernel you follow the same steps as building a modularized kernel with a few exceptions.

- When configuring the kernel only answer **Yes** and **No** to the questions (don't make anything modular).

- Omit the steps:

```
make modules
make modules_install
```

- Edit the file /etc/rc.d/rc.sysinit and comment out the line depmod -a by inserting a "#" at the beginning of the line.

11.5   Sendmail

A default sendmail.cf file will be installed in /etc. The default configuration should work for most SMTP-only sites. It will *not* work for UUCP sites; you will need to generate a new sendmail.cf if you need to use UUCP mail transfers. To generate a new sendmail.cf, you will need to install m4 and the sendmail source package. Read the README file in the sendmail sources for more details on creating sendmail configuration files. Also, O'Reilly & Associates publishes a good sendmail reference entitled *sendmail* by Bryan Costales.

One common sendmail configuration is to have a single machine act as a mail gateway for all the machines on your network. For instance, at Red Hat Software we have a machine mail.redhat.com that does all our mail. On that machine we simply need to add the names of machines for which mail.redhat.com will handle mail to /etc/sendmail.cw. Here is an example:

```
# sendmail.cw - include all aliases for your machine
# here.
torgo.redhat.com
poodle.redhat.com
devel.redhat.com
```

Then on the other machines, torgo, poodle, and devel, we need to edit
/etc/sendmail.cf to "masquerade" as mail.redhat.com when sending mail, and to forward any local mail processing to redhat.com. Find the DH and DM lines in
/etc/sendmail.cf and edit them thusly:

```
# who I send unqualified names to
# (null means deliver locally)
DRmail.redhat.com

# who gets all local email traffic
DHmail.redhat.com

# who I masquerade as (null for no masquerading)
DMredhat.com
```

With this type of configuration, all mail sent will appear as if it were sent from redhat.com, and
any mail sent to torgo.redhat.com or the other hosts will be delivered to mail.redhat.com.

Please be aware that if you configure your system to masquerade as another any email sent from
your system to your system will be sent to the machine you are masquerading as. For example,
in the above illustration, log files that are periodically sent to root@poodle.redhat.com by
the cron daemon would be sent to root@mail.redhat.com.

11.6 Controlling Access to Services

As a security measure, most network services are managed by a protective program called a *TCP
wrapper*. The protected services are those listed in
/etc/inetd.conf that specify /usr/sbin/tcpd. tcpd can allow or deny access to a service
based on the origin of the request, and the configuration in
/etc/hosts.allow and /etc/hosts.deny. By default Red Hat Linux allows all service
requests. To disable or limit services you can edit /etc/hosts.allow. Here is an example
/etc/hosts.allow file:

```
ALL: redhat.com .redhat.com
in.talkd: ALL
in.ntalkd: ALL
in.fingerd: ALL
in.ftpd: ALL
```

This configuration allows all connections from `redhat.com` and `*.redhat.com` machines. It also allows talk, finger, and ftp requests from all machines.

`tcpd` allows much more sophisticated access control, using a combination of `/etc/hosts.allow` and `/etc/hosts.deny`. Read the tcpd(8) and hosts_access(5) man pages for complete details.

11.7   Anonymous FTP

Setting up anonymous FTP is simple. All you need to do is install the `anon-ftp` rpm package (which you may have already done at install time). Once it is installed, anonymous FTP will be up and running.

There are a few files you might wish to edit to configure your FTP server.

/etc/ftpaccess   This file defines most of the access control for your ftp server. Some of the things that you can do are: set up logical "groups" to control access from different sites, limit the number of simultaneous FTP connections, configure transfer logging, and much more. Read the ftpaccess man page for complete details.

/etc/ftphosts   The ftphosts file is used to allow or deny access to certain accounts from various hosts. Read the ftphosts man page for details.

/etc/ftpusers   This file lists all the users that are *not* allowed to ftp into your machine. For example, `root` is listed in /etc/ftpusers by default. That means that you can not ftp to your machine and log in as root. This is a good security measure, but some administrators prefer to remove `root` from this file.

11.8   NFS Configuration

NFS stands for Network File System, and is a way to share files between machines as if they were on your local hard drive. Linux can be both an NFS server and an NFS client, which means that it can *export* filesystems to other systems, and *mount* filesystems exported from other machines.

11.8.1   Mounting NFS Filesystems

Use the `mount` command to mount a NFS filesystem from another machine:

```
mkdir /mnt/local # Only required if /mnt/local doesn't exist
mount bigdog:/mnt/export /mnt/local
```

In this command, `porky` is the hostname of the NFS fileserver, `/mnt/export` is the filesystem that porky is exporting, and `/mnt/local` is a directory on my local machine where we want to mount the filesystem. After the `mount` command runs (and if we have the proper permissions from porky) we can enter `ls /mnt/local` and get a listing of the files in `/mnt/export` on porky.

11.8.2 Exporting NFS Filesystems

The file that controls what filesystems you wish to export is `/etc/exports`. Its format is:

```
directory        hostname(options)
```

the `(options)` are optional. For example:

```
/mnt/export     speedy.redhat.com
```

would allow `speedy.redhat.com` to mount `/mnt/export`, but:

```
/mnt/export     speedy.redhat.com(ro)
```

would just allow `speedy` to mount `/mnt/export` read-only.

Each time you change `/etc/exports`, you need to tell the NFS daemons to examine it for new information. One simple way to accomplish this is to just stop and start the daemons:

```
/etc/rc.d/init.d/nfs stop
/etc/rc.d/init.d/nfs start
```

The following will also work:

```
killall -HUP rpc.nfsd rpc.mountd
```

See the following man pages for more details: nfsd(8), mountd(8), and exports(5). Another good reference is *Managing NFS and NIS Services* by Hal Stern, published by O'Reilly & Associates.

11.9 The Boot Process, Init, and Shutdown

This section contains information on what happens when a Red Hat Linux system is booted and shut down. Let's start with information on the files in `/etc/sysconfig`.

11.9.1   Sysconfig Information

The following information outlines the various files in /etc/sysconfig, their function, and their contents.

Files in /etc/sysconfig

The following files are normally found in /etc/sysconfig:

- /etc/sysconfig/clock
- /etc/sysconfig/keyboard
- /etc/sysconfig/mouse
- /etc/sysconfig/network
- /etc/sysconfig/pcmcia
- /etc/sysconfig/amd
- /etc/sysconfig/tape

Let's take a look at each one.

/etc/sysconfig/clock – The /etc/sysconfig/clock file controls the interpretation of values read from the system clock. Earlier releases of Red Hat Linux used the following values (which is deprecated):

- **CLOCKMODE=*mode***, where ***mode*** is one of the following:
    - **GMT** – indicates that the clock is set to UTC.
    - **ARC** – on alpha only indicates the ARC console's 42-year time offset is in effect.

Currently, the correct values are:

- **UTC=*boolean***, where ***boolean*** is one of the following:
    - **true** – indicates that the clock is set to UTC. Any other value indicates that it is set to local time.
- **ARC=*boolean***, where ***boolean*** is one of the following:
    - **true** – (for Alpha-based systems only) Indicates the ARC console's 42-year time offset is in effect; Any other value indicates that the normal Unix epoch is assumed.

/etc/sysconfig/keyboard – The /etc/sysconfig/keyboard files controls the behavior of the keyboard. The following values may be used:

- **KEYTABLE=*file*,** where *file* is the name of a keytable file. For example:
  KEYTABLE="/usr/lib/kbd/keytables/us.map"

/etc/sysconfig/mouse – The /etc/sysconfig/mouse file is used to specify information about the available mouse. The following values may be used:

- **MOUSETYPE=*type*,** where type is one of the following:

  - **microsoft** – A Microsoft mouse.
  - **mouseman** – A MouseMan mouse.
  - **mousesystems** – A Mouse Systems mouse.
  - **ps/2** – A PS/2 mouse.
  - **msbm** – A Microsoft bus mouse.
  - **logibm** – A Logitech bus mouse.
  - **atibm** – An ATI bus mouse.
  - **logitech** – A Logitech mouse.
  - **mmseries** – A older MouseMan mouse.
  - **mmhittab** – A mmhittab mouse.

- **XEMU3=*emulation*,** where *emulation* is one of the following:

  - **yes** – Three mouse buttons should be emulated.
  - **no** – The mouse already has three buttons.

In addition, /dev/mouse is a symlink that points to the actual mouse device.

/etc/sysconfig/network – The /etc/sysconfig/network file is used to specify information about the desired network configuration. The following values may be used:

- **NETWORKING=*answer*,** where *answer* is one of the following:

  - **yes** – Networking should be configured.
  - **no** – Networking should not be configured.

- **HOSTNAME=*hostname*,** where *hostname* should be the FQDN (Fully Qualified Domain Name), but can be whatever hostname you want.

  Please Note: For compatibility with older software that people might install (such as trn), the /etc/HOSTNAME file should contain the same value as here.

- **FORWARD_IPV4=*answer***, where **answer** is one of the following:

  - **yes** – Perform IP forwarding.
  - **no** – Do not perform IP forwarding.

  (The current Red Hat Linux installation sets this to "no" by default (for RFC compliance), but if FORWARD_IPV4 is not set at all, forwarding is *enabled* for compatibility with the configuration files used on Red Hat Linux versions 4.2 and earlier.)

- **GATEWAY=*gw-ip***, where **gw-ip** is the IP address of the network's gateway.

- **GATEWAYDEV=*gw-dev***, where **gw-dev** is the gateway device (e.g. eth0).

- **NISDOMAIN=*dom-name***, where **dom-name** is the NIS domain name.

/etc/sysconfig/pcmcia – The `/etc/sysconfig/pcmcia` file is used to specify PCMCIA configuration information. The following values may be used:

- **PCMCIA=*answer***, where **answer** is one of the following:

  - **yes** – PCMCIA support should be enabled.
  - **no** – PCMCIA support should not be enabled.

- **PCIC=*pcic-type***, where **pcic-type** is one of the following:

  - **i82365** – The computer has an i82365-style PCMCIA socket chipset.
  - **tcic** – The computer has a tcic-style PCMCIA socket chipset.

- **PCIC_OPTS=*option***, where **option** is the socket driver (i82365 or tcic) timing parameters.

- **CORE_OPTS=*option***, where **option** is the list of pcmcia_core options.

- **CARDMGR_OPTS=*option***, where **option** is the list of options for the PCMCIA cardmgr.

/etc/sysconfig/amd – The `/etc/sysconfig/amd` file is used to specify operational parameters for amd. The following values may be used:

- **ADIR=*path***, where **path** is the amd directory. It should be "`/.automount`", and is normally never changed.

- **MOUNTPTS=*mountpts***, where **mountpts** is, for example, "`/net /etc/amd.conf`"

- **AMDOPTS=*options***, where **options** are any extra options for AMD.

/etc/sysconfig/tape – The /etc/sysconfig/tape file is used to specify tape-related configuration information. The following values may be used:

- **DEV=*devnam***, where ***devnam*** is the tape device (for example, "/dev/nst0)". Use the non-rewinding device for these scripts.

    For SCSI tapes this is "/dev/nst#", where "#" is the number of the tape drive you want to use. If you only have one, then use "/dev/nst0".

    For IDE tapes you use "/dev/ht#", where "#" is the number of the tape drive you want to use. If you only have one, then use "/dev/ht0".

    For floppy tape drives use "/dev/ftape".

- **ADMIN=*account***, where ***account*** is the user account to send mail to if the backup fails for any reason. Normally set to "root".

- **SLEEP=*time***, where ***time*** is the time to sleep between tape operations. Some drives need a bit more than others, but "5" seems to work for 8mm, 4mm, and DLT.

- **BLOCKSIZE=*size***, where ***size*** is the tape drive's optimal block size. A value of "32768" worked fine for 8mm, then 4mm, and now DLT. An optimal setting is probably however much data your drive writes at one time.

- **SHORTDATE=*date***, where ***date*** is a string that evaluates to a short date string, to be used in backup log filenames. The default setting is: "$(date +%y:%m:%d:%H:%M)"

- **DAY=*date***, where ***date*** is a string that evaluates to a date string, to be used for the log file directory. The default setting is: "$(date +log-%y:%m:%d)"

- **DATE=*date***, whre ***date*** is a string that evaluates to a reguarl date string, to be used in log files. The default setting is: "$(date)"

- **LOGROOT=*path***, where ***path*** is the root of the logging directory.

- **LIST=*file***, where ***file*** is the file name the incremental backup will use to store the incremental list. It will be followed by a sequence number.

- **DOTCOUNT=*count***, where ***count*** is the name of a file used for counting as you go, to know which incremental list to use.

- **COUNTER=*count-file***, where ***count-file*** is used for rewinding when done (might not use).

- **BACKUPTAB=*file***, where ***file*** is the name of the file in which we keep our list of backup(s) we want to make.

Files in /etc/sysconfig/network-scripts/

The following files are normally found in /etc/sysconfig/network-scripts:

- /etc/sysconfig/network-scripts/ifup
- /etc/sysconfig/network-scripts/ifdown
- /etc/sysconfig/network-scripts/network-functions
- /etc/sysconfig/network-scripts/ifcfg-<*interface-name*>
- /etc/sysconfig/network-scripts/ifcfg-<*interface-name*>-<*clone-name*>
- /etc/sysconfig/network-scripts/chat-<*interface-name*>
- /etc/sysconfig/network-scripts/dip-<*interface-name*>
- /etc/sysconfig/network-scripts/ifup-post
- /etc/sysconfig/network-scripts/ifdhcpc-done

Let's take a look at each one.

/etc/sysconfig/network-scripts/ifup, /etc/sysconfig/network-scripts/ifdown – Symlinks to /sbin/ifup and /sbin/ifdown, respectively. These are the only two scripts in this directory that should be called directly; these two scripts call all the other scripts as needed. These symlinks are here for legacy purposes only – they will probably be removed in future versions, so only /sbin/ifup and /sbin/ifdown should currently be used.

These scripts take one argument normally: the name of the device (e.g. "eth0"). They are called with a second argument of "boot" during the boot sequence so that devices that are not meant to be brought up on boot (ONBOOT=no, see below) can be ignored at that time.

/etc/sysconfig/network-scripts/network-functions – Not really a public file. Contains functions which the scripts use for bringing interfaces up and down. In particular, it contains most of the code for handling alternative interface configurations and interface change notification through netreport.

/etc/sysconfig/network-scripts/ifcfg-<*interface-name*>, /etc/sysconfig/network-scripts/ifcfg-<*interface-name*>-<*clone-name*> – The first file defines an interface, while the second file contains only the parts of the definition that are different in a "clone" (or alternative) interface. For example, the network numbers might be different, but everything else might be the same, so only the network numbers would be in the clone file, while all the device information would be in the base ifcfg file.

The items that can be defined in an ifcfg file depend on the interface type.

The following values are common to all base files:

- **DEVICE=*name***, where *name* is the name of the physical device (except dynamically-allocated PPP devices where it is the "logical name").

- **IPADDR=*addr***, where *addr* is the IP address.

- **NETMASK=*mask***, where *mask* is the netmask value.

- **NETWORK=*addr***, where *addr* is the network address.

- **BROADCAST=*addr***, where *addr* is the broadcast address.

- **GATEWAY=*addr***, where *addr* is the gateway address.

- **ONBOOT=*answer***, where *answer* is one of the following:

  - **yes** – This device should be activated at boot-time.
  - **no** – This device should not be activated at boot-time.

- **USERCTL=*answer***, where *answer* is one of the following:

  - **yes** – Non-root users are allowed to control this device.
  - **no** – Non-root users are not allowed to control this device.

- **BOOTPROTO=*proto***, where *proto* is one of the following:

  - **none** – No boot-time protocol should be used.
  - **bootp** – The bootp protocol should be used.
  - **dhcp** – The dhcp protocol should be used.

The following values are common to all PPP and SLIP files:

- **PERSIST=*answer***, where *answer* is one of the following:

  - **yes** – This device should be kept active at all times, even if deactivated after a modem hangup.
  - **no** – This device should not be kept active at all times.

- **MODEMPORT=*port***, where *port* is the modem port's device name (for exmaple, "/dev/modem").

- **LINESPEED=*baud***, where *baud* is the modem's linespeed (for example, "115200").

- **DEFABORT=*answer***, where *answer* is one of the following:

  - **yes** – Insert default abort strings when creating/editing the script for this interface.
  - **no** – Do not insert default abort strings when creating/editing the script for this interface.

The following values are common to all PPP files:

- **DEFROUTE=*answer*,** where **answer** is one of the following:

    - **yes** – Set this interface as the default route.
    - **no** – Do not set this interface as the default route.

- **ESCAPECHARS=*answer*,** where **answer** is one of the following:

    - **yes** – Use the pre-defined asyncmap.
    - **no** – Do not use the pre-defined asyncmap.

    (This represents a simplified interface; it doesn't let people specify which characters to escape. However, almost everyone can use an asyncmap of 00000000 anyway, and it's possible to set PPPOPTIONS to use an arbitrary asyncmap if so desired.)

- **HARDFLOWCTL=*answer*,** where **answer** is one of the following:

    - **yes** – Use hardware flow control.
    - **no** – Do not use hardware flow control.

- **PPPOPTIONS=*options*,** where **options** is an arbitrary option string. It is placed last on the command line so it can override other options (such as asyncmap) that were specified previously.

- **PAPNAME=*name*,** where **name** is used as part of "name $PAPNAME" on the pppd command line.

    note that the "remotename" option is always specified as the logical ppp device name, like "ppp0" (which might perhaps be the physical device ppp1 if some other ppp device was brought up earlier...), which makes it easy to manage pap/chap files – name/password pairs are associated with the logical ppp device name so that they can be managed together.

    In principal, there shouldn't anything that would keep the logical PPP device names from being "worldnet" or "myISP" instead of "ppp0" – "pppN".

- **REMIP=*addr*,** where **addr** is the remote ip address (which is normally unspecified).

- **MTU=*value*,** where **value** is the value to be used as MTU.

- **MRU=*value*,** where **value** is the value to be used as MRU.

- **DISCONNECTTIMEOUT=*value*,** where **value** represents the number of seconds to wait before re-establishing the connection after a successfully-connected session terminated.

- **RETRYTIMEOUT=*value*,** where **value** represents the number of seconds to wait before re-attempting to establish a connection after a previous attempt has failed.

/etc/sysconfig/network-scripts/chat-<*interface-name*> – This file is a chat script for PPP or SLIP connections, and is intended to establish the connection. For SLIP devices, a DIP script is written from the chat script; for PPP devices, the chat script is used directly.

/etc/sysconfig/network-scripts/dip-<*interface-name*> – This write-only script is created from the chat script by netcfg. Do not modify this file. In the future, this file may disappear and instead will be created on-the-fly from the chat script.

/etc/sysconfig/network-scripts/ifup-post – This file is called when any network device (except a SLIP device) comes up. Calls `/etc/sysconfig/network-scripts/ifup-routes` to bring up static routes that depend on that device. Brings up aliases for that device. Sets the hostname if it is not already set and a hostname can be found for the IP for that device. Sends SIGIO to any programs that have requested notification of network events.

Could be extended to fix up nameservice configuration, call arbitrary scripts, etc, as needed.

/etc/sysconfig/network-scripts/ifdhcpc-done – This file is called by dhcpcd once dhcp configuration is complete; sets up `/etc/resolv.conf` from the version dhcpcd dropped in `/etc/dhcpc/resolv.conf`.

11.9.2 System V Init

This section is a brief description of the internals of the boot process. It basically covers in detail how the machine boots using SysV init, as well as the differences between the init used in older Linux releases, and SysV init.

Init is the program that gets run by the kernel at boot time. It is in charge of starting all the normal processes that need to run at boot time. These include the gettys that allow you to log in, NFS daemons, FTP daemons, and anything else you want to run when your machine boots.

SysV init is fast becoming the standard in the Linux world to control the startup of software at boot time. This is because it is easier to use and more powerful and flexible than the traditional BSD init.

SysV init also differs from BSD init in that the config files are in a subdirectory of `/etc` instead of residing directly in `/etc`. This directory is called `rc.d`. In there you will find `rc.sysinit` and the following directories:

```
init.d
rc0.d
rc1.d
rc2.d
rc3.d
```

```
rc4.d
rc5.d
rc6.d
```

`init.d` contains a bunch of scripts. Basically, you need one script for each service you may need to start at boot time or when entering another runlevel. Services include things like networking, nfs, sendmail, httpd, etc. Services do not include things like setserial that must only be run once and then exited. Things like that should go in `rc.local` or `rc.serial`.

If you want `rc.local`, it should be in `/etc/rc.d`. Most systems include one even though it doesn't do much. You can also include an rc.serial in `/etc/rc.d` if you need to do serial port specific things at boot time.

The chain of events is as follows:

- The kernel looks in several places for `init` and runs the first one it finds
- `init` runs `/etc/rc.d/rc.sysinit`
- `rc.sysinit` does a bunch of necessary things and then runs `rc.serial` (if it exists)
- `init` runs all the scripts for the default runlevel.
- `init` runs `rc.local`

The default runlevel is decided in `/etc/inittab`. You should have a line close to the top like:

```
id:3:initdefault:
```

From this, you'd look in the second column and see that the default runlevel is 3, as should be the case for most systems. If you want to change it, you can edit `/etc/inittab` by hand and change the 3. Be very careful when you are messing with the inittab. If you do mess up, you can fix it by rebooting and doing:

```
LILO boot:   linux single
```

This *should* allow you to boot into single user mode so you can fix inittab.

Now, how does it run all the right scripts? If you enter `ls -l` on `rc3.d`, you might see something like:

```
lrwxrwxrwx 1 root root 17 3:11 S10network -> ../init.d/network
lrwxrwxrwx 1 root root 16 3:11 S30syslog -> ../init.d/syslog
lrwxrwxrwx 1 root root 14 3:32 S40cron -> ../init.d/cron
lrwxrwxrwx 1 root root 14 3:11 S50inet -> ../init.d/inet
```

```
lrwxrwxrwx 1 root root 13 3:11 S60nfs -> ../init.d/nfs
lrwxrwxrwx 1 root root 15 3:11 S70nfsfs -> ../init.d/nfsfs
lrwxrwxrwx 1 root root 18 3:11 S90lpd -> ../init.d/lpd.init
lrwxrwxrwx 1 root root 11 3:11 S99local -> ../rc.local
```

What you'll notice is that there are no real "files" in the directory. Everything there is a link to one of the scripts in the init.d directory. The links also have an "S" and a number at the beginning. The "S" means to start this particular script and a "K" would mean to stop it. The number is there just for ordering purposes. Init will start all the services based on the order they appear. You can duplicate numbers, but it will only confuse you somewhat. You just need to use a two digit number only, along with an upper case "S" or "K" to start or stop the services you need to.

How does init start and stop services? Simple. Each of the scripts is written to accept an argument which can be "start" and "stop". You can execute those scripts by hand in fact with a command like:

```
/etc/rc.d/init.d/httpd.init stop
```

to stop the httpd server. Init just reads the name and if it has a "K", it calls the script with the "stop" argument. If it has an "S" it calls the script with a "start" argument. Why all these runlevels? Some people want an easy way to set up machines to be multi-purpose. I could have a "server" runlevel that just runs httpd, sendmail, networking, etc. Then I could have a "user" runlevel that runs xdm, networking, etc.

11.9.3   Init Runlevels

Generally, Red Hat Linux runs in run level 3—full multiuser mode. The following runlevels are used in Red Hat Linux:

0 Halt.

1 Single user mode.

2 Multiuser mode, without NFS.

3 Full multiuser mode.

6 Reboot.

If your machine gets into a state where it will not boot due to a bad /etc/inittab, or will not let you log in because you have a corrupted /etc/passwd or have simply forgotten your password, boot into single user mode by typing linux 1 at the LILO boot prompt. A very bare system will come up and you will be given a shell from which you can fix things.

11.9.4 Initscript Utilities

The chkconfig utility provides a simple command-line tool for maintaining the /etc/rc.d directory hierarchy. It relieves system administrators from having to directly manipulate the numerous symlinks in /etc/rc.d.

In addition, there is the ntsysv utility, that provides a screen-oriented interface, versus chkconfig's command-line interface.

Please see the chkconfig and ntsysv man pages for more information.

11.9.5 Running Programs at Boot Time

The file /etc/rc.d/rc.local is executed at boot time, after all other initialization is complete, and whenever you change runlevels. You can add additional initialization commands here. For instance, you may want to start up additional daemons, or initialize a printer. In addition, if you require serial port setup, you can edit /etc/rc.d/rc.serial, and it will be executed automatically at boot time.

The default /etc/rc.d/rc.local simply creates a nice login banner with your kernel version and machine type.

11.9.6 Shutting Down

To shut down Red Hat Linux, issue the shutdown command. You can read the shutdown man page for complete details, but the two most common usages are:

```
shutdown -h now
shutdown -r now
```

Each will cleanly shutdown the system. After shutting everything down, the first will halt the machine, and the second will reboot.

Although the reboot and halt commands are now "smart" enough to invoke shutdown if run while the system is in runlevels 1-5, it is a bad habit to get into, as not all Linux-like operating systems have this feature.

11.10 Rescue Modes

When things go wrong, there are several ways to work on fixing them. However, they require that you understand the system well. This manual can't teach you what to do, but we will present the ways that you can use our products to get into rescue modes where you can use your own knowledge to rescue the system.

11.10.1 Through LILO

If your system boots, but does not allow you to log in when it has completed booting, you can use the single or emergency boot option. At the LILO boot: prompt, type linux single in order to boot in single-user mode. In single-user mode, your local filesystems will be mounted, but your network will not be activated. In emergency mode, almost nothing will be set up. Only the root filesystem will be mounted, and it will be mounted read-only.

11.10.2 Emergency Boot Diskettes

The boot diskette created during installation of Red Hat Linux 5.1 may be used as part of a rescue diskette set. For more information, please read the file rescue.txt in the /doc on your Red Hat Linux 5.1 CD-ROM.

A Handy Trick

Have you ever rebuilt a kernel and, eager to try out your new handiwork, rebooted before running LILO? And you didn't have an entry for an older kernel in lilo.conf? Read on...

Here's a handy trick. In many cases, it's possible to boot your Red Hat Linux/Intel from the Red Hat Linux boot diskette with your root filesystem mounted and ready to go. Here's how:

Enter the following command at the boot diskette's boot: prompt:

```
linux single root=/dev/hdXX initrd=
```

(Replace the XX in /dev/hdXX with the appropriate letter and number for your root partition.)

What does this do? First, it starts the boot in single-user mode, with the root partition set to your root partition. The empty initrd specification bypasses the installation-related image on the boot diskette, which will cause you to enter single-user mode immediately.

Is there a downside to this trick? Unfortunately, yes. Because the kernel on the Red Hat Linux boot diskette only has support for IDE built-in, those of you with SCSI-based systems won't be able to use this trick. In that case, you'll have to use the boot/rescue diskette combination mentioned above.

Getting Technical Support

This chapter discusses Red Hat Software's support:

- What it is
- How to get it
- Frequently asked questions

A.1 An Overview of Our Support Policy

Red Hat Software provides 90-day installation support for people that have purchased the Official Red Hat Linux product.

Red Hat will provide support to registered purchasers of the Red Hat Linux Boxed Set. This support will be provided by means of electronic mail. In the case that the user doesn't have access to e-mail, fax support will be provided for those requests submitted with complete registration numbers.

In order to receive support it is necessary to register the product via the World Wide Web at http://www.redhat.com/support/register or by sending mail including the registration number to register@redhat.com.

After registering successfully, support may be obtained by sending a specially formatted message to support@redhat.com. The message format is described in the support HOW-TO, located at:

http://www.redhat.com/support/register/support-how2.html

This e-mail will then be delivered to Red Hat Software support where it will be distributed to a Red Hat Support Engineer.

As the name implies, installation support centers on helping you successfully install Red Hat Linux on your computer. This includes support in three distinct areas:

- Answering questions you may have prior to installation, such as:
  - Hardware compatibility issues.
  - Basic approaches to partitioning your hard drive.

- Helping you get through the installation process:
  - Getting any supported hardware necessary for installation recognized by the installation program.
    (See http://www.redhat.com/hardware/)
  - Assisting with the creation of a root and swap partition using the free space available on your hard drive.
  - Using the installation program to configure LILO to boot Red Hat Linux, and one other operating system (such as DOS, Windows 95, or Windows NT) already residing on your hard drive.

- Assisting with final configuration tasks, such as:
  - The successful configuration of the X window system on supported hardware, using either the Metro-X or XFree86 software. (Additional configuration, such as automatically starting X on reboot, or changing/customizing window managers is your responsibility.)
  - Configuring a printer connected directly to the Red Hat Linux system, enabling it to print text.
  - Setting up a mouse to be used with the text-based console, or with the X window system.
  - Getting access to the CD-ROM, so that information can be read from it.

Naturally, although our installation support service will get your system running Red Hat Linux, there are many other optional tasks that you might want to undertake, such as compiling a customized kernel, adding support for devices not included in the installation process, and so on.

For assistance with these tasks, please consider the many books on Linux at your local bookstore, or various on-line resources. A starting point in your on-line search for Linux information should always be:

```
http://www.redhat.com/support/
```

for information specific to Red Hat Linux, or:

```
http://www.redhat.com/linux-info/
```

for more general Linux information. Another good resource is
`http://www.linux.org/`.

Red Hat Software can only support customers that have purchased the official Red Hat Linux Box set. If you have obtained Red Hat from any other publisher, you must contact them for support. Examples of other publishers would be:

- Macmillan/Sams
- Cheapbytes
- Pacific Hi-Tech (PHT)
- Infomagic
- Linux Systems Labs (LSL)
- ADRAS Computing

Also, RHL-Intel obtained via any of the following methods does not qualify for support from Red Hat Software:

- Red Hat Linux PowerTools Archive
- Downloaded via FTP on the Internet.
- Included in a package such as Applixware or Motif.
- Copied or installed from another user's CD.

A.2   Getting Support

As of July 1996, Red Hat Software put a new Technical Support system online. The support system automatically routes questions to support technicians. This document describes how to use the Red Hat Software technical support system.

A.2.1   Registration

In order to receive technical support for your Red Hat Software product, you have to register it. Every official Red Hat product comes with a Registration Card. Your product registration number appears on both the detachable mail-in portion and on the top portion of this card. The product registration number uniquely identifies a product which you have purchased (such as Red Hat Linux) that includes 90 days of free installation technical support by fax or email.

Registering via the Web

Registering via the Web

You can register your Red Hat Software product online at Red Hat's World Wide Web site at http://www.redhat.com/support/register/. Choose **Register a Product**. Please enter all applicable information, and please be accurate with the system information. This information will aid in solving problems and answering questions more quickly and easily, and incorrect information benefits neither us nor our customers. Also, make sure the electronic mail address you give is correct. All support correspondence will be sent to that address. If this should change, please login to the registration pages and edit this information.

Registration has changed. There will be no more annoying support ID numbers to remember. If you don't have a current login to the support database, you will need to create one. Simply enter a name at the **Support Login** and click on the **Create Login** button to begin registration of your product. If you were already registered for support before August 14, 1997 you can login in by using your email address as your Support Login and your former support/customer ID as the password. The password can be changed once logged in. If you don't remember it, follow the steps as if you never had a login, and re-enter the registration numbers and information.

Registering via Email

If you don't have access to the World Wide Web, but you do have access to Internet mail, you can send registration details to register@redhat.com. Please include the following information:

- Contact Information: name, address, city, state/province, country, zip/postal code, and telephone and fax numbers; also, your support ID if you have one;

- Product Information: name of product you are registering, product registration number (very important!), architecture you're using the product on (Intel, Alpha/AXP, or Sparc), and what you're using the product for (File Server, Internet Server, Workstation, Home Computer, or Other);

- System Information: CPU (i386, i486, i586, i686/PentiumPro, AXP21164, AXP21064, Sparc4C, Sparc4M), CPU speed (MHz), amount of RAM (MB), hard drives (number, size, type, partitions), video card, CD-ROM drive, any network card, and other hardware components (SCSI or ISDN adaptors, etc.).

Registering via Fax or Snail Mail

Although a mail-in portion is provided with your registration card, we do not recommend registering via fax or snail mail if you have access to either the World Wide Web or Internet mail; if you do so, your registration is likely to be delayed considerably. If you do wish to register via fax, fax a copy of your registration card to Red Hat Software at +1-919-361-2711.

A.2.2   Support Questions

Technical support is a black art: in most cases, support technicians rely solely on communication with the customer to solve installation problems on hardware the technicians have never physically seen. It is extremely important, therefore, to state your question clearly and concisely, including detailed information such as:

- symptoms of the problem ("Red Hat Linux 5.1 doesn't recognize my CD-ROM drive.")

- when the problem began ("It stopped working yesterday ...")

- what changes you have made to your system around the time of the problem ("... after I disconnected it from the IDE controller.")

- any diagnostic output specifically related to the problem ("In the bootup messages, it says 'Cannot find /dev/hdb; device disconnected'.") however, this can be taken overboard; don't send us your system logs unless we ask you for them.

- other relevant information ("I'm using the floppy installation method, from the CD.")

How to Send Them

Red Hat's support system is email-based and is partially automated; for this reason, it is important to make sure you send support questions in the correct format, so that your message will be recognized and routed to an appropriate support technician. In order to receive technical support for your Red Hat Software product, you must first register it.

Submitting trouble tickets can be sent in the traditional email way, or can be initiated via the World Wide Web. After providing the information for the registration, you will have a new menu allowing you to edit your registration information or open a trouble ticket. Hurry and login now to open a ticket on the Web! http://www.redhat.com/support/register/

To open a support ticket via email, all you need to do is send the support system a message with a Subject: of [registration #nnnn nnnn nnnn nnnn], where nnnn nnnn nnnn nnnn is the registration number of the product for which you are requesting support. For example, if your registration number is fffe 0fff ff00 ff00, the subject line should read:

```
Subject: [registration #fffe 0fff ff00 ff00]
```

The square brackets, the number sign, and the word 'registration' must be present. If you wish, you may add explanatory text to the subject line:

```
Subject: [registration #fffe 0fff ff00 ff00] CD-ROM problem
```

Once you've opened a ticket, support responses come to you with the support ticket number in the subject line:

```
Subject: [ticket #12015] CD-ROM problem
```

To correspond about the same problem, simply send a reply with the same subject:

```
Subject: Re: [ticket #12015] CD-ROM problem
```

If you feel that the problem has been solved the ticket can also be closed by you. Simply add close to the same subject:

```
Subject: Re: [close ticket #12015] CD-ROM problem
```

Once your problem is solved or your question answered, the technician handling your support ticket can close the ticket. This can also be done by you via the website. Either method will result in a message from the support system stating the ticket is closed and contain a summary of the problem and the solution. You can open a new ticket for your next support question. All past correspondence will be saved in the database under the old ticket number and can be accessed with your account at any time.

Where to Send Them

The address for Red Hat's Technical Support System is support@redhat.com; all support questions should go there. There are also several related addresses:

- For a copy of the Red Hat FAQ (Frequently Asked Questions, with answers), send mail to faq@redhat.com.

- For a copy of the Red Hat PPP Tips (tips on setting up a PPP connection), send mail to ppp-tips@redhat.com.

- To report a bug, send mail to bugs@redhat.com.

A.3   Support FAQ (Frequently Asked Questions)

Here are a few questions that the Red Hat Support Staff see frequently, along with the answers:

Question – I've sent several messages to the Red Hat Support System, and I've gotten absolutely no response. Is anybody there?

Answer – Check your registration information to make sure your email address is correct. You can check it by logging in at
`http://www.redhat.com/support/register/`.

Question – I know I have already registered, but I keep getting a message from the support system telling me I'm not registered. Is the system broken?

Answer – Make sure to register via the World Wide Web at
`http://www.redhat.com/support/register/`. If you didn't please do so, by first accessing the registration page. Next, input a login name and click on **Create Login**. After this you will be prompted to input some personal information. When finished click on the **Submit** button and then enter your registration number which should look something like `fffe 0fff ff00 ff00`. Then be sure to enter all the information about your system. This information can be maintained by logging in and accessing your registration information from
`http://www.redhat.com/support/register/`.

Question – But I registered via email. Why isn't the support system working?

Answer – When you register via email, your message goes to an actual human who registers you manually; this can delay your registration anywhere from several hours to several days.

Question – I've done everything perfectly for my registration, but I'm still getting messages telling me I have an invalid registration number.

Answer – Please make sure you're using a valid product registration number. If you have not purchased the official box set from Red Hat Software or a Vendor that sells the official version (it will say 'official' on the box) you will not be able to register, as Red Hat Software cannot support products packaged and sold by other software publishers.

Question – I see this thing on the registration page that asks me what my login is? What is my login anyway?

Answer – If you are a first time user of the the support system or accessed the support system after August 15, 1997 then the Login can be whatever you want it to be. It must be all one word and if there is already a duplicate you will be warned of an error. If you accessed the system before this time and have a valid registration, your login will be the email address you had when registering and the password will be the old Support ID number. You can change the password if you like; however the login cannot be changed.

Question – I've tried entering a login and password but it won't accept it. Why won't it accept the password I'm trying to enter?

Answer – The password must be a minimum of 5 alphanumeric characters long and no more than 8. Make sure you typed in the exact same password both times for both password fields on the registration page.

Question – I hear that it's possible to change my registration information and view all my old tickets and the past correspondence. How do I do that?

Answer – Simply login to the registration page at
`http://www.redhat.com/support/register` and all these options will be available to you. If you need to reference an old trouble ticket, change your system information, or just check up on the status of a trouble ticket, visit this page. You can also open a trouble ticket with valid registration numbers directly from the web from these pages.

Making Installation Diskettes

It is sometimes necessary to create a diskette from an *image file* (for example, you might need to use updated diskette images obtained from the Red Hat Linux Errata).

As the name implies, an image file is a file that contains an exact copy (or image) of a diskette's contents. Since a diskette contains filesystem information in addition to the data contained in files, the image file is not usable until it has been written to a diskette.

To start, you'll need a blank, formatted, high-density (1.44 MB), 3.5-inch diskette. You'll need access to a computer with a 3.5-inch diskette drive, and capable of running a DOS program, or the dd utility program found on most Linux-like operating systems.

The image files are found in the following directories on your Red Hat Linux CD:

- images – Contains the boot and supplemental images for Red Hat Linux/Intel.

Once you've selected the proper image, it's time to transfer the image file onto a diskette. As mentioned previously, this can be done on a DOS-capable system, or on a system running a Linux-like operating system.

B.1   Making a Diskette Under MS-DOS

To make a diskette under MS-DOS, use the rawrite utility included on the Red Hat Linux CD in the dosutils directory. First, label a blank, formatted 3.5-inch diskette appropriately (eg. "Boot Diskette", "Supplemental Diskette", etc). Insert it into the diskette drive. Then, use the following commands (assuming your CD is drive d:):

```
C:\> d:
D:\> cd \dosutils
D:\dosutils> rawrite
Enter disk image source file name:  ..\images\boot.img
Enter target diskette drive:  a:
Please insert a formatted diskette into drive A: and
press --ENTER-- :  Enter
D:\dosutils>
```

rawrite first asks you for the filename of a diskette image; enter the directory and name of the image you wish to write (for example, ..\images\boot.img). Then rawrite asks for a diskette drive to write the image to; enter a:. Finally, rawrite asks for confirmation that a formatted diskette is in the drive you've selected. After pressing Enter to confirm, rawrite copies the image file onto the diskette. If you need to make another diskette, label another diskette, and run rawrite again, specifying the appropriate image file.

B.2   Making a Diskette Under a Linux-like O/S

To make a diskette under Linux (or any other Linux-like operating system), you must have permission to write to the device representing a 3.5-inch diskette drive (known as /dev/fd0 under Linux). First, label a blank, formatted diskette appropriately (eg. "Boot Diskette", "Supplemental Diskette", etc). Insert it into the diskette drive (but don't issue a mount command). After mounting the Red Hat Linux CD, change directory to the directory containing the desired image file, and use the following command (changing the name of the image file and diskette device as appropriate):

```
# dd if=boot.img of=/dev/fd0 bs=1440k
```

If you need to make another diskette, label another diskette, and run dd again, specifying the appropriate image file.

C

Package List

This appendix lists the packages that make up Red Hat Linux. In each entry, you'll find the following information:

- The name of the package

- The packaged software's version number

- The size of the packaged software, in kilobytes

- A short description of the software

Please Note: This package list was automatically generated right before Red Hat Linux 5.1 went into production. Because of the short timeframes involved, you might find minor typesetting problems in the package lists. However, we felt that an up-to-date package list was more important than a picture-perfect package list. We hope you'll agree...

You may also notice that some packages have different versions, and that packages listed here are not mentioned in the installation program (and vice versa). Any differences in package versions are normally due to the normal bug fixing process. It's possible that "missing" or "extra" packages are the result of last-minute changes prior to pressing CDROMs. Also note that all the packages in the "Base" group (and subgroups) are always installed, therefore you will not see them mentioned explicitly during the installation process.

Using the Package List After Installation   This list can come in handy even after you've installed Red Hat Linux. You can use it search for documentation. Here's how:

1. Find the package in this list.

2. Note the package name (The very first thing listed in bold at the start of each package description).

3. Enter the following command, taking care to enter the package name *exactly* as it is shown in the list (the package name is case-sensitive):

   ```
   rpm -qd package-name
   ```

   (Replacing package-name with the actual name of the package, of course.)

If you installed the package, you should get a list of filenames. Each file contains documentation relating to the package you specified. Here are some of the types of filenames you'll see:

- **/usr/man... something.n** – This is a man page. You can view it by using the man command (for example, man something. You might also need to include the file's ending number in the man command (as in man n something.

- **/usr/X11R6/man... something.nx** – This is a man page for part of the X Window System. View these files the same way as a regular man page.

- **/usr/doc/something...** – Files under /usr/doc can be in any number of different formats. Sometimes the end of the filename can provide a clue as to how it should be viewed:

  - **.html** – An HTML file. View with the web browser of your choice.
  - **.txt** – A text file. View with cat or less.
  - **.ps** – A Postscript file. You can print it to a Postscript printer, or you can view it with gv.
  - **.gz** – A file compressed with gzip. If you make a copy of the original file, you can use gunzip to decompress it (you'll probably want to keep the original file compressed to save space). You can then view the file as you would normally. The zless command combines gunzip and less, and makes it possible to read compressed text files without making interim copies. There are other, more elegant ways to work with compressed files, but this approach will work for those just starting to use Linux.

  In general, most of the documentation files you'll find will be one of those listed above. If in doubt, it's a good bet that the file is text. You can always try the file command to see if the file's contents can be identified.

- **/usr/info...** – Files in /usr/info are meant to be viewed using the info (or Emacs' Info mode). If you use Emacs, press [Ctrl]-[I], followed by [I] to view the main Info screen.

C.1 Applications

As this section's name implies, this is where you can find most of the applications available with Red Hat Linux. We've split the applications into several different categories to make finding things a bit easier.

(If you noticed that we said *"most* of the applications" above, you can find more apps by looking at X11's application section towards the end of the appendix.)

C.1.1 Communications

This section contains packages that help you communicate – either via fax, on-line chat, or simple terminal emulation.

efax – (Version 0.8a, 205K)   This is a program to send and receive faxes over class 1 or class 2 fax modems. It has a nice interface to help facilitate faxing.

ircii – (Version 4.4, 1,223K)   This is a popular Internet Relay Chat (IRC) client. It is a program used to connect to IRC servers around the globe so that the user can "chat" with others.

ircii-help – (Version 4.4, 455K)   This package contains the help files and other documentation for the ircii client package.

lrzsz – (Version 0.12.14, 340K)   This collection of commands can be used to download and upload files using the Z, X, and Y protocols. Many terminal programs (like minicom) make use of these programs to transfer files.

minicom – (Version 1.81, 268K)   Minicom is a communications program that resembles the MSDOS Telix somewhat. It has a dialing directory, color, full ANSI and VT100 emulation, an (external) scripting language and more.

C.1.2 Databases

This section contains packages that provide basic database support for Red Hat Linux.

postgresql – (Version 6.3.2, 9,268K)   PostgreSQL Data Base Management System (formerly known as Postgres, then as Postgres95).

PostgreSQL is an enhancement of the POSTGRES database management system, a next-generation DBMS research prototype. While PostgreSQL retains the powerful data model and rich data types of POSTGRES, it replaces the PostQuel query language with an extended subset of SQL. PostgreSQL is free and the complete source is available.

PostgreSQL development is being performed by a team of Internet developers who all subscribe to the PostgreSQL development mailing list. The current coordinator is Marc G. Fournier (scrappy@postgreSQL.org). This team is now responsible for all current and future development of PostgreSQL.

The authors of PostgreSQL 1.01 were Andrew Yu and Jolly Chen. Many others have contributed to the porting, testing, debugging and enhancement of the code. The original Postgres code, from which PostgreSQL is derived, was the effort of many graduate students, undergraduate students, and staff programmers working under the direction of Professor Michael Stonebraker at the University of California, Berkeley.

The original name of the software at Berkeley was Postgres. When SQL functionality was added in 1995, its name was changed to Postgres95. The name was changed at the end of 1996 to PostgreSQL.

PostgreSQL runs on Solaris, SunOS, HPUX, AIX, Linux, Irix, FreeBSD, and most flavours of Unix.

postgresql-clients – (Version 6.3.2, 942K)   This package includes only the clients and client libraries needed to access an PostgreSQL server. The server is included in the main package. If all you need is to connect to another PostgreSQL server, the this is the only package you need to install.

In this package there are client libraries available for C, C++ and PERL, as well as several command-line utilities you can use to manage your databases on a remote PostgreSQL server.

postgresql-data – (Version 6.3.2, 876K)   This packages includes an initial database structure directory for PostgreSQL. For a quick startup on PostegreSQL, it is recommended to install this package with your PostgreSQL backend server (altough it is not required).

If you choose to not install this package you will have to create the initial database yourself using 'initdb' command and possibly modify the postgresql startup script if you choose a directory other than /var/lib/pgsql for storing your databases.

C.1.3   Editors

In this section, we have an assortment of packages that provide basic (and in some cases not so basic) file editing capabilities.

ed – (Version 0.2, 104K)   This is the GNU line editor. It is an implementation of one of the first editors under *nix. Some programs rely on it, but in general you probably don't *need* it.

emacs – (Version 20.2, 10,602K)   Emacs is the extensible, customizable, self-documenting real-time display editor. Emacs has special code editing modes, a scripting language (elisp), and comes with many packages for doing mail, news, and more, all in your editor.

This package includes the libraries necessary to run the emacs editor - the actual program can be found in either the emacs-nox or emacs-X11 packages, depending on whether you use X Windows or not.

emacs-X11 – (Version 20.2, 2,327K)   This package contains an emacs binary built with support for X Windows. It will still work fine outside of X Windows (on the console, for instance) but supports the mouse and GUI elements when used inside of X Windows.

emacs-el – (Version 20.2, 14,718K)   This package contains the emacs-lisp sources for many of the elisp programs included with the main emacs package. You do not need this package unless you want to modify these packages, or see some elisp examples.

emacs-nox – (Version 20.2, 1,995K)   This package contains an emacs binary built without support for X Windows. While the emacs binary in the main emacs package will work fine outside of X Windows (on the console, for instance), the one in this package has a smaller memory image.

jed – (Version 0.98.4, 1,193K)   Jed is a fast compact editor based on the slang screen library. It has special editing modes for C, C++, and other languages. It can emulate Emacs, Wordstar, and other editors, and can be customized with slang macros, colors, keybindings, etc.

jed-xjed – (Version 0.98.4, 153K)   Xjed is the same editor as jed, it just runs in its own X Window.

joe – (Version 2.8, 283K)   Joe is a friendly and easy to use editor. It has a nice interface and would be a good choice for a novice needing a text editor. It uses the same WordStar keybindings which are also used by Borland's development enbironment.

vim – (Version 5.1, 3,780K)   The VIsual editor iMproved is an updated and feature-added clone of the 'vi' editor that comes with almost all UN*X systems. It adds multiple windows, multi-level undo, block highliting, and many other features to the standard vi program.

vim-X11 – (Version 5.1, 451K)   This package is a version of VIM with the X-Windows libraries linked in, allowing you to run VIM as an X-Windows application with a full GUI interface and mouse support. You just run 'gvim'.

C.1.4   Emulators

In this section are packages that let your Red Hat Linux system run programs meant for other operating systems.

dosemu – (Version 0.66.7, 3,269K)   This package enables you to run a number of DOS programs under Linux. This package includes an image with DOS-C kernel (MS DOS 3.31 compatible) and FreeDos utilities. You should be able to start up the DOS emulator by logging in as root and typing 'dos' at the prompt.

xdosemu – (Version 0.66.7, 26K)   This is a version of the DOS emulator that is designed to run in an X windows session. It provides VGA graphics support as well as mouse support.

C.1.5 Engineering

This section contains packages for those of you that are into engineering.

spice – (Version 2g6, 431K) SPICE is a general-purpose circuit simulation program for nonlinear dc, nonlinear transient, and linear ac analyses. Circuits may contain resistors, capacitors, inductors, mutual inductors, independent voltage and current sources, four types of dependent sources, transmission lines, and the four most common semiconductor devices: diodes, BJT's, JFET's, and MOSFET's.

units – (Version 1.0, 24K) The units program converts quantities expression in various scales to their equivalents in other scales. The units program can only handle multiplicative scale changes.

C.1.6 Graphics

This section contains packages that help you work with graphics-related material.

ghostscript – (Version 3.33, 1,867K) Ghostscript is a PostScript interpretor. It can render both PostScript and PDF compliant files to devices which include an X window, many printer formats (including support for color printers), and popular graphics file formats.

ghostscript-fonts – (Version 4.0, 2,188K) These fonts can be used by the GhostScript interpreter during text rendering.

giftrans – (Version 1.12.2, 20K) This program can convert and manipulate GIF images from the command line. It is most useful for making a color transparent for web sites.

libgr-progs – (Version 2.0.13, 1,397K) This package includes various utility programs for manipulating JPEG files for use by libgr programs.

xfig – (Version 3.2, 685K) This program gives you all the features you need to create basic-to intermediate-level vector graphics, including bezier curves, lines, rulers, and more.

zgv – (Version 3.0, 172K) Zgv is a picture viewer capable of displaying GIF files as defined by CompuServe, with the exceptions listed in the RESTRICTIONS section. It is also capable of displaying JPEG/JFIF files using the Independant JPEG Group's JPEG software, PBM/PGM/PPM files as used by pbmplus and netpbm, Microsoft Windows and OS/2 BMP files, Targa (TGA) files, and the new PNG format.

C.1.7 Mail

This section contains several of the more popular e-mail-related programs.

elm – (Version 2.4.25, 479K)   ELM is one of the most popular terminal mode mail handling programs. It is powerful, easy to use, and easy to find help on. It has all the mail handling features you would expect, including MIME support (via metamail).

exmh – (Version 2.0.2, 1,814K)   exmh is a graphical interface to the MH mail system. It includes MIME support, faces, glimpse indexing, color highlighting, PGP interface, and more. Requires sox (or play) for sound support.

fetchmail – (Version 4.4.4, 462K)   Fetchmail is a program that is used to retrieve mail from a remote mail server. It can use the Post Office Protocol (POP) or IMAP (Internet Mail Access Protocol) for this, and delivers the mail through the local SMTP server (normally sendmail).

mailx – (Version 5.5.kw, 83K)   The /bin/mail program can be used to send quick mail messages, and is often used in shell scripts.

metamail – (Version 2.7, 333K)   Metamail is an implementation of MIME, the Multipurpose Internet Mail Extensions, a proposed standard for multimedia mail on the Internet. Metamail implements MIME, and also implements extensibility and configuration via the "mailcap" mechanism described in an informational RFC that is a companion to the MIME document.

mutt – (Version 0.91.1, 463K)   Mutt is a small but very poweful full-screen Unix mail client. Features include MIME support, color, POP3 support, message threading, bindable keys, and threaded sorting mode.

nmh – (Version 0.24, 4,293K)   nmh mail handling system (with POP support). nmh is a popular mail handling system but includes only a command line interface. It is an important base, however, for programs like xmh and exmh.

pine – (Version 3.96, 2,367K)   Pine is a very full featured text based mail and news client. It is aimed at both novice and expert users. It includes an easy to use editor, pico, for composing messages. Pico has gained popularity as a stand alone text editor in it's own right. It features MIME support, address books, and support for IMAP, mail, and MH style folders.

C.1.8 Math

This section contains packages of interest to the mathematician in all of us.

bc – (Version 1.04, 125K)   bc is a text mode calculator of sorts. It has many extended features such as base translation. It can also accept input from stdin and return output. dc is the RPN version.

gnuplot – (Version 3.5, 495K)   This is the GNU plotting package. It can be used to graph data in an X window or to a file.

C.1.9 Networking

This section contains network-related packages.

lynx – (Version 2.8, 1,916K) This a terminal based WWW browser. While it does not make any attempt at displaying graphics, it has good support for HTML text formatting, forms, and tables.

ncftp – (Version 2.4.3, 170K) Ncftp is a ftp client with many advantageous over the standard one. It includes command line editing, command histories, support for recurisive gets, automatic logins, and much more.

tcpdump – (Version 3.4a5, 186K) Tcpdump prints out the headers of packets on a network interface. It is very useful for debugging network problems and security operations.

wget – (Version 1.5.0, 346K) GNU Wget is a freely available network utility to retrieve files from the World Wide Web using HTTP and FTP, the two most widely used Internet protocols. It works non-interactively, thus enabling work in the background, after having logged off.

The recursive retrieval of HTML pages, as well as FTP sites is supported – you can use Wget to make mirrors of archives and home pages, or traverse the web like a WWW robot (Wget understands /robots.txt).

Wget works exceedingly well on slow or unstable connections, keeping getting the document until it is fully retrieved. Re-getting files from where it left off works on servers (both HTTP and FTP) that support it. Matching of wildcards and recursive mirroring of directories are available when retrieving via FTP. Both HTTP and FTP retrievals can be time-stamped, thus Wget can see if the remote file has changed since last retrieval and automatically retrieve the new version if it has.

By default, Wget supports proxy servers, which can lighten the network load, speed up retrieval and provide access behind firewalls. However, if you are behind a firewall that requires that you use a socks style gateway, you can get the socks library and compile wget with support for socks.

Most of the features are configurable, either through command-line options, or via initialization file .wgetrc. Wget allows you to install a global startup file (/usr/local/lib/wgetrc by default) for site settings.

C.1.10 News

This section contains packages that you can use to read on-line newsgroups.

slrn – (Version 0.9.4.3, 303K) Slrn is an easy to use but powerful full-screen NNTP based newsreader. It relies extensively on the S-Lang programmer's library for many of its features. Slrn works particularly well over slow network connections.

tin – (Version 1.22, 538K)   Tin is a full-screen easy to use Netnews reader. It can read news locally (i.e. /usr/spool/news) or remotely (rtin or tin -r option) via a NNTP (Network News Transport Protocol) server.

trn – (Version 3.6, 436K)   'trn' is one of the original threaded news readers. this version is configured to read news from an NNTP news server.

C.1.11   Productivity

This section contains packages aimed at helping you keep track of time, and staying productive.

ical – (Version 2.2, 676K)   ical is a popular X-based calendar/scheduler application which can help you keep track of single events and recurring events (daily, weekly, monthly, or yearly), and sets off alarms to warn you of appointments.

C.1.12   Publishing

This section contains packages that turn your Red Hat Linux system into a high-quality typesetting workstation. (In fact, the printed version of this document is produced using many of these tools!)

groff – (Version 1.11a, 2,957K)   The groff text formatting system can be used to create professional looking documents on both paper and a computer screen. All the man pages are processed with groff, so you'll need this package to read man pages.

groff-gxditview – (Version 1.11a, 71K)   The package contains the gxditview program, which can be used to format and view groff documents in X Windows. For example, man pages can be read using gxditview.

lout – (Version 3.08, 3,429K)   The Lout system reads a high-level description of a document similar in style to LaTeX and produces a PostScript file which can be printed on many laser printers and graphic display devices. Plain text output is also available.

Lout offers an unprecedented range of advanced features, including optimal paragraph and page breaking, automatic hyphenation, PostScript EPS file inclusion and generation, equation formatting, tables, diagrams, rotation and scaling, sorted indexes, bibliographic databases, running headers and odd-even pages, automatic cross referencing, multilingual documents including hyphenation (most European languages are supported, including Russian), formatting of C/C++ programs, and much more, all ready to use. Furthermore, Lout is easily extended with definitions which are very much easier to write than troff of TeX macros because Lout is a high-level language, the outcome of an eight-year research project that went back to the beginning.

lout-doc – (Version 3.08, 2,069K)   This package includes the complete Lout documentation, including the "user" and "expert" manuals, written in Lout and with PostScript output. Good examples of writing large docs with Lout.

sgml-tools – (Version 1.0.6, 1,884K) SGML-Tools is a SGML-based text formatter which allows you to produce a variety of output formats. You can create PostScript and dvi (with LaTeX), plain text (with groff), HTML, and texinfo files from a single SGML source file.

tetex – (Version 0.4pl8, 26,966K) TeX formats a file of interspersed text and commands and outputs a typesetter independent file (called DVI, which is short for DeVice Independent). TeX capabilities and language are described in The TeXbook, by Knuth.

tetex-afm – (Version 0.4pl8, 763K) PostScript fonts are (or should be) accompanied by font metric files such as Times-Roman.afm, which describes the characteristics of the font called Times-Roman. To use such fonts with TeX, we need TFM files that contain similar information. afm2tfm does that conversion.

tetex-dvilj – (Version 0.4pl8, 270K) Dvilj and siblings convert TeX-output .dvi files into HP PCL (i.e. HP Printer Control Language) commands suitable for printing on a HP LaserJet+, HP LaserJet IIP (using dvilj2p), HP LaserJet 4 (using dvilj4), and fully compatible printers.

tetex-dvips – (Version 0.4pl8, 553K) The program dvips takes a DVI file file[.dvi] produced by TeX (or by some other processor such as GFtoDVI) and converts it to PostScript, normally sending the result directly to the laserprinter.

tetex-latex – (Version 0.4pl8, 9,678K) LaTeX is a TeX macro package. The LaTeX macros encourage writers to think about the content of their documents, rather than the form. The ideal, very difficult to realize, is to have no formatting commands (like "switch to italic" or "skip 2 picas") in the document at all; instead, everything is done by specific markup instructions: "emphasize", "start a section".

tetex-texmf-src – (Version 0.4pl8, 18,054K) This package contains the source for the documents and TeX components in the teTeX distribution. This package IS NOT REQUIRED to use teTeX, but is useful for those who need to customize it. The documented source file (*.dtx) are an example of what this package contains.

tetex-xdvi – (Version 0.4pl8, 140K) xdvi is a program which runs under the X window system. It is used to preview dvi files, such as are produced by tex and latex.

texinfo – (Version 3.12, 501K) The GNU project uses the texinfo file format for much of its documentation. This package includes the tools necessary to create .info files from .texinfo source files, as well as an emacs interface to all these tools.

C.1.13 Sound

This section contains packages that let you use your Red Hat Linux system's sound capabilities.

aumix – (Version 1.8, 30K) This program provides a tty based, interactive method of controlling a sound cards mixer. It lets you adjust the input levels from the CD, microphone, and on board synthesizers as well as the output volume.

cdp – (Version 0.33, 37K)   This program allows you to play audio CD's on your computers CDROM drive. It provides a version with a full screen interface as well as a command line version.

maplay – (Version 1.2, 70K)   This program plays MPEG 2 format audio files through your PC's sound card. MPEG audio files are popular for sending high fidelity music over the Internet, and http://www.iuma.com contains a large archive of MPEG 2 sound files.

playmidi – (Version 2.3, 129K)   Plays MIDI sound files through a sound card synthesizer. It includes basic drum samples for use with simple FM synthesizers.

playmidi-X11 – (Version 2.3, 36K)   X program for playing MIDI sound files through a sound card sProgramme X pour jouer des fichiers MIDI par le synthtiseur d'une carte son. Il contient des exemples de batterie de base pour les synthtiseurs FM simples.

sox – (Version 11g, 97K)   The self described "swiss army knife of sound tools", sox can convert between many different digitized sound formats and perform simple sound manipulation functions.

tracker – (Version 4.3, 80K)   Amiga MOD files are a very popular format for distributing sound files and the digital samples that are required to play them. Tracker can play a wide range of .mod files through any sound card supported by Linux.

C.2   Base

This section contains the packages that are consider basic to every Red Hat Linux system. You will normally will not see them during the installation process, but they're included here for your information.

C.2.1   Kernel

This section contains packages related to your Red Hat Linux system's kernel. This part of the Linux operating system is central to all system operations.

kernel – (Version 2.0.34, 4,180K)   This package contains the Linux kernel that is used to boot and run your system. It contains few device drivers for specific hardware. Most hardware is instead supported by modules loaded after booting.

kernel-headers – (Version 2.0.34, 1,349K)   These are the C header files for the Linux kernel, which define structures and constants that are needed when building most standard programs under Linux, as well as to rebuild the kernel.

kernel-ibcs – (Version 2.0.34, 211K)   This package allows you to run programs in the iBCS2 (Intel Binary Compatibility Standard, version 2) and related executable formats.

kernel-source – (Version 2.0.34, 27,183K) This is the source code for the Linux kernel. It is required to build most C programs as they depend on constants defined in here. You can also build a custom kernel that is better tuned to your particular hardware.

basesystem – (Version 4.9, 0K) While this package does not contain any files, it does perform an important function. It defines the components of a basic Red Hat system, as the package installation order to use during bootstrapping. It should be the first package installed on a system, and it should never be removed.

crontabs – (Version 1.7, 4K) The root crontab file is used to schedule execution of various programs.

dev – (Version 2.5.9, 0K) Unix and unix like systems (including Linux) use file system entries to represent devices attached to the machine. All of these entries are in the /dev tree (though they don't have to be), and this package contains the most commonly used /dev entries. These files are essential for a system to function properly.

etcskel – (Version 1.3, 5K) This is part of the Base Red Hat system. It contains the files that go in /etc/skel, which are in turn placed in every new user's home directory when new accounts are created.

filesystem – (Version 1.3.1, 79K) This package contains the basic directory layout for a Linux system, including the proper permissions for the directories. This layout conforms to the Linux Filesystem Standard (FSSTND) 1.3.

initscripts – (Version 3.64, 91K) This package contains the scripts use to boot a system, change run levels, and shut the system down cleanly. It also contains the scripts that activate and deactivate most network interfaces.

mailcap – (Version 1.0, 29K) This is the Red Hat Mailcap package. Installing it will allow programs like lynx to automatically use zgv to display pictures (provided zgv is installed).

pam – (Version 0.64, 1,637K) PAM (Pluggable Authentication Modules) is a powerful, flexible, extensible authentication system which allows the system administrator to configure authentication services individually for every pam-compliant application without recompiling any of the applications.

pamconfig – (Version 0.51, 2K) This package has been made obsolete by pam-0.56, and is provided for compatibility purposes only. If the command:

rpm -q –whatrequires pamconfig

returns no package names, you may remove this package with:

rpm -e pamconfig

passwd – (Version 0.50, 17K) This password-changing program uses PAM (Pluggable Authentication Modules) to set or change a password. Like all PAM-capable applications, it can be configured using a file in the /etc/pam.d/ directory.

pwdb – (Version 0.54, 1,256K) pwdb (Password Database Library) allows configurable access to and management of /etc/passwd, /etc/shadow, and network authentication systems including NIS and Radius.

redhat-release – (Version 5.1, 0K) Red Hat Linux release file

rootfiles – (Version 1.5, 2K) This package contains all the startup files for the root user. These are basically the same files that are in the etcskel package.

setup – (Version 1.9.1, 8K) This package contains a number of very important configuration and setup files, including the passwd, group, profile files, etc.

termcap – (Version 9.12.6, 424K) The /etc/termcap file is a database defining the capabilities of various terminals and terminal emulators. Programs use /etc/termcap to gain access to various features of terminals such as the bell, color, and graphics.

C.3 Daemons

This section contains packages for all the daemons available for your Red Hat Linux system. Daemons are programs that run automatically, and perform various system functions for you.

SysVinit – (Version 2.74, 141K) SysVinit is the first program started by the Linux kernel when the system boots, controlling the startup, running, and shutdown of all other programs.

at – (Version 3.1.7, 60K) at and batch read commands from standard input or a specified file which are to be executed at a later time, using /bin/sh.

bdflush – (Version 1.5, 9K) This program flushes the disk buffers the kernel keeps to prevent them from growing too stale.

gpm – (Version 1.13, 193K) GPM adds mouse support to text-based Linux applications such as emacs, Midnight Commander, and more. It also provides console cut-and-paste operations using the mouse. Includes a program to allow pop-up menus to appear at the click of a mouse button.

kernel-pcmcia-cs – (Version 2.0.34, 677K) Many laptop machines (and some others) support PCMCIA cards for expansion. Also known as "credit card adapters", PCMCIA cards are small cards for everything from SCSI support to modems. They are hot swappable (they can be exchanged without rebooting the system) and quite convienent. This package contains support for numerous PCMCIA cards of all varieties and supplies a daemon which allows them to be hot swapped.

procmail – (Version 3.10, 180K) Red Hat Linux uses procmail for all local mail delivery. In addition to regluar mail delivery duties, procmail can be used to do many different automatic filtering, presorting, and mail handling jobs. It is the basis for the SmartList mailing list processor.

sendmail-cf – (Version 8.8.7, 611K)   This package contains all the configuration files used to generate the sendmail.cf file distributed with the base sendmail package. You'll want this package if you need to reconfigure and rebuild your sendmail.cf file. For example, the default sendmail.cf is not configured for UUCP. If you need to send and receive mail over UUCP, you may need this package to help you reconfigure sendmail.

sendmail-doc – (Version 8.8.7, 1,219K)   This package includes release notes, the sendmail FAQ, and a few papers written about sendmail. The papers are available in PostScript and troff.

sysklogd – (Version 1.3, 105K)   This is the Linux system and kernel logging program. It is run as a daemon (background process) to log messages to different places. These are usually things like sendmail logs, security logs, and errors from other daemons.

uucp – (Version 1.06.1, 2,012K)   UUCP is a Unix to Unix transfer mechanism. It is used primarily for remote sites to download and upload email and news files to local machines. If you didn't already know that, you probably don't need this package installed. :-)

vixie-cron – (Version 3.0.1, 54K)   cron is a standard UNIX program that runs user-specified programs at periodic scheduled times. vixie cron adds a number of features to the basic UNIX cron, including better security and more powerful configuration options.

C.4   Development

This section contains packages of interest to programmers. Red Hat Linux comes with a very powerful and rich set of tools for the programmer, so there are several different subsections here.

C.4.1   Building

This section contains packages that help programmers easily build programs.

autoconf – (Version 2.12, 524K)   GNU's "autoconf" is a tool for source and Makefile configuration. It assists the programmer in creating portable and configurable packages, by allowing the person building the package to specify various configuration options.

"autoconf" is not required for the end user - it is needed only to generate the configuration scripts.

automake – (Version 1.3, 777K)   Automake is an experimental Makefile generator. It was inspired by the 4.4BSD make and include files, but aims to be portable and to conform to the GNU standards for Makefile variables and targets.

libtool – (Version 1.0h, 379K)   GNU libtool is a set of shell scripts to automatically configure UNIX architectures to build shared libraries in generic fashion.

make – (Version 3.76.1, 247K)   The program make is used to coordinate the compilation and linking of a set of sources into a program, recompiling only what is necessary, thus saving a developer a lot of time. In fact, make can do a lot more - read the info docs.

pmake – (Version 1.0, 126K)   The program make is used to coordinate the compilation and linking of a set of sources into a program, recompiling only what is necessary, thus saving a developer a lot of time. In fact, make can do a lot more - read the info docs.

Pmake is a particular version of make which supports some additional syntax not in the standard make program. Some berkeley programs have Makefiles written for pmake.

C.4.2   Debuggers

This section contains a number of packages that make it easier to find bugs in a program.

ElectricFence – (Version 2.0.5, 44K)   Electric Fence is a libary that can be used for C programming and debugging. You link it in at compile time and it will warn you of possible problems such as free'ing memory that doesn't exist, etc.

gdb – (Version 4.17, 1,236K)   This is a full featured, command driven debugger. It allows you to trace the exectuion of programs and examine their internal state at any time. It works for C and C++ compiled with the GNU C compiler gcc.

strace – (Version 3.1, 113K)   Strace prints a record of each system call another program makes, including all of the arguments passed to it and the system call's return value.

xxgdb – (Version 1.12, 95K)   xxgdb is a graphical interface to GNU's debugger. It has the ability to display source files as they are executed, set breakpoints, and singlestep through or over commands - all with an easy-to-use graphical X Windows interface.

C.4.3   Languages

This section lists the packages containing various programming languages.

basic – (Version 1.20, 53K)   This is a BASIC language interpreter. You can use it to run programs written in BASIC. For those who may not know, BASIC is an archaic language used only to learn early fundamentals of programming, and it isn't very good for that, either. :-)

bin86 – (Version 0.4, 70K)   This package provides an assembler and linker for real mode 80x86 instructions. Programs that run in real mode, including LILO and the kernel's bootstrapping code, need to have this package installed to be built from the sources.

ctags – (Version 2.0.3, 77K)   A better ctags which generates tags for all possible tag types: macro definitions, enumerated values (values inside enum...), function and method definitions, enum/struct/union tags, external function prototypes (optional), typedefs, and variable declarations. It is far less easily fooled by code containing #if preprocessor conditional constructs, using a conditional path selection algorithm to resolve complicated choices, and a fall-back algorithm when this one fails. Can also be used to print out a list of selected objects found in source files.

egcs – (Version 1.0.2, 2,968K)   A compiler aimed at integrating all the optimizations and features necessary for a high-performance and stable development environment.

egcs-c++ – (Version 1.0.2, 1,965K)   This package adds C++ support to the GNU C compiler. It includes support for most of the current C++ specification, including templates and exception handling. It does not include a standard C++ library, which is available separately.

egcs-g77 – (Version 1.0.2, 2,569K)   This apckage adds support for compiling Fortran 77 programs with the GNU compiler.

egcs-objc – (Version 1.0.2, 1,648K)   This package adds Objective C support to the GNU C compiler. Objective C is a object oriented derivative of the C language, mainly used on systems running NeXTSTEP. This package does not include the standard objective C object library.

expect – (Version 5.24, 2,297K)   Expect is a tool for automating interactive applications such as telnet, ftp, passwd, fsck, rlogin, tip, etc. It makes it easy for a script to control another program and interact with it.

f2c – (Version 19970805, 819K)   f2c is a Fortran to C translation and building program. It can take fortran source code, convert it to C, and then use gcc to compile it into an executable.

fort77 – (Version 1.14a, 11K)   This is the driver for f2c, a fortran to C translator.

gcc – (Version 2.7.2.3, 2,046K)   The GNU C compiler – a full featured ANSI C compiler, with support for K&R C as well. GCC provides many levels of source code error checking tradionaly provided by other tools (such as lint), produces debugging information, and can perform many different optimizations to the resulting object code. This contains the back end for C++ and Objective C compilers as well.

guavac – (Version 1.1, 2,537K)   Guavac is a standalone compiler for the Java programming language. It was written entirely in C++, and should be portable to any platform supporting Gnu's C++ compiler or a similarly powered system.

kaffe – (Version 0.10.0, 591K)   This is Kaffe, a virtual machine design to execute Java bytecode. This machine can be configured in two modes. In one mode it operates as a pure bytecode interpreter (not unlike Javasoft's machine); in the second mode if performs "just-in-time" code conversion from the abstract code to the host machine's native code. This will ultimately allow execution of Java code at the same speed as standard compiled code but while maintaining the advantages and flexibility of code independence.

p2c-devel – (Version 1.20, 507K)   This is the development kit for the Pascal to C translator. It contains the header files and some other programs that might be useful to someone using the translator.

python – (Version 1.5.1, 5,320K)   Python in an interpreted, object orientated scripting language. If contains support for dynamic loading of objects, classes, modules, and exceptions.

Adding interfaces to new system libraries through C code is straightforward, making Python easy to use in custom settings.

This Python package includes most of the standard Python modules, along with modules for interfacing to the Tix widget set for Tk and RPM.

python-devel – (Version 1.5.1, 2,878K) The Python interpreter is relatively easy to extend with dynamically loaded extensions and to embed in other programs. This packages contains the header files and libraries which are needed to do both of these tasks.

python-docs – (Version 1.5.1, 2,611K) This package contains documentation on the Python language and interpretor as a mix of plain ASCII files and LaTeX sources.

tcl – (Version 8.0.2, 5,438K) TCL is a simple scripting language that is designed to be embedded in other applications. This package includes tclsh, a simple example of a tcl application. TCL is very popular for writing small graphical applications because of the TK widget set which is closely tied to it.

tclx – (Version 8.0.2, 1,938K) TclX is a set of extensions to make it more suitable for common Unix programming tasks. It adds or enhances support for files, network access, debugging, math, lists, and message catalogs. It can be used with both tcl and tcl/tk applications.

tix – (Version 4.1.0.6, 2,706K) Tix is a add on for the tk widget set which adds many complex widgets which are built from tk building blocks. The extra widgets include combo box, file selection, notebooks, paned windows, spin controls, and hierarchical list boxes.

tk – (Version 8.0.2, 5,214K) Tk is a X Windows widget set designed to work closely with the tcl scripting language. It allows you to write simple programs with full featured GUI's in only a little more time then it takes to write a text based interface. Tcl/Tk applications can also be run on Windows and Macintosh platforms.

tkinter – (Version 1.5.1, 639K) A graphical interface for Python, based on Tcl/Tk, and used by many of the configuration tools.

umb-scheme – (Version 3.2, 1,212K) UMB Scheme is an implementation of the language described in the IEEE Standard for the Scheme Programming Language (December, 1990).

xlispstat – (Version 3.50, 2,751K) An implementation of the Lisp programming language for X-Windows, with extensions for advanced statistics computations.

C.4.4 Libraries

This section contains packages of the various libraries. Some libraries are required for normal system operation, while others are only needed if you will be using their features in a program you're writing.

cracklib – (Version 2.7, 69K) Checks passwords for security related characteristics - length, uniqueness, whether they are in a word database, etc.

e2fsprogs-devel – (Version 1.10, 225K)   Libraries and header files needed to develop ext2 filesystem-specific programs.

faces-devel – (Version 1.6.1, 22K)   This is the xface development environment. It contains the static libraries and header files for doing xface development.

gdbm-devel – (Version 1.7.3, 70K)   These are the development libraries and header files for gdbm, the GNU database system. These are required if you plan to do development using the gdbm database.

giflib – (Version 3.0, 2,047K)   GIF loading and saving shared library and tools.

glibc – (Version 2.0.7, 15,304K)   Contains the standard libraries that are used by multiple programs on the system. In order to save disk space and memory, as well as to ease upgrades, common system code is kept in one place and shared between programs. This package contains the most important sets of shared libraries, the standard C library and the standard math library. Without these, a Linux system will not function. It also contains national language (locale) support and timezone databases.

glibc-debug – (Version 2.0.7, 2K)   These libraries have the debugging information debuggers use for tracing the execution of programs. These are only needed when the shared libraries themselves are being debugged – they are not needed to debug programs which use them.

glibc-devel – (Version 2.0.7, 11,612K)   To develop programs which use the standard C libraries (which nearly all programs do), the system needs to have these standard header files and object files available for creating the executables.

glibc-profile – (Version 2.0.7, 9,982K)   When programs are being profiled used gprof, they must use these libraries instrad of the standard C libraries for gprof to be able to profile them correctly.

gpm-devel – (Version 1.13, 23K)   This package allows you to develop your own text-mode programs that take advantage of the mouse.

inn-devel – (Version 1.7.2, 129K)   This library is needed by several programs that interface to INN, such as newsgate or tin.

libgr-devel – (Version 2.0.13, 307K)   This package is all you need to develop programs that handle the various graphics file formats supported by libgr.

libjpeg-devel – (Version 6b, 228K)   This package is all you need to develop programs that manipulate jpeg images, including documentation.

libpng-devel – (Version 1.0.1, 227K)   The header files and static libraries are only needed for development of programs using the PNG library.

libstdc++-devel – (Version 2.8.0, 1,107K)   This is the GNU implementation of the standard C++ libraries. This package includes the header files and libraries needed for C++ development.

libtiff-devel – (Version 3.4, 1,372K) This package is all you need to develop programs that manipulate tiff images.

ncurses-devel – (Version 4.2, 5,795K) This package includes the header files and libraries necessary to develop applications that use ncurses.

newt-devel – (Version 0.25, 66K) These are the header files and libraries for developing applications which use newt. Newt is a windowing toolkit for text mode, which provides many widgets and stackable windows.

postgresql-devel – (Version 6.3.2, 1,003K) This package contains header files and libraries required to compile applications that are talking directly to the PostgreSQL backend server.

pythonlib – (Version 1.22, 236K) This package contains code used by a variety of Red Hat programs. It includes code for multifield listboxes and entry widgets with non-standard keybindings, among others.

readline-devel – (Version 2.2, 256K) The "readline" library will read a line from the terminal and return it, using prompt as a prompt. If prompt is null, no prompt is issued. The line returned is allocated with malloc(3), so the caller must free it when finished. The line returned has the final newline removed, so only the text of the line remains.

rpm-devel – (Version 2.5, 204K) The RPM packaging system includes a C library that makes it easy to manipulate RPM packages and databases. It is intended to ease the creation of graphical package managers and other tools that need intimate knowledge of RPM packages.

slang-devel – (Version 0.99.38, 472K) This package contains the slang static libraries and header files required to develop slang-based applications. It also includes documentation to help you write slang-based apps.

svgalib-devel – (Version 1.2.13, 407K) These are the libraries and header files that are needed to build programs which use SVGAlib. SVGAlib allows programs to use full screen graphics on a variety of hardware platforms and without the overhead X requires.

xpm-devel – (Version 3.4j, 217K) Allows you to develop applications that display bitmaps in X-Windows.

zlib-devel – (Version 1.1.2, 159K) The 'zlib' compression library provides in-memory compression and decompression functions, including integrity checks of the uncompressed data. This version of the library supports only one compression method (deflation) but other algorithms may be added later and will have the same stream interface.

This package contains the header files and libraries needed to develop programs that use these zlib.

C.4.5 Tools

This section contains packages that provide the usual assortment of tools that programmers require.

binutils – (Version 2.9.1.0.4, 4,530K)   Binutils is a collection of utilities necessary for compiling programs. It includes the assembler and linker, as well as a number of other miscellaneous programs for dealing with executable formats.

bison – (Version 1.25, 158K)   This is the GNU parser generator which is mostly compatible with yacc. Many programs use this as part of their build process. Bison is only needed on systems that are used for development.

byacc – (Version 1.9, 54K)   This is a public domain yacc parser. It is used by many programs during their build process. You probably want this package if you do development.

cdecl – (Version 2.5, 74K)   This is a package to translate English to C/C++ function declarations and vice versa. It is useful for programmers.

cproto – (Version 4.4, 92K)   Cproto generates function prototypes for functions defined in the specified C source files to the standard output. The function definitions may be in the old style or ANSI C style. Optionally, cproto also outputs declarations for variables defined in the files. If no file argument is given, cproto reads its input from the standard input.

flex – (Version 2.5.4a, 291K)   This is the GNU fast lexical analyzer generator. It generates lexical tokenizing code based on a lexical (regular expression based) description of the input. It is designed to work with both yacc and bison, and is used by many programs as part of their build process.

gettext – (Version 0.10, 443K)   The gettext library provides an easy to use library and tools for creating, using, and modifying natural language catalogs. It is a powerfull and simple method for internationalizing programs.

indent – (Version 1.9.1, 81K)   This is the GNU indenting program. It is used to beautify C program source files.

xwpe – (Version 1.4.2, 713K)   XWPE is actually a package of four programs: we, wpe, xwe, and xwpe. They are different versions of the same basic programmers editor and development environment. If you have used some of the Micro$oft Windows programming IDE's and longed for an X Windows equivalent, this is what you have been looking for! Also included are the text-mode equivalents of the X programs, enabling you to use xwpe no matter what your development environment may be.

This package includes the basic xwpe libraries and the text-mode programs; the X Windows programs are contained in the 'xwpe-X11' package.

C.4.6   Version Control

This section contains packages that allow the programmer to implement various forms of version control over their programs.

cvs – (Version 1.9, 1,543K)   CVS is a front end to the rcs(1) revision control system which extends the notion of revision control from a collection of files in a single directory to a hierarchical collection of directories consisting of revision controlled files. These directories and files can be combined together to form a software release. CVS provides the functions necessary to manage these software releases and to control the concurrent editing of source files among multiple software developers.

rcs – (Version 5.7, 497K)   The Revision Control System (RCS) manages multiple revisions of files. RCS automates the storing, retrieval, logging, identification, and merging of revisions. RCS is useful for text that is revised frequently, for example programs, documentation, graphics, papers, and form letters.

C.5   Documentation

This section lists packages that contain a variety of Linux-related information. There is a lot of good information here; unless you are low on disk space, you should install these packages. (Note, however, that you probably don't need all the HOWTO packages; in most cases howto and howto-html will probably suffice.)

faq – (Version 5.1, 1,084K)   This is a package of the Frequently Asked Questions (FAQ) about Linux from sunsite.unc.edu. It is one of the best sources of information about Linux.

howto – (Version 5.1, 8,580K)   This is the best collection of Linux documentation there is. It was put together on Apr 15 1998. If you want to find newer versions of these documents, see http://sunsite.unc.edu/linux. For the versions in this package, see /usr/doc/HOWTO.

howto-chinese – (Version 5.1, 1,683K)   This package contains translated versions of the Linux HOWTO into chinese. Please note that not all the files have been translated, so you most likely will need the english version installed if you want to have a complete HOWTO install.

howto-dvi – (Version 5.1, 2,739K)   These are the dvi versions of the HOWTOs. Probably only useful to TeX hackers.

howto-french – (Version 5.1, 33,266K)   This package contains translated versions of the Linux HOWTO into french. Please note that not all the files have been translated, so you most likely will need the english version installed if you want to have a complete HOWTO install.

howto-german – (Version 5.1, 8,476K)   This package contains translated versions of the Linux HOWTO into german. Please note that not all the files have been translated, so you most likely will need the english version installed if you want to have a complete HOWTO install.

howto-greek – (Version 5.1, 891K)   This package contains translated versions of the Linux HOWTO into greek. Please note that not all the files have been translated, so you most likely will need the english version installed if you want to have a complete HOWTO install.

howto-html – (Version 5.1, 9,572K)   These are the html versions of the HOWTOs. You can view them with your favorite web browser.

howto-indonesian – (Version 5.1, 3,812K)   This package contains translated versions of the Linux HOWTO into indonesian. Please note that not all the files have been translated, so you most likely will need the english version installed if you want to have a complete HOWTO install.

howto-italian – (Version 5.1, 4,348K)   This package contains translated versions of the Linux HOWTO into italian. Please note that not all the files have been translated, so you most likely will need the english version installed if you want to have a complete HOWTO install.

howto-japanese – (Version 5.1, 24,746K)   This package contains translated versions of the Linux HOWTO into japanese. Please note that not all the files have been translated, so you most likely will need the english version installed if you want to have a complete HOWTO install.

howto-korean – (Version 5.1, 5,952K)   This package contains translated versions of the Linux HOWTO into korean. Please note that not all the files have been translated, so you most likely will need the english version installed if you want to have a complete HOWTO install.

howto-polish – (Version 5.1, 9,853K)   This package contains translated versions of the Linux HOWTO into polish. Please note that not all the files have been translated, so you most likely will need the english version installed if you want to have a complete HOWTO install.

howto-ps – (Version 5.1, 5,505K)   These are the PostScript versions of the HOWTOs. You can view them with ghostview or print them on PostScript printers.

howto-sgml – (Version 5.1, 2,469K)   These are the SGML versions of the HOWTOs. They are the "source" files that the HOWTOs are built from (using linuxdoc-sgml).

howto-spanish – (Version 5.1, 14,175K)   This package contains translated versions of the Linux HOWTO into spanish. Please note that not all the files have been translated, so you most likely will need the english version installed if you want to have a complete HOWTO install.

howto-swedish – (Version 5.1, 397K)   This package contains translated versions of the Linux HOWTO into swedish. Please note that not all the files have been translated, so you most likely will need the english version installed if you want to have a complete HOWTO install.

howto-turkish – (Version 5.1, 689K)   This package contains translated versions of the Linux HOWTO into turkish. Please note that not all the files have been translated, so you most likely will need the english version installed if you want to have a complete HOWTO install.

indexhtml – (Version 5.1, 6K)   Red Hat html index page

install-guide – (Version 2.3, 1,520K)   A general guide for installing and getting started with Linux. The installation sections should be ignored, in favor of the Red Hat Linux manual. Although, there is overlap, there is other useful information in this guide.

lpg – (Version 0.4, 1,739K)   This is a generic guide to the Programming on Linux systems. Check http://sunsite.unc.edu/LDP for more information about the Linux Documentation Project, and possible updates to this version.

man-pages – (Version 1.19, 1,538K)   A large collection of man pages covering programming APIs, file formats, protocols, etc.

Section 1 = user commands (intro only) Section 2 = system calls Section 3 = libc calls Section 4 = devices (e.g., hd, sd) Section 5 = file formats and protocols (e.g., wtmp, /etc/passwd, nfs) Section 6 = games (intro only) Section 7 = conventions, macro packages, etc. (e.g., nroff, ascii) Section 8 = system administration (intro only)

nag – (Version 1.0, 1,217K)   This is a generic guide to the Network Administration of Linux systems. Check http://sunsite.unc.edu/LDP for more information about the Linux Documentation Project, and possible updates to this version.

rhl-alpha-install-addend-en – (Version 5.1, 196K)   This is a local copy of the HTML version of the Red Hat Linux 5.1 Alpha Installation Addendum.

rhl-install-guide-en – (Version 5.1, 1,472K)   This is a local copy of the HTML version of the Red Hat Linux 5.1 Installation Guide. An online copy can be found at http://www.redhat.com.

sag – (Version 0.5, 603K)   This is a generic guide to the System Administration of Linux systems. Check http://sunsite.unc.edu/LDP for more information about the Linux Documentation Project, and possible updates to this version.

C.6   Extensions

This section lists packages that provide language-specific extensions to Red Hat Linux.

C.6.1   Japanese

This section lists packages that provide Japanese-specific extensions to Red Hat Linux.

kterm – (Version 6.2.0, 147K)   kterm is the Kanji Terminal Emulator. It uses the Kanji character set instead of the normal english set for those who prefer Kanji.

C.7 Games

This section lists the packages that provide fun and entertainment to Red Hat Linux system owners the world over. Game packages that run under the X window system can be found in the X11 section near the end of this appendix.

bsd-games – (Version 2.1, 1,791K) This is a bunch of games. Highlights include backgammon, cribbage, hangman, monop, primes, trek, and battlestar.

christminster – (Version 3, 223K) This is a text adventure game for use with xzip.

colour-yahtzee – (Version 1.0, 19K) This is a terminal mode version of the popular game, yahtzee. It is a dice and board game.

fortune-mod – (Version 1.0, 2,337K) This is the ever popular fortune program. It will gladly print a random fortune when run. Is usually fun to put in the .login for your users on a system so they see something new every time they log in.

gnuchess – (Version 4.0.pl77, 1,330K) This is the famous GNU chess program. It is text based, but can be used in conjunction with xboard to play X based chess.

mysterious – (Version 1.0, 163K) Brian Howarth's Mysterious Adventure game series. This is a text based adventure game.

pinfocom – (Version 3.0, 169K) 'pinfocom' is an interpreter for those old Infocom-compatible text adventure games (remember those?).

scottfree – (Version 1.14, 31K) 'scottfree' is an interpreter for Scott-Adams-format text adventure games (remember those?).

trojka – (Version 1.1, 15K) The aim of this game is to control and to place the falling blocks, so that at least three blocks horizontally or diagonally, or both, have matching patterns. This sequence is then removed, and the above blocks will coll you reach the top of the screen, the game is finished.

vga_cardgames – (Version 1.3.1, 110K) A number of various card games for the Linux console, including Klondike, 'Oh Hell', Solitaire, and Spider, as we

vga_gamespack – (Version 1.3, 54K) A number of various mind games for the Linux console using SVGAlib. The selection includes such faJeux de rflexion pour la console Linux, utilisant SVGAlib. Inclus Othello Dmineur et Connect 4.

C.8 Libraries

This section lists packages that contain various libraries. These libraries are used by other program to support various functions, such as image manipulation, compatibility with older binary program formats, and screen handling.

aout-libs – (Version 1.4, 3,663K) Old Linux systems used a format for programs and shared libraries called a.out while newer ones use the ELF format. In order to run old a.out format programs, you need the a.out format libraries which this package provide. With it, you are to run most a.out format packages for text, X, and SVGAlib modes.

gdbm – (Version 1.7.3, 25K) This is a database indexing library. It is useful for those who need to write C applications and need access to a simple and efficient database or build C applications which use it.

glib – (Version 1.0.1, 51K) Handy library of utility functions. Development libs and headers are in gtk+-devel.

ld.so – (Version 1.9.5, 242K) This package contains the shared library configuration tool, ldconfig, which is required by many packages. It also includes the shared library loader and dynamic loader for Linux libc 5.

libc – (Version 5.3.12, 5,293K) Older Linux systems (including all Red Hat Linux releases between 2.0 and 4.2, inclusive) were based on libc 5. This package includes these libraries and other libraries based on libc 5, allowing old applcications to run on glibc (libc 6) based systems.

libelf – (Version 0.6.4, 74K) This library gives you access to the internals of the ELF object file format. It lets you poke around in the various different sections of an ELF file, check out the symbols, etc.

libg++ – (Version 2.7.2.8, 1,897K) This is the GNU implementation of the standard C++ libraries, along with additional GNU tools. This package includes the shared libraries necessary to run C++ applications.

libgr – (Version 2.0.13, 210K) This package is a library for handling various graphics file formats, including FBM, PBM, PGM, PNM, PPM, and REL.

libjpeg – (Version 6b, 245K) This package is a library of functions that manipulate jpeg images, along with simple clients for manipulating jpeg images.

libpng – (Version 1.0.1, 217K) The PNG library is a collection of routines used to crate and manipulate PNG format graphics files. The PNG format was designed as a replacement for GIF, with many improvements and extensions.

libstdc++ – (Version 2.8.0, 385K) This is the GNU implementation of the standard C++ libraries, along with additional GNU tools. This package includes the shared libraries necessary to run C++ applications.

libtermcap – (Version 2.0.8, 11K) This is the library for accessing the termcap database. It is necessary to be installed for a system to be able to do much of anything.

libtermcap-devel – (Version 2.0.8, 11K) This is the package containing the development libaries and header files for writing programs that access the termcap database. It may be necessary to build some other packages as well.

libtiff – (Version 3.4, 607K)   This package is a library of functions that manipulate TIFF images.

ncurses – (Version 4.2, 2,290K)   The curses library routines give the user a terminal-independent method of updating character screens with reasonable optimization. This implementation is "new curses" (ncurses) and is the approved replacement for 4.4BSD classic curses, which is being discontinued.

ncurses3 – (Version 1.9.9e, 317K)   The curses library routines give the user a terminal-independent method of updating character screens with reasonable optimization. This implementation is "new curses" (ncurses) and is the approved replacement for 4.4BSD classic curses, which is being discontinued.

newt – (Version 0.25, 96K)   Newt is a windowing toolkit for text mode built from the slang library. It allows color text mode applications to easily use stackable windows, push buttons, check boxes, radio buttons, lists, entry fields, labels, and displayable text. Scrollbars are supported, and forms may be nested to provide extra functionality. This pacakge contains the shared library for programs that have been built with newt as well as a /usr/bin/dialog replacement called whiptail.

p2c – (Version 1.20, 14K)   p2c is the Pascal to C translation system. It is used to convert Pascal source code into C source code so that it can be compiled using a standard C compiler (such as gcc).

readline – (Version 2.2, 251K)   The "readline" library will read a line from the terminal and return it, allowing the user to edit the line with the standard emacs editing keys. It allows the programmer to give the user an easier-to-use and more intuitive interface.

slang – (Version 0.99.38, 164K)   Slang (pronounced "sssslang") is a powerful stack based interpreter that supports a C-like syntax. It has been designed from the beginning to be easily embedded into a program to make it extensible. Slang also provides a way to quickly develop and debug the application embedding it in a safe and efficient manner. Since slang resembles C, it is easy to recode slang procedures in C if the need arises.

svgalib – (Version 1.2.13, 579K)   SVGAlib is a library which allows applications to use full screen graphics on a variety of hardware platforms. Many games and utilities are avaiable which take advantage of SVGAlib for graphics access, as it is more suitable for machines with little memory then X Windows is.

zlib – (Version 1.1.2, 57K)   The 'zlib' compression library provides in-memory compression and decompression functions, including integrity checks of the uncompressed data. This version of the library supports only one compression method (deflation) but other algorithms may be added later and will have the same stream interface.

This library is used by a number of different system programs.

C.9 Networking

This section lists packages that are related to networking. It has been split into several subsections for easier browsing.

C.9.1 Admin

This section lists packages that provide basic network administrative functions.

anonftp – (Version 2.5, 1,019K)   Contains the files needed for allowing anonymous ftp access to your machine. This lets any user get files from your machine without having an account, which is a popular way of making programs available on the Internet.

caching-nameserver – (Version 5.1, 3K)   Includes configuration files for bind (the DNS nameserver) which make it behave as a simple caching nameserver. Many users on dialup connections use this package (along with bind) and make the it's own nameserver to speed up name resoultions.

net-tools – (Version 1.33, 149K)   This is a collection of the basic tools necessary for setting up networking on a Linux machine. It includes ifconfig, route, netstat, rarp, and some other minor tools.

nfs-server-clients – (Version 2.2beta29, 10K)   This package contains client programs that interact with NFS servers. It is not needed to mount NFS volumes. At the moment the only program in it is showmount, which can be used to show exported and mounted filesystems.

tcp_wrappers – (Version 7.6, 245K)   With this package you can monitor and filter incoming requests for the SYSTAT, FINGER, FTP, TELNET, RLOGIN, RSH, EXEC, TFTP, TALK, and other network services.

C.9.2 Daemons

This section lists packages that provide various network-related daemons. Daemons are programs that are run automatically to perform various system functions.

am-utils – (Version 6.0a16, 1,976K)   Am-utils is the"next generation" of the popular BSD Automounter, Amd. Am-utils includes many additional updates, ports, programs, features, bug fixes, and more.

Amd is the Berkeley automount daemon. It has the ability to automatically mount filesystems of all types, including NFS filesystems, CD-ROM's, and local drives, and unmount them when they are not being used any more.

The default setup allows you to 'cd /net/[hostname]' and get a list of directories exported from that host.

apache – (Version 1.2.6, 1,121K)   Apache is a full featured web server that is freely available, and also happens to be the most widely used.

autofs – (Version 3.1.1, 100K)   autofs is a daemon which automatically mounts filesystems when you use them, and unmounts them later when you are not using them. This can include network filesystems, CD-ROMs, floppies, and so forth.

bind – (Version 4.9.6, 288K)   Includes the named name server, which is used to define host name to IP address translations (and vice versa). It can be used on workstations as a caching name server, but is generally only needed on one machine for an entire network.

bootp – (Version 2.4.3, 101K)   This is a server for the bootp protocol; which allows network administrators to setup networking information for clients via an /etc/bootptab on a server so that the clients can automatically get their networking information. While this server includes rudimentary DHCP support as well, we suggest using the dhcpd package if you need DHCP support, as it is much more complete.

cleanfeed – (Version 0.95.5a, 62K)   Cleanfeed is an automatic filter for INN that removes spam from incoming newsfeeds.

cmu-snmp – (Version 3.5, 310K)   This is a derivative of the original Carnegie Mellon University Simple Network Management Protocol. It is useful for managing networks and doing accounting.

dhcp – (Version 2.0b1pl0, 814K)   This is the second release of the dhcp package from the Internet Software Consortium. It provides a server and a relay agent.

gated – (Version 3.5.9, 2,260K)   GateD is a routing daemon that handles multiple routing protocols and replaces routed and egpup. GateD currently handles the RIP, BGP, EGP, HELLO, and OSPF routing protocols. The gated process can be configured to perform all routing protocols or any subset of them. It is curently maintained by Merit.

imap – (Version 4.1.BETA, 1,353K)   IMAP is a server for the POP (Post Office Protocol) and IMAP mail protocols. The POP protocol allows a "post office" machine to collect mail for users and have that mail downloaded to the user's local machine for reading. The IMAP protocol provides the functionality of POP, and allows a user to read mail on a remote machine without moving it to his local mailbox.

inn – (Version 1.7.2, 3,199K)   INN is a news server, which can be set up to handle USENET news, as well as private "newsfeeds". There is a *LOT* of information about setting up INN in /usr/doc – read it.

intimed – (Version 1.10, 94K)   intimed is a server that will tell networked machines what time it currently has. It is useful for keeping networks of machines in synintimed est un serveur qui indique aux machines connectes l'heure qu'il est. Utile pour synchroniser les rseaux de machines sur l'heure correcte.

mars-nwe – (Version 0.99pl6, 508K)   MARS is a NetWare compatible file and printer server. It lets you use a Linux machine as a file and print server for NetWare based clients using NetWare's native IPX protocol suite.

mod_perl – (Version 1.11, 1,269K)   mod_perl is a powerful Apache module that enables the use of the PERL language within HTML files and more.

mod_php – (Version 2.0.1, 657K)   PHP is a powerful apache module that adds scripting and database connection capabilities to the apache server.

nfs-server – (Version 2.2beta29, 126K)   The NFS and mount daemons are used to create an NFS server which can export filesystems to other machines. This package is not needed to mount NFS filesystems – that functionality is already in the Linux kernel.

pnserver – (Version 5.0, 5,604K)   Real Audio/Video server with a 5 stream license. This is the basic server and is upgradable from Progressive Networks. It also includes the Real Audio encoder, which encodes audio files and live audio streams for use with the Real Audio server.

pnserver-docs – (Version 5.0, 5,139K)   WANGER will fill in the desc

portmap – (Version 4.0, 44K)   The portmapper manages RPC connections, which are used by protocols such as NFS and NIS. The portmap server must be running on machines which act as servers for protocols which make use of the RPC mechanism. This portmapper supports hosts.allow,deny type access control.

ppp – (Version 2.3.3, 272K)   This is the daemon and documentation for PPP support. It requires a kernel greater than 2.0 which is built with PPP support. The default Red Hat kernels include PPP support as a module.

sendmail – (Version 8.8.7, 552K)   Sendmail is a Mail Transport Agent, which is the program that moves mail from one machine to another. Sendmail implements a general internetwork mail routing facility, featuring aliasing and forwarding, automatic routing to network gateways, and flexible configuration.

If you need the ability to send and receive mail via the internet you'll need sendmail.

squid – (Version 1.1.21, 514K)   Squid is a high-performance proxy caching server for web clients, supporting FTP, gopher, and HTTP data objects. Unlike traditional caching software, Squid handles all requests in a single, non-blocking, I/O-driven process.

Squid keeps meta data and especially hot objects cached in RAM, caches DNS lookups, supports non-blocking DNS lookups, and implements negative caching of failed requests. If you are tight on memory, check out the NOVM version of this package.

Squid supports SSL, extensive access controls, and full request logging. By using the lightweight Internet Cache Protocol, Squid caches can be arranged in a hierarchy or mesh for additional bandwidth savings.

Squid consists of a main server program squid, a Domain Name System lookup program dnsserver, a program for retrieving FTP data ftpget, and some management and client tools. When squid starts up, it spawns a configurable number of dnsserver processes, each of which can perform a single, blocking Domain Name System (DNS) lookup. This reduces the amount of time the cache waits for DNS lookups.

Squid is derived from the ARPA-funded Harvest project.

squid-novm – (Version 1.1.21, 505K)   The NOVM version of the squid will use less memory to do the proxy job, at the expense of file descriptors. (NOVM stands for NO Virtual Memory). If you are tight on memory on your proxy/cache server, this might be for you.

Squid is a high-performance proxy caching server for web clients, supporting FTP, gopher, and HTTP data objects. Unlike traditional caching software, Squid handles all requests in a single, non-blocking, I/O-driven process.

Squid keeps meta data and especially hot objects cached in RAM, caches DNS lookups, supports non-blocking DNS lookups, and implements negative caching of failed requests.

Squid supports SSL, extensive access controls, and full request logging. By using the lightweight Internet Cache Protocol, Squid caches can be arranged in a hierarchy or mesh for additional bandwidth savings.

Squid consists of a main server program squid, a Domain Name System lookup program dnsserver, a program for retrieving FTP data ftpget, and some management and client tools. When squid starts up, it spawns a configurable number of dnsserver processes, each of which can perform a single, blocking Domain Name System (DNS) lookup. This reduces the amount of time the cache waits for DNS lookups.

Squid is derived from the ARPA-funded Harvest project.

wu-ftpd – (Version 2.4.2b16, 275K)   wu-ftpd is the daemon (background) program which serves FTP files to ftp clients. It is useful if you wish to exchange programs between computers without running a network filesystem such as NFS, or if you with to run an anonymous FTP site (in which case, you will want to install the anonftp package).

xntp3 – (Version 5.93, 997K)   This package contains utilities and daemons to help synchronize your computer's time to UTC standard time. It includes ntpdate, a program similar to rdate, and xntpd, a daemon which adjusts the system time continuously.

ypserv – (Version 1.3.1, 261K)   ypserv is an implementation of the standard NIS/YP networking protocol. It allows network-wide distribution of hostname, username, and other information databases. This is the NIS server, and is not needed on NIS clients.

C.9.3   News

This section lists packages related to Usenet news.

inews – (Version 1.7.2, 47K)   The inews program is used by some news readers to post news. It does some consistency checking and header reformatting, and forwards the article on to the news server specified in inn.conf.

C.9.4   Utilities

This section lists packages that provide handy utilities related to networking.

bind-utils – (Version 4.9.6, 311K)   Collection of utilities for querying name servers and looking up hosts. These tools let you determine the IP addresses for given host names, and find information about registered domains and network addresses.

bootpc – (Version 061, 35K)   bootpc is the bootp client for Linux that will allow a linux machine to retrieve it's networking information from a server via the network. It sends out a general broadcast asking for the information which is returned.

cmu-snmp-devel – (Version 3.5, 115K)   These are the development libraries and header files for CMU SNMP. This will allow the network administrator to write programs for use with network management.

cmu-snmp-utils – (Version 3.5, 174K)   These are the various utilities for use with CMU SNMP. Contains utils such as snmpwalk, snmptest, and more.

comanche – (Version 0.4, 182K)   Comanche stands for COnfiguration MANager for apaCHE. It is a front end for the Apache Configuration Server Project Apache is the most popular, fast, reliable Web server on the internet. You can find more about Apache at www.apache.org

This package is working with RCS to provide you with accurate history of the changes for the apache config files.

dip – (Version 3.3.7o, 86K)   dip is a program to allow for automatic scripting of modem dialing. It's useful for setting up PPP and SLIP connections, but isn't required for either. It is used by netcfg for setting up SLIP connections.

fwhois – (Version 1.00, 7K)   This is the "whois" program. It will allow you to find out information on people stored in the whois databases around the world.

ipxutils – (Version 1.0, 44K)   This package includes utilities necessary for configuring and debugging IPX interfaces and networks under Linux. IPX is the low-level protocol used by NetWare to transfer data.

mgetty – (Version 1.1.14, 1,158K)   This package contains an intelligent getty for allowing logins over a serial line (such as through a modem). It allows automatic callback and includes fax support (though mgetty-sendfax needs to be installed to make full use of it's fax support).

mgetty-sendfax – (Version 1.1.14, 251K)   This package includes support for FAX Class 2 modems to send and receive faxes. It also includes simple FAX queueing support.

mgetty-voice – (Version 1.1.14, 623K)   This package includes support for some modems which have voice mail extensions.

ncpfs – (Version 2.0.11, 378K)   This package contains tools to help configure and use the ncpfs filesysten, which is a linux filesystem which understands the NCP protocol. This protocol is used by Novell NetWare clients use to talk to NetWare servers.

rdate – (Version 0.960923, 5K)   rdate is a program that can retrieve the time from another machine on your network. If run as root, it will also set your local time to that of the machine you queried. It is not super accurate; get xntpd if you are really worried about milliseconds.

rdist – (Version 1.0, 118K)   Rdist is a program to maintain identical copies of files over multiple hosts. It preserves the owner, group, mode, and mtime of files if possible and can update programs that are executing.

traceroute – (Version 1.4a5, 30K)   Traceroute prints the route packets take across a TCP/IP. The names (or IP numbers if names are not available) of the machines which are routing packets from the machine traceroute is running on to the destination machine are printed, along with the time is took to receive a packet acknowledgement from that machine. This tool can be very helpfull in diagnosing networking problems.

yp-tools – (Version 1.4.1, 92K)   This implementation of NIS for linux is based on the YP stuff for FreeBSD. It is a special port for glibc 2.x and libc $¿$ = 5.4.21.

This implementation only provides NIS _clients_. You must already have a NIS server running somewhere. You can find one for linux on http://www-vt.uni-paderborn.de/ kukuk/linux/nis.html. Please read the NIS-HOWTO, too.

biff – (Version 0.10, 16K)   The biff client and comsat server are an antiquated method of asynchronous mail notification. Although they are still supported, most users use their shells MAIL variable (or mail under csh variants) to check for mail, or a dedicated application such as xbiff or xmailbox.

bootparamd – (Version 0.10, 17K)   Some (notably Sun's) network boot loaders rely on special boot server code on the server, in addition to rarp and tftp servers. This server is compatible with the SunOS bootparam clients and servers.

finger – (Version 0.10, 31K)   Finger is a simple protocol which allows users to find information about users on other machines. This package includes a standard finger client and server. The server runs from /etc/inetd.conf, which must be modified to disable finger requests.

ftp – (Version 0.10, 84K)   This provides the standard Unix command-line ftp client. ftp is the standard Internet file transfer protocol, which is extremely popular for both file archives and file transfers between individuals.

netkit-base – (Version 0.10, 53K)   This package provides the ping and inetd programs, which are both used for basic networking.

ntalk – (Version 0.10, 31K)   This package provides a client and daemon for the Internet talk protocol, which allows one-on-one chatting between users on different systems.

pidentd – (Version 2.7, 116K)   identd is a program that implements the RFC1413 identification server. identd operates by looking up specific TCP/IP connections and returning the user name of the process owning the connection.

routed – (Version 0.10, 38K)   A number of protocols are available for automatic updating of TCP/IP routing tables. RIP is the simplest of those, and this package includes a daemon which broadcasts RIP routing notification and handles incoming RIP packets.

rsh – (Version 0.10, 95K)   Rsh, rlogin, and rcp are a suite of programs which allow users to run commands on remote machines, login into other machines, and copy files between machines. All of these commands use rhosts style authentication. This package includes the client and servers needed for all of these services, as well as a server for rexec, which is an alternate method of executing remote commands. All of these servers are run from inetd and configured through /etc/inetd.conf and PAM. The rexecd server is disabled by default, but the rest are enabled.

rusers – (Version 0.10, 36K)   The rusers server and client, both included in this package, allow users to find out what users are logged into various machines on the local network.

rwall – (Version 0.10, 17K)   The rwall client sends a message to an rwall daemon running on a remote machine, which relays the message to all of the users on the remote machine. The rwall daemon is run from /etc/inetd.conf, and is disabled by default on Red Hat systems.

rwho – (Version 0.10, 23K)   The rwho program displays what users are logged into all of machines on the local network which are running the rwho daemon. Both the rwho client and daemon are provided in this package.

samba – (Version 1.9.18p5, 2,422K)   Samba provides an SMB server which can be used to provide network services to SMB (sometimes called "Lan Manager") clients, including various versions of MS Windows, OS/2, and other Linux machines. Samba also provides some SMB clients, which complement the built-in SMB filesystem in Linux.

Samba uses NetBIOS over TCP/IP (NetBT) protocols and does NOT need NetBEUI (Microsoft Raw NetBIOS frame) protocol.

telnet – (Version 0.10, 176K)   Telnet is a popular protocol for remote logins across the Internet. This package provides a command line telnet client as well as a telnet daemon which allows remote logins into the machine it is running on. The telnet daemon is enabled by default, and may be disabled by editing /etc/inetd.conf.

tftp – (Version 0.10, 33K)   The trivial file transfer protocol (tftp) is normally used only for booting diskless workstations. It provides very little security, and should not be enabled unless it is needed. The tftp server is run from /etc/inetd.conf, and is disabled by default on Red Hat systems.

timed – (Version 0.10, 60K)   This timed server allows remote machines to query the time-of-day of the machine the server is running on. This allows for simple time syncronization across a network.

ypbind – (Version 3.3, 37K)   This is a daemon which runs on NIS/YP clients and binds them to a NIS domain. It must be running for systems based on glibc to behave as NIS clients.

ytalk – (Version 3.0.3, 72K)   ytalk is an extension of the standard Internet 'talk' protocol that allows more than two users per conversation, redirection of program output to others, as well as an easy-to-use menu of commands. It uses the same talk daemon as the standard talk program.

C.10   Shells

This section lists packages that provide a wide variety of shells for your Red Hat Linux system.

ash – (Version 0.2, 245K)   ash is a bourne shell clone from Berkeley. It supports all of the standard Bourne shell commands and has the advantage of supporting them while remaining considerably smaller than bash.

bash – (Version 1.14.7, 476K)   Bash is an sh-compatible command language interpreter that executes commands read from the standard input or from a file. Bash also incorporates useful features from the Korn and C shells (ksh and csh).

Bash is ultimately intended to be a conformant implementation of the IEEE Posix Shell and Tools specification (IEEE Working Group 1003.2).

mc – (Version 4.1.33, 792K)   Midnight Commander is a visual shell much like a file manager, only with way more features. It is text mode, but also includes mouse support if you are running GPM. Its coolest feature is the ability to ftp, view tar and zip files, and poke into RPMs for specific files. :-)

pdksh – (Version 5.2.12, 391K)   pdksh, a reimplementation of ksh, is a command interpreter that is intended for both interactive and shell script use. Its command language is a superset of the sh(1) shell language.

tcsh – (Version 6.07, 476K)   'tcsh' is an enhanced version of csh (the C shell), with additional features such as command history, filename completion, and fancier prompts.

zsh – (Version 3.0.5, 957K)   zsh is an enhanced version of the bourne shell with these features: - very close to ksh/sh grammar, with csh additions - most features of ksh, bash, and tcsh - 75 builtins, 89 options, 154 key bindings - short for loops, ex: for i (*.c) echo $i - select - shell functions ...and many more

C.11   Utilities

This section lists packages that provide various utilities for your Red Hat Linux system. Because there are so many, we've split them into different subsections.

C.11.1   Archiving

This section lists packages that provide utilities for data archiving.

bzip2 – (Version 0.1pl2, 78K)   Bzip2 compresses files using the Burrows-Wheeler block-sorting text compression algorithm, and Huffman coding. Compression is generally considerably better than that achieved by more conventional LZ77/LZ78-based compressors, and approaches the performance of the PPM family of statistical compressors.

The command-line options are deliberately very similar to those of GNU Gzip, but they are not identical.

cpio – (Version 2.4.2, 60K) cpio copies files into or out of a cpio or tar archive, which is a file that contains other files plus information about them, such as their file name, owner, timestamps, and access permissions. The archive can be another file on the disk, a magnetic tape, or a pipe. cpio has three operating modes.

dhcpcd – (Version 0.65, 31K) dhcpcd is an implementation of the DHCP client specified in draft-ietf-dhc-dhcp-09 (when -r option is not speci- fied) and RFC1541 (when -r option is specified).

It gets the host information (IP address, netmask, broad- cast address, etc.) from a DHCP server and configures the network interface of the machine on which it is running. It also tries to renew the lease time according to RFC1541 or draft-ietf-dhc-dhcp-09.

gzip – (Version 1.2.4, 227K) This is the popular GNU file compression and decompression program, gzip.

lha – (Version 1.00, 51K) This is an archiving and compression utility. It is mostly used in the DOS world, but can be used under Linux to extract DOS files from LHA archives.

ncompress – (Version 4.2.4, 30K) ncompress is a utility that will do fast compression and decompression compatible with the original *nix compress utility (.Z extensions). It will not handle gzipped (.gz) images (although gzip can handle compress images).

tar – (Version 1.12, 213K) GNU 'tar' saves many files together into a single tape or disk archive, and can restore individual files from the archive. It includes multivolume support, the ability to archive sparse files, automatic archive compression/decompression, remote archives and special features that allow 'tar' to be used for incremental and full backups. If you wish to do remote backups with tar, you will need to install the 'rmt' package as well.

unarj – (Version 2.41a, 25K) The unarj program is used to uncompress .arj format archives, which were somewhat popular on DOS based machines.

unzip – (Version 5.31, 336K) unzip will list, test, or extract files from a ZIP archive, commonly found on MS-DOS systems. A companion program, zip, creates ZIP archives; both programs are compatible with archives created by PKWARE's PKZIP and PKUNZIP for MS-DOS, but in many cases the program options or default behaviors differ.

zip – (Version 2.1, 218K) zip is a compression and file packaging utility for Unix, VMS, MSDOS, OS/2, Windows NT, Minix, Atari and Macintosh. It is analogous to a combination of the UNIX commands tar(1) and compress(1) and is compatible with PKZIP (Phil Katz's ZIP for MSDOS systems).

BRU2000 – (Version 15.0P, 400K) BRU 2000 PE - RedHat Edition. BRU is the Backup and Restore Utility from EST. It's a powerful program that can be used to backup any or all of your Red Hat Linux system.

The Red Hat distribution has had the suid bit removed. In this configuration only root may use it.

BRU2000-X11 – (Version 15.0P, 457K)   BRU X11 is an X windows interface to BRU, the popular Backup and Restore Utility from EST. This is an intuitive graphical user interface that allows anyone to quickly setup their backup system.

The Red Hat distribution has had the suid bit removed. In this configuration only root may use it.

C.11.2   Console

This section lists packages that provide utilities that manage your Red Hat Linux system's console.

SVGATextMode – (Version 1.8, 845K)   SVGATextMode allows the screen mode of the Linux console to be controlled in detail. This allows more characters on screen, more stable text, less characters on screen, less stable text, etc. also, on badly designed hardware, you could sometimes achieve a melted monitor.

Extra fonts are required to work fully, though without them useful effects can still be achieved.

open – (Version 1.4, 12K)   This program runs a command on an given virtual console number. It can also run the program on the first virtual console which isn't already in use.

vlock – (Version 1.2, 9K)   vlock either locks the current terminal (which may be any kind of terminal, local or remote), or locks the entire virtual console system, completely disabling all console access. vlock gives up these locks when either the password of the user who started vlock or the root password is typed.

C.11.3   File

This section lists packages containing file-related utility programs.

file – (Version 3.24, 185K)   This package is useful for finding out what type of file you are looking at on your system. For example, if an fsck results in a file being stored in lost+found, you can run file on it to find out if it's safe to 'more' it or if it's a binary. It recognizes many file types, including ELF binaries, system libraries, RPM packages, and many different graphics formats.

fileutils – (Version 3.16, 870K)   These are the GNU file management utilities. It includes programs to copy, move, list, etc, files.

The ls program in this package now incorporates color ls!

findutils – (Version 4.1, 157K)   This package contains programs to help you locate files on your system. The find program can search through a hierarchy of directories looking for files matching a certain set of criteria (such as a filename pattern). The locate program searches a database (create by updatedb) to quickly find a file matching a given pattern.

git – (Version 4.3.17, 698K)   GIT is a file system browser for UNIX systems. An interactive process viewer/killer, a hex/ascii file viewer, an auto-mount shell script and a per file type action script are also available.

The standard ANSI color sequences are used where available. Manual pages and info documentation are also provided.

macutils – (Version 2.0b3, 201K)   This is a set of utilities for manipulating files from the Macintosh. Popular utilities like macunpack, hexbin, and binhex are included.

mtools – (Version 3.8, 414K)   Mtools is a collection of utilities to access MS-DOS disks from Unix without mounting them. It supports Win'95 style long file names, OS/2 Xdf disks, ZIP/JAZ disks and 2m disks (store up to 1992k on a high density 3 1/2 disk).

sharutils – (Version 4.2, 218K)   The shar utilities can be used to encode and package a number of files, binary and/or text, in a special plain text format. This format can safely be sent through email or other means where sending binary files is difficult.

smbfs – (Version 2.0.1, 50K)   This package includes the tools necessary to mount filesystems from SMB servers.

stat – (Version 1.5, 6K)   The stat program prints out filesystem level information about a file, including permissions, link count, inode, etc.

symlinks – (Version 1.2, 96K)   This program check for a number of problems with symlinks on a system, including symlinks which point to nonexistant files (dangling symlinks). It can also automatically convert absolute symlinks to relative symlinks.

tree – (Version 1.2, 18K)   This program is basically a UNIX port of the very useful DOS utility 'tree', which prints out a view of the specified directory tree, along with the files it owns. Includes support for 'color ls'-style listings.

which – (Version 1.0, 7K)   Give it a program name, and it tells you if it is on your 'PATH'.

For example, 'which ls' would print '/bin/ls', because the ls program, which is in one of the directories listed in your PATH environment variable, is located in the /bin directory.

C.11.4   Printing

This section lists packages that provide utility programs related to printing.

mpage – (Version 2.4, 84K)   mpage formats multiple pages of ASCII text onto a single page of PostScript. It supports many different layouts for the final pages.

C.11.5 System

This section lists packages that provide utilities that perform various system-related functions.

MAKEDEV – (Version 2.3.1, 24K) The /dev tree holds special files, each of which corresponds to a type of hardware device that Linux supports. This package contains a script which makes it easier to create and maintain the files which fill the /dev tree.

adjtimex – (Version 1.3, 22K) adjtimex is a kernel clock management system. It is useful in adjusting the system clock for accuracy.

apmd – (Version 2.4, 63K) This is a Advanced Power Management daemon and utilities. It can watch your notebook's battery and warn all users when the battery is low.

I have added an unofficial patch for shutting down the PCMCIA sockets before a suspend.

cabaret – (Version 0.5, 59K) cabaret is a friendly text-mode program for manipulating /etc/fstab. It allows you to add, delete, and modify mount points. It also lets you mount and unmount partitions through its graphical interface.

chkconfig – (Version 0.9.3, 57K) chkconfig provides a simple command-line tool for maintaining the /etc/rc.d directory hierarchy by relieving system administrators of directly manipulating the numerous symbolic links in that directory.

control-panel – (Version 3.7, 211K) The Red Hat control panel is an X program launcher for various configuration tools. Other packages provide information which allow them to show up on the control panel's menu of available tools.

cracklib-dicts – (Version 2.7, 227K) Includes the cracklib dictionaries for the standard /usr/dict/words, as well as utilities needed to create new dictionaries.

dump – (Version 0.3, 123K) dump and restore can be used to backup extended 2 (ext2) partitions in a variety of ways.

e2fsprogs – (Version 1.10, 798K) This package includes a number of utilities for creating, checking, and repairing ext2 filesystems.

eject – (Version 1.5, 34K) This program allows the user to eject media that is autoejecting like CD-ROMs, Jaz and Zip drives, and floppy drives on SPARC machines.

ext2ed – (Version 0.1, 283K) This is a package to allow for hacking of your extended two file systems. It is for hackers *only* and should only be used by experienced personnel. If you aren't sure if this is you, it isn't. Also, do not smoke near this software. You have been warned. This is not a recording.

fstool – (Version 2.6, 72K) The fstool is a X program for manipulating /etc/fstab. It allows you to add, delete, and modify amount points. It also lets you mount and unmount partitions through its graphical interface.

getty_ps – (Version 2.0.7j, 122K) getty and uugetty are used to accept logins on the console or a terminal. They can handle answer a modem for dialup connections (although mgetty is recommended for that purpose).

glint – (Version 2.5, 429K) Glint is a graphical interface to the RPM package management tool. It allows you to browse packages installed on your system, verify and query those package. It allows allows you to update packages with new versions and install new packages.

hdparm – (Version 3.3, 36K) This is a utility for setting Hard Drive parameters. It is useful for tweaking performance and for doing things like spinning down hard drives to conserve power.

helptool – (Version 2.4, 23K) The help tool provides a unified graphical interface for searching through many of the help sources available, including man pages and GNU texinfo documents.

info – (Version 3.12, 132K) The GNU project uses the texinfo file format for much of its documentation. This package includes a standalone browser program to view these files.

ipfwadm – (Version 2.3.0, 85K) This is the IP firewall and accounting administration tool. It is useful if you need to run a firewall (a machine that acts as a secure gateway to the Internet).

isapnptools – (Version 1.11, 99K) These programs allow ISA Plug-And-Play devices to be configured on a Linux machine.

This program is suitable for all systems, whether or not they include a PnP BIOS. In fact, a PnP BIOS adds some complications because it may already activate some cards so that the drivers can find them, and these tools can unconfigure them, or change their settings causing all sorts of nasty effects. If you have (for example) plug and play network cards that already work, I suggest you read section 4 on the format of the configuration file below very carefully.

kbd – (Version 0.95, 1,308K) This package contains utilities to load console fonts and keyboard maps. It also includes a number of different fonts and keyboard maps.

kbdconfig – (Version 1.6, 15K) This is a terminal mode program for setting the keyboard map for your system. Keyboard maps are necessary for using non US default keyboards. Kbdconfig loads the selected keymap before exiting and configures your machine to use that keymap automatically after rebooting.

kernelcfg – (Version 0.4, 57K) Red Hat Linux kernelcfg provides a GUI interface which allows you to easily administrate your kerneld configuration.

ldconfig – (Version 1.9.5, 105K) ldconfig scans a running system and sets up the symbolic links that are used to load shared libraries properly. It also creates /etc/ld.so.cache which speeds the loading programs which use shared libraries.

lilo – (Version 0.20, 1,437K) Lilo is repsonsible for loading your linux kernel from either a floppy or a hard drive and giving it control of the system. It can also be used to boot many other operating sysetms, including the BSD variants, DOS, and OS/2.

linuxconf – (Version 1.11r11, 6,749K)   Linuxconf has an easy-to-navigate user interface that is accessible from a text console, a web interface, and a GUI interface.

Linuxconf has the ability to manage:

Networking: Host information: IP Address, Hostname etc. IP Subnet allocation Resolving Name Servers Routing and Gateways NIS IPX Interface Setup PPP and Slip Dialout NFS File Systems Named (DNS) Zones and Secondaries Reverse Lookup Sendmail Virtual Email Domains UUCP IP Aliasing DCHP/BOOTP Server RARP Server Input Firewalling Output Firewalling Blocking Firewalling IP Masquerading Packet Accounting Mail to Fax Gateway User Accounts: User and Group management PPP Acounts Slip Accounts UUCP Accounts POP Only Accounts Virtual Email Domain Accounts Email Aliases For Normal and Virtual Domains Policies For Passwords and User Accounts Available User Shells Crontab Management Shadow Management File Systems: Local Partition Management (/etc/fstab) NFS Volume Management (Samba Volume Management coming soon) Swap File and Partition Management User and Group Disk Quotas File Permissions Boot Mode: Lilo Configuration Default Boot Mode Runlevel Definitions

And more...

logrotate – (Version 2.6, 40K)   Logrotate is designed to ease administration of systems that generate large numbers of log files. It allows automatic rotation, compression, removal, and mailing of log files. Each log file may be handled daily, weekly, monthly, or when it grows too large.

losetup – (Version 2.7l, 7K)   Linux supports a special block device called the loopback device, which maps a normal file onto a virtual block device. This package contains programs for setting up and removing the mapping between files and loopback devices.

Block loopback devices should not be confused with the networking loopback device, which is configured with the normal ifconfig command.

lpr – (Version 0.31, 169K)   This package manages printing services. It manages print queues, sends jobs to local printers and remote pritners, and accepts jobs from remote clients.

man – (Version 1.5d, 88K)   The man page suite, including man, apropos, and whatis. These programs are used to read most of the documentation available on a Linux system. The whatis and apropos programs can be used to find documentation related to a particular subject.

mingetty – (Version 0.9.4, 32K)   mingetty, by Florian La Roche, is a lightweight, minimalist getty for use on virtual consoles only. mingetty is not suitable for serial lines (the author recommends using 'mgetty' for that purpose).

mkbootdisk – (Version 1.0, 5K)   This package creates a self-contained boot disk for booting a system. It assumes that the boot disk should use the root partition mentioned in /etc/fstab. The resultant boot disk includes all of the SCSI modules needed to use the system.

mkdosfs-ygg – (Version 0.3b, 15K)   This is the mkdosfs package. You can use this under Linux to create MS-DOS FAT file systems.

mkinitrd – (Version 1.8, 6K) Generic kernels can be built without drivers for any SCSI adapters which load the SCSI driver as a module. To solve the problem of allowing the kernel to read the module without being able to address the SCSI adapter, an initial ramdisk is used. That ramdisk is loaded by the operating system loader (such as lilo) and is available to the kernel as soon as it is loaded. That image is resonsible for loading the proper SCSI adapter and allowing the kernel to mount the root filesystem. This program creates such a ramdisk image using information found in /etc/conf.modules.

mkisofs – (Version 1.11.2, 121K) This is the mkisofs package. It is used to create ISO 9660 file system images for creating CD-ROMs. Now includes support for making bootable "El Torito" CD-ROMs.

mktemp – (Version 1.4, 7K) mktemp is a small utility that interfaces to the mktemp() function call to allow shell scripts and other programs to use files in /tmp safely.

modemtool – (Version 1.21, 15K) The modem tool is a graphical simple configuration tool for selecting which of your serial ports is connected to a modem.

modutils – (Version 2.1.85, 573K) The Linux kernel allows new kernel pieces to be loaded and old ones to be unloaded while the kernel continues to run. These loadable piecs are called modules, and can include device drivers and filesystems among other things. This package includes program to load and unload programs both automatically and manually.

mount – (Version 2.7l, 104K) Mount is used for adding new filesystems, both local and networked, to your current directory structure. The filesystems must already exist for this to work. It can also be used to change the access types the kernel uses for already-mounted filesystems.

This package is critical for the functionality of your system.

mouseconfig – (Version 2.6, 48K) This is a text based mouse configuration tool. You can use it to set the proper mouse type for programs like 'gpm'. It also can be used in conjunction with the Red Hat Xconfigurator to setup the mouse for the X Window System.

mt-st – (Version 0.4, 22K) The mt program can be used to perform many operations on tapes, including rewind, eject, skipping files and blocks, etc.

netcfg – (Version 2.19, 165K) Red Hat Linux netcfg provides a GUI interface which allows you to easily administrate your network setup.

popt – (Version 1.1.1, 10K) Popt is a C library for pasing command line parameters. It was heavily influenced by the getopt() and getopt_long() functions, but it allows more powerfull argument expansion. It can parse arbitrary argv[] style arrays and automatically set variables based on command line arguments. It also allows command line arguments to be aliased via configuration files and includes utility functions for parsing arbitrary strings into argv[] arrays using shell-like rules.

printtool – (Version 3.28, 105K) The printtool provides a graphical interface for setting up printer queue. It manages both local printers and remote printers. Windows (SMB) printers can also be configured.

procinfo – (Version 13, 41K)   procinfo is a package to allow you to get useful information from /proc. /proc is the kernel filesystem. This is a place you can go to acquire information from your running kernel.

procps – (Version 1.2.7, 212K)   A package of utilities which report on the state of the system, including the states of running processes, amount of memory available, and currently-logged-in users.

psacct – (Version 6.3, 80K)   The tools necessary for accounting the activities of processes are included here.

psmisc – (Version 17, 41K)   This package contains programs to display a tree of processes, find out what users have a file open, and send signals to processes by name.

quota – (Version 1.55, 80K)   Quotas allow the system administrator to limit disk usage by a user and/or group per filesystem. This package contains the tools which are needed to enable, modify, and update quotas.

rhbackup – (Version 0.2, 29K)   rhbackup is a backup utility that can be used for local and remote backups. This should be considered alpha quality software and should be used with care.

rhmask – (Version 1.0, 9K)   rhmaskR is intended to allow the distribution of files as masks against other files. This lets new versions of software be freely distributed on public internet servers but limits their usefulness to those who already have a copy of the package. It uses a simple XOR scheme for creating the file mask and uses file size and md5 sums to ensure the integrity of the result.

rhs-hwdiag – (Version 0.20, 70K)   A package of utilities which report on the devices of the system. PnP probing of serial and parallel devices is supported. Useful for reporting errors to Red Hat concerning hardware.

rhs-printfilters – (Version 1.44, 88K)   The Red Hat print filter system provides an easy way to handle the printing of numerous file formats. Meant primarily to be used in conjuction with the Red Hat printtool.

rhsound – (Version 1.5, 9K)   The fake "service" created by rhsound allows sound modules to be loaded in contrallable runlevels and preserves mixer settings on shutdown/restarts

rmt – (Version 0.3, 12K)   rmt provides remote access to tape devices for programs like dump, restore, and tar.

rpm – (Version 2.5, 830K)   RPM is a powerful package manager, which can be used to build, install, query, verify, update, and uninstall individual software packages. A package consists of an archive of files, and package information, including name, version, and description.

setconsole – (Version 1.0, 4K)   setconsole sets up /etc/inittab, /dev/systty, and /dev/console for a new console. The console may be either the local terminal (directly attached to the system via a video card) or a serial console.

setserial – (Version 2.12, 31K) Setserial is a program which allows you to look at and change various attributes of a serial device, including its port, its IRQ, and other serial port options.

setuptool – (Version 1.0, 9K) setup is a friendly text-mode menu program that gives you easy, instant access to all the text-mode configuration programs in Red Hat Linux.

sh-utils – (Version 1.16, 339K) The GNU shell utilities provide many of the basic common commands used (among other things) for shell programming, hence the name. Nearly all shell scripts use at least one of these programs.

shadow-utils – (Version 980403, 585K) This package includes the programs necessary to convert standard UNIX password files to the shadow password format, as well as programs for command-line management of the user's accounts. - 'pwconv' converts everything to the shadow password format. - 'pwunconv' unconverts from shadow passwords, generating a file in the current directory called npasswd that is a standard UNIX password file. - 'pwck' checks the integrity of the password and shadow files. - 'lastlog' prints out the last login times of all users. - 'useradd', 'userdel' and 'usermod' for accounts management. - 'groupadd', 'groupdel' and 'groupmod' for group management.

A number of man pages are also included that relate to these utilities, and shadow passwords in general.

sliplogin – (Version 2.1.1, 52K) Attaches a SLIP interface to standard input. This is often used to allow dialin SLIP connections.

sndconfig – (Version 0.21, 69K) The Red Hat sound package includes the sndconfig tool whichs is a text based sound configuration tool. You can use it to set the proper sound type for programs which use the devices /dev/dsp, /dev/audio, and /dev/mixer. Sound settings are saved via the use of aumix and sysV runlevel scripts.

Currently only supports sound blaster type cards.

statserial – (Version 1.1, 166K) Statserial displays a table of the signals on a standard 9-pin or 25-pin serial port, and indicates the status of the handshaking lines. It can be useful for debugging problems with serial ports or modems.

swatch – (Version 2.2, 129K) Swatch is used to monitor log files. When it sees a line matching a pattern you specify, it can highlight it and print it out, or run external programs to notify you through mail or some other means.

taper – (Version 6.8.4, 846K) This is a tape backup and restore program that provides a friendly user interface to allow backing/restoring files to a tape drive. Alternatively, files can be backed up to hard disk files. Selecting files for backup and restore is very similar to the Midnight Commander interface and allows easy traversal of directories. Recursively selected directories are supported. Incremental backup and automatic most recent restore are defaults settings. SCSI, ftape, zftape, and removable drives are supported

time – (Version 1.7, 17K) The 'time' utility is used as a sort of 'stopwatch' to time the execution of a specified command. It can aid in the optimization of programs for maximum speed, as well as a number of other uses.

timeconfig – (Version 2.2, 35K) This is a simple tool for setting both the timezone and the way your system clock stores the time. It runs in text mode using a simple windowing system.

timetool – (Version 2.3, 22K) Timetool is a graphical interface for setting the current date and time for your system.

tksysv – (Version 1.0, 35K) This is a graphical tool for manipulating run levels. It allows you to control what services get started and stopped for every run level.

tmpwatch – (Version 1.5, 8K) This package provides a program that can be used to clean out directories. It recursively searches the directory (ignoring symlinks) and removes files that haven't been accessed in a user-specified amount of time.

tunelp – (Version 1.3, 9K) 'tunelp' aids in configuring the kernel parallel port driver.

usercfg – (Version 3.5, 94K) The User and Group Configurator Tool provides a graphical user interface which allows you to add users to your system, remove them, edit their characteristics, and manage groups of users.

usernet – (Version 1.0.7, 59K) A program that makes it easy for users to bring user-controllable network devices up and down, and to check on the status of those devices.

util-linux – (Version 2.7, 824K) util-linux contains a large variety of low-level system utilities necessary for a functional Linux system. This includes, among other things, configuration tools such as fdisk and system programs such as login.

C.11.6   Terminal

This section lists packages that provide utilities related to terminal handling.

dialog – (Version 0.6, 88K) Dialog is a utility that allows you to build user interfaces in a TTY (text mode only). You can call dialog from within a shell script to ask the user questions or present with choices in a more user friendly manner. See /usr/doc/dialog-*/samples for some examples.

screen – (Version 3.7.4, 348K) Screen is a program that allows you to have multiple logins on one terminal. It is useful in situations where you are telnetted into a machine or connected via a dumb terminal and want more than just one login.

C.11.7   Text

This section lists packages that provide utilities related to the handling and manipulation of text.

diffstat – (Version 1.25, 13K) 'diffstat' provides a number of statistics on a patch generated by diff, including number of additions, number of removals, and total number of changes. It can be useful, for example, to find out what changes have been made to a program, just by feeding the update patch to diffstat.

diffutils – (Version 2.7, 149K) The diff utilities can be used to compare files, and generate a record of the "differences" between files. This record can be used by the patch program to bring one file up to date with the other. All these utilities (except cmp) only work on text files.

faces – (Version 1.6.1, 139K) The faces package is for use mainly with exmh. You can take a photo of something and turn it into a "face" which can be transmitted in all email and will show up in exmh and other mailers.

faces-xface – (Version 1.6.1, 20K) These are the utilities to handle X-Face mail headers. They are called by mail readers to display an face from a message.

gawk – (Version 3.0.3, 2,288K) This is GNU Awk. It should be upwardly compatible with the Bell Labs research version of awk. It is almost completely compliant with the 1993 POSIX 1003.2 standard for awk.

Gawk can be used to process text files and is considered a standard Linux tool.

gecko – (Version 1.5, 66K) newt-based front end for the linuxconf system.

This is the default interface to linuxconf on a Red Hat system if the X Window System is not available (that is, if the DISPLAY environment variable is not set).

grep – (Version 2.2, 258K) This is the GNU implementation of the popular 'grep' *nix utility. It allows for the fast locating of strings in text files.

ispell – (Version 3.1.20, 2,480K) This is the GNU interactive spelling checker. You can run it on text files and it will interactively spell check. This means it will tell you about words it doesn't know, and will suggest alternatives when it can.

less – (Version 332, 138K) less is a text file viewer much like 'more', only better.

m4 – (Version 1.4, 118K) This is the GNU Macro processing language. It is useful for writing text files that can be parsed logically. Many programs use it as part of their build process.

mawk – (Version 1.2.2, 126K) Mawk is a version of awk, which is a powerful text processing program. In some areas mawk can outperform gawk, which is the standard awk program on Linux.

nenscript – (Version 1.13++, 24K) nenscript is a print filter. It can take ASCII input and format it into PostScript output and at the same time can do nice transformations like putting 2 ASCII pages on one physical page (side by side).

patch – (Version 2.5, 95K) Patch is a program to aid in patching programs. :-) You can use it to apply 'diff's. Basically, you can use diff to note the changes in a file, send the changes to someone who has the original file, and they can use 'patch' to combine your changes to their original.

perl – (Version 5.004, 11,422K)   Perl is an interpreted language optimized for scanning arbitrary text files, extracting information from those text files, and printing reports based on that information. It's also a good language for many system management tasks. The language is intended to be practical (easy to use, efficient, complete) rather than beautiful (tiny, elegant, minimal).

perl-MD5 – (Version 1.7, 29K)   Provides access to the md5 algorithm from RSA.

sed – (Version 2.05, 31K)   Sed copies the named files (standard input default) to the standard output, edited according to a script of commands.

textutils – (Version 1.22, 683K)   These are the GNU text file (actually, file contents) processing utilities. They include programs to split, join, compare, and modify files.

words – (Version 2, 414K)   This package contains the english dictionary in /usr/dict. It is used by programs like ispell as a database of words to check for spelling and so forth.

rgrep – (Version 0.98.4, 17K)   a recursive 'grep' utility that can highlight the matching expression, by the author of Jed.

C.12   X11

This section lists packages related to the X Window System. If you'd like your Red Hat Linux system to have a spiffy graphical user interface, this is where you'll need to look. Since there are so many X-related packages, we've divided them into subsections to make it easier to browse.

C.12.1   Amusements

This section lists packages containing various amusing programs that run under X.

multimedia – (Version 2.1, 325K)   This package contains XPlaycd, XMixer and XGetfile. XPlaycd is a program to play audio cd's using a cdrom drive. XMixer is used to control the mixer on a soundcard. XGetfile is a versatile file browser, made for use in shell-scripts.

xbanner – (Version 1.31, 648K)   XBanner displays text, patterns, and images on the root window. This allows users to customize both their normal X background and the background used on xdm style login screens.

xearth – (Version 1.0, 188K)   Xearth displays a pseudo-3D globe that rotates to show the earth as it actually is, including markers for major cities and Red Hat Software :-).

xfishtank – (Version 2.0, 386K)   Enjoy an animated aquarium background on your screen, with a variety of tropical fish swimming in it.

xsnow – (Version 1.40, 28K) A continual gentle snowfall is accompanied by Santa Claus flying his sleigh around your screen. Don't forget to shake the snow off those windows every now and then!

C.12.2 Applications

This section lists packages containing various applications that run under X.

ImageMagick – (Version 4.0.5, 2,384K) ImageMagick is an image display, conversion, and manipulation tool. It runs under X windows. It is very powerful in terms of it's ability to allow the user to edit images. It can handle many different formats as well.

gimp – (Version 0.99.28, 11,412K) The GIMP is an image manipulation program suitable for photo retouching, image composition and image authoring. Many people find it extremely useful in creating logos and other graphics for web pages. The GIMP has many of the tools and filters you would expect to find in similar commercial offerings, and some interesting extras as well.

The GIMP provides a large image manipulation toolbox, including channel operations and layers, effects, sub-pixel imaging and anti-aliasing, and conversions, all with multi-level undo.

This version of The GIMP includes a scripting facility, but many of the included scripts rely on fonts that we cannot distribute. The GIMP ftp site has a package of fonts that you can install by yourself, which includes all the fonts needed to run the included scripts. Some of the fonts have unusual licensing requirements; all the licenses are documented in the package. Get ftp://ftp.gimp.org/pub/gimp/fonts/freefonts-0.10.tar.gz and ftp://ftp.gimp.org/pub/gimp/fonts/sharefonts-0.10.tar.gz if you are so inclined. Alternatively, choose fonts which exist on your system before running the scripts.

gimp-data-extras – (Version 0.99a, 7,826K) Patterns, gradients etc. for gimp. This package isn't required, but contains lots of goodies for gimp.

gimp-devel – (Version 0.99.28, 229K) Static libraries and header files for writing GIMP plugins and extensions.

gimp-libgimp – (Version 0.99.28, 162K) Libraries used to communicate between The GIMP and other programs which may function as "GIMP plugins".

gv – (Version 3.5.8, 411K) gv allows to view and navigate through PostScript and PDF documents on an X display by providing a user interface for the ghostscript interpreter. gv is based upon an earlier program known as ghostview.

mxp – (Version 1.0, 53K) This is a very fast Mandelbrot set generator for X Windows. It lets you select regions to zoom in on and allows you to control other aspects of fractal generation.

netscape-common – (Version 4.05, 4,586K) Files shared between the Netscape Navigator and Netscape Communicator web browsers.

netscape-communicator – (Version 4.05, 9,892K)   Netscape Communicator is the industry-leading web browser. It supports the latest HTML standards, Java, and JavaScript. It also includes full-featured Usenet news reader as well as a complete email client.

Information on the Netscape Communicator license may be found in the file /usr/doc/netscape-4-4/LICENSE.update.

netscape-navigator – (Version 4.05, 6,720K)   Netscape Navigator is the industry-leading web browser. It supports the latest HTML standards, Java, and JavaScript. It also includes full-featured Usenet news reader as well as a complete email client.

Information on the Netscape Navigator license may be found in the file /usr/doc/netscape-4-4/LICENSE.update.

rvplayer – (Version 5.0, 3,692K)   Real Media client

seyon – (Version 2.14c, 215K)   Seyon is a complete full-featured telecommunications package for the X Window System. Some of its features are a dialing directory that supports an unlimited number of entries, terminal emulation window supporting DEC VT02, Tektronix 4014, and ANSI, script language to automate tedious tasks such as logging into remote hosts, unlimited number of slots for external file transfer protocols, support for Zmodem auto-download, and more.

transfig – (Version 3.2, 248K)   TransFig is a set of tools for creating TeX documents with graphics which are portable, in the sense that they can be printed in a wide variety of environments.

usermode – (Version 1.4.1, 639K)   Several graphical tools, including a tool to help users manage floppies (and other removable media) and a tool to help the user change his or her finger information.

x3270 – (Version 3.1.1.6, 553K)   This program emulates an IBM 3270 terminal, commonly used with mainframe applications, in an X window.

xanim – (Version 27064, 502K)   Viewer for various animated graphic formats, including QuickTime and FLiC.

xfm – (Version 1.3.2, 680K)   xfm is a file manager for X windows that allows you to manipulate files and directories in an intuitive, easy-to-understand manner, as well as allowing you to extend itself with other programs.

xgopher – (Version 1.3.3, 277K)   Gopher, a method of accessing information on the Internet, is made easy with this X-Windows gopher client. Although gopher is less up-to-date than the WWW, Xgopher can still open up a portal to the vast storehouse of information available on the Internet.

xloadimage – (Version 4.1, 237K)   Xloadimage displays images in an X11 window, loads them onto the root window, or writes them into a file. Many image types are recognized.

xmorph – (Version 1996.07.12, 124K)   xmorph allows you to create fascinating "morphs" - animated changes between two different images - and provides the tools to do so in an intuitive and easy-to-comprehend manner.

xpaint – (Version 2.4.9, 409K)   XPaint is a color image editing tool which features most standard paint program options, as well as advanced features such as image processing algorithms. It allows for the editing of multiple images simultaneously and supp

xpdf – (Version 0.7a, 746K)   Xpdf is a viewer for Portable Document Format (PDF) files. (These are also sometimes also called 'Acrobat' files, from the name of Adobe's PDF software.) Xpdf is designed to be small and efficient. It does not use the Motif or Xt libraries. It uses standard X fonts. Xpdf is quite usable on a 486-66 PC running Linux.

xrn – (Version 8.02, 190K)   This is an X program for reading USENET news. It allows point and click reading, replying, and posting or news as well as simple group selections.

xterm-color – (Version 1.1, 191K)   xterm-color displays the ANSI color codes in addition to performing as a standard xterm/VT100 terminal emulator.

xv – (Version 3.10a, 4,486K)   This is the famous 'xv' by John Bradley. It is shareware, but we ship it with the permission of the authors. It is a graphics viewer for many file types, including gif, jpg, tiff, xwd, etc. It also have manipulation features such as cropping, expanding, etc.

xwpe-X11 – (Version 1.4.2, 682K)   Includes the 'xwpe' and 'xwe' programs from the xwpe package that are specific to X Windows.

C.12.3   Games

This section lists packages that contain various games capable of running under X.

acm – (Version 4.7, 3,438K)   ACM is an X based flight simulator. It also have network cabailities for multiple player games.

cxhextris – (Version 1.0, 38K)   cxhextrix is a color version of the popular hextris. Both are a close of the popular T*tris video game, a game where one must try to stack odd shaped blocks together perfectly. This game requires X Windows to work properly.

flying – (Version 6.20, 212K)   This is a package of games that run under X Windows. It contains pool, snooker, air hockey, and other table games. WARNING: This software could become addictive and could cause serious levels of sleep deprivation or loss of mobility in the legs if used at extreme levels.

paradise – (Version 2.3p19, 413K)   Netrek is a very popular Internet based arcade game. You fly around with a team of players shooting at and capturing planets from the enemy (another team). A good way to drop out of college.

spider – (Version 1.0, 51K)   spider is a particularly challenging double-deck solitaire. Unlike most solitaires, it provides extraordinary opportunities for the skillful player to overcome bad luck in the deal by means of careful analysis and complex manipulations.

xbill – (Version 2.0, 184K)   This package has seen increased popularity with the dawn of the Linux age. Very popular at Red Hat.

The object of the game? To seek out and destroy all forms of Bill, to disestablish new and alien operating systems, and to boldly go where no geek has gone before.

xbl – (Version 1.0h, 176K)   A three dimensional version of a popular arcade game.

xboard – (Version 3.2.pl0, 316K)   xboard gives you an easy-to-use, graphical interface to the GNU chess program, allowing you to enjoy hours of mind-boggling chess action without having to learn complicated commands. It may also be used as a front end for playing chess with other people across the Internet.

xboing – (Version 2.4, 1,021K)   xboing is an X-Windows game in the tradition of the classic 'Breakout' arcade game. The object is to keep a ball bouncing on the bricks until they break down. Even more fun comes in later levels when you have to handle multiple balls and ball traps.

xchomp – (Version 1.0, 36K)   The classic arcade action game comes to your screen with xchomp, the PacMan-like game. Not as extensive as the original game, but still lots of fun!

xdemineur – (Version 1.1, 26K)   This is a game of intense concentration, where you must successfully determine the locations of mines through logic and deduction.

xevil – (Version 1.5, 527K)   An action/adventure game for X-Windows in which you, as a Ninja warrior, kill everything in sight, and explore if you survive.

xgalaga – (Version 1.6c, 366K)   A clone of the old space arcade game 'Galaga'. (It's Galaga, you know how to play Galaga! Ship follows the mouse, button fires. Auto-fire by holding it down, so no-one accuses us of breaking their mouse!)

xgammon – (Version 0.98, 3,277K)   This version of the popular card/board game 'backgammon' allows you to play either against the computer or another human.

xjewel – (Version 1.6, 49K)   Jewel is a game much like Domain/Jewelbox which is a puzzle game like Tetris.

It is played by controling the motion of blocks which continue to fall from the top of the screen. One can move them left and right, as well as rotate the jewel segments. The object is to get the most points before the grim reaper ends the fun.

xlander – (Version 1.2, 23K)   A very hard game, but lots of fun nonetheless. Try to manuver the lunar lander to a safe-and-nonviolent landing.

xpat2 – (Version 1.04, 459K)   In 1989, Dave Lemke, Heather Rose, Donald R. Woods and Sun Microsystems, Inc., created the xsol solitaire game (also known as klondike under DOS) and the rules of some other patience games. Its main features are variable rule sets and different card sets for different resolution monitors.

xpat2 (X Patience) is a collection of these assorted solitaire card games that will truly "try your patience".

xpilot – (Version 3.6.2, 1,576K)   xpilot is a fast-paced action game with multiplayer networking capabilities that make it full of hours of enjoyment. The basic object of them game is to kill and fly - need more be said?

xpuzzles – (Version 5.4.1, 498K)   An assortment of geometric puzzles and toys, including an electronic version of Rubik's cube, and a "dinosaur cube" program.

xtrojka – (Version 1.2.3, 181K)   Similar to xjewels or tetris, this game presents you with the challenge of keeping the playing area clear of falling blocks.

A variation on the addictive classic.

xzip – (Version 161, 91K)   Now all your favorite text adventure games can take on a new dimension with this X Windows interpreter for them.

C.12.4   Libraries

This section lists packages containing various X-related system libraries.

ImageMagick-devel – (Version 4.0.5, 1,366K)   This is the ImageMagick development package. It includes the static libraries and header files for use in developing your own applications that make use of the ImageMagick code and/or APIs.

Xaw3d – (Version 1.3, 278K)   Xaw3d is an enhanced version of the MIT Athena Widget set for X Windows that adds a 3-dimensional look to the applications with minimal or no source code changes.

Xaw3d-devel – (Version 1.3, 644K)   Xaw3d is an enhanced version of the MIT Athena Widget set for X Windows that adds a 3-dimensional look to the applications with minimal or no source code changes. This package includes the header files and static libraries for developing programs that take full advantage of Xaw3d's features.

gnome-core – (Version 0.13, 540K)   Basic programs and libraries that are virtually required for any GNOME installation.

GNOME is the GNU Network Object Model Environment. That's a fancy name but really GNOME is a nice GUI desktop environment. It makes using your computer easy, powerful, and easy to configure.

gnome-graphics – (Version 0.13, 688K)   GNOME graphics programs.

GNOME is the GNU Network Object Model Environment. That's a fancy name but really GNOME is a nice GUI desktop environment. It makes using your computer easy, powerful, and easy to configure.

gtk+ – (Version 1.0.1, 1,063K)   The X libraries originally written for the GIMP, which are now used by several other programs as well.

gtk+-devel – (Version 1.0.1, 1,573K)   Static libraries and header files for the GIMP's X libraries, which are available as public libraries. GLIB includes generally useful data structures, GDK is a drawing toolkit which provides a thin layer over Xlib to help automate things like dealing with different color depths, and GTK is a widget set for creating user interfaces.

imlib – (Version 1.4, 645K)   Imlib is an advanced replacement library for libraries like libXpm that provides many more features with much greater flexability and speed.

imlib-devel – (Version 1.4, 430K)   Headers, static libraries and documentation for Imlib.

nls – (Version 1.0, 4K)   This is a package of files used by some older X11R5 binaries such at Netscape. It isn't required by versions of Netscape greater than 3.0, however.

xpm – (Version 3.4j, 56K)   Allows applications to display color, bitmapped pictures. Used by a large number of popular X Windows programs to enhance the user interface.

C.12.5   Shells

This section lists packages containing various graphically-oriented shells.

mcserv – (Version 4.1.33, 19K)   mcserv is the server program for the Midnight Commander networking file system. It provides access to the host file system to clients running the Midnight file system (currently, only the Midnight Commander file manager).

tkmc – (Version 4.1.33, 558K)   Midnight Commander is a visual shell much like a file manager, only with way more features. It is tk X window wersion. Its coolest feature is the ability to ftp, view tar and zip files, and poke into RPMs for specific files. The tk version of Midnight Commander is not yet finished, though. :-(

C.12.6   Utilities

This section lists packages containing utilities related to the X window system.

Xconfigurator – (Version 3.57, 208K)   This is the Red Hat X Configuration tool. It is based on the sources for xf86config, a utility from XFree86. It has a nicer user interface added to make it easier for the end user.

NOTE - use mouseconfig to change your mouse type, then re-run Xconfigurator to set X up for your new mouse type.

gnome-linuxconf – (Version 0.13, 68K)   GNOME front end for the linuxconf system.

GNOME is the GNU Network Object Model Environment. That's a fancy name but really GNOME is a nice GUI desktop environment. It makes using your computer easy, powerful, and easy to configure.

mkxauth – (Version 1.7, 15K) 'mkxauth' aids in the creation and maintenance of X authentication databases (.Xauthority files). Use it to create a /.Xauthority file or merge keys from another local or remote .Xauthority file. Remote .Xauthority files can be retrieved via ftp (using ncftp) or via rsh. For security, mkxauth does not create any temporary files containing authentication keys.

moonclock – (Version 1.0, 25K) Displays the time of day and the current moon phase. Colors change depending on time of day (day/night) and the moon is displayed in a neat little wedge with a star field.

procps-X11 – (Version 1.2.7, 21K) A package of X-based utilities which report on the state of the system. These utilities generally provide graphical presentations of information available from tools in the procps suite.

rxvt – (Version 2.20, 246K) Rxvt is a VT100 terminal emulator for X. It is intended as a replacement for xterm(1) for users who do not require the more esoteric features of xterm. Specifically rxvt does not implement the Tektronix 4014 emulation, session logging and toolkit style configurability. As a result, rxvt uses much less swap space than xterm - a significant advantage on a machine serving many X sessions.

xdaliclock – (Version 2.10, 73K) The xdaliclock program displays a digital clock; when a digit changes, it "melts" into its new shape.

It can display in 12 or 24 hour modes, and displays the date when a mouse button is held down. It has two large fonts built into it, but it can animate other fonts.

xlockmore – (Version 4.09, 1,323K) An enhanced version of the standard xlock program which allows you to keep other users locked out of an X session while you are away from the machine. It runs one of many provided screensavers while waiting for you to type your password, unlocking the session and letting you at your X programs.

xmailbox – (Version 2.5, 30K) This program will notify you when new mail arrives. It is similar to xbiff, but offers more features and fancier notification options.

xosview – (Version 1.5.1, 94K) xosview provides a convenient bar graph of the current system state - memory usage, CPU load, and network usage. Very useful for monitoring status.

xscreensaver – (Version 2.16, 11,180K) Screen savers of every sort are included in this package, guaranteeing hours of enjoyment˘H˘H˘H˘H˘H˘H˘Hmonitor saving. And if you are bent on really saving your monitor, there's that old classic, the plain black screen.

xsysinfo – (Version 1.6, 21K) Many aspects of system performance can be monitored with xsysinfo, including network traffic, CPU load, disk space, disk usage, and more. Displays a history of performance in a window so you can easily see changes.

xtoolwait – (Version 1.1, 9K) Utility to start a program and wait for it to map a window. Not an end-user program, but useful for writing scripts that run X Windows programs.

xwpick – (Version 2.20, 44K)   Xwpick lets you pick an image from an arbitrary window or rectangular area of an X11-server and write it to a file in a variety of formats.

C.12.7   Window Managers

This section lists packages containing various window managers (and related files). Unlike other graphical user interfaces on other operating systems, your Red Hat Linux system lets you choose which window manager you'd like to run on top of X. The packages in this section let you choose from several window manager styles.

AfterStep – (Version 1.4.5.3, 2,425K)   AfterStep is a continuation of the BowMan window manager which was originally put together by Bo Yang. BowMan was based on the fvwm window manager, written by Robert Nation. Fvwm was based on code from twm. And so on... It was originally designed to emulate some of the look and feel of the NEXTSTEP user interface, but has since taken steps towards adding more useful, requested, and neat features especially in 1.4 version ! The changes which comprise AfterStep's personality were originally part of bowman development, but due to a desire to move past simple emulation and into a niche as its own valuable window manager, AfterStep designers decided to change the project name and move on.

Important features of AfterStep include:

1. Wharf: a free-floating application loader which can "Swallow" running programs and also can contain "Folders" of more applications. 2. Gradient filled TitleBars with 5 button : help/zap, action/tasks, iconize/maximise, shade/stick & close/destroy buttons 3. Gradient filled root window PopUp menus which can be configured to accomodate different tastes and styles of management 4. NEXTSTEP style icons which give a consistent look to the entire desktop 5. Pixmapped Pager with desktop pixmmaping 6. Easy to use look files, to share you desktop appearance with your friends 7. Start menu entries in a hierarchy of directories 8. WinList : a tasklist which can be horizontal or vertical 9. Many modules & asapps to give a good look to your X window station

AnotherLevel – (Version 0.6.8, 308K)   AnotherLevel is the next version of TheNextLevel. TheNextLevel desktop was created by Greg J. Badros and was the winning entry in the 1996 Red Hat Desktop Contest. It features a powerful and attractive fvwm configuration that works with fvwm2. That version suffered a number of enhancements and transformations, so we called it AnotherLevel. Some documentation is available in /usr/doc/AnotherLevel in html format.

This desktop is defined to be easily reconfigured. Most attributes may be redefined by copying /etc/X11/AnotherLevel/fvwm2rc.defines to a user's home directory as .fvwm2rc.defines and modifying the copied file appropriately.

fvwm – (Version 1.24r, 550K)   fvwm is a small, fast, and very flexible window manager. It can be configured to look like Motif, and has a useful "button bar".

fvwm2 – (Version 2.0.46, 1,483K)   fvwm is a version of the popular "Feeble Virtual Window Manager"

fvwm2-icons – (Version 2.0.46, 599K)   This package contains icons, bitmaps and pixmaps for fvwm and fvwm2.

wmconfig – (Version 0.4.1, 47K)   This is a program that will generate menu configurations for different window managers available for the X11 system. It is an attempt to gain some form of abstractization of the menu configuration across some window managers. Currently it supports: FVWM2, FVWM95, Afterstep, MWM, IceWM, KDE

C.12.8   XFree86

This section lists packages containing part of XFree86, a freely available version of the X Window System. In order to use X, you must install an X server capable of driving your Red Hat Linux system's video card. As you can see, XFree86 has a number of servers from which to choose.

X11R6-contrib – (Version 3.3.2, 447K)   This is a collection of X programs from X11R6's contrib tape, which contains programs contributed by various users. It includes listres, xbiff, xedit, xeyes, xcalcm, xload, and xman amoung others.

XFree86-100dpi-fonts – (Version 3.3.2, 1,228K)   The 100dpi fonts used on most Linux systems. Users with high resolution displays may prefer the 100dpi fonts available in a separate package.

XFree86 – (Version 3.3.2, 16,142K)   X Windows is a full featured graphical user interface featuring multiple windows, multiple clients, and different window styles. It is used on most Unix platforms, and the clients can also be run under other popular windowing systems. The X protocol allows applications to be run on either the local machine or across a network, providing flexibility in client/server mplementations.

This package contains the basic fonts, programs and documentation for an X workstation. It does not provide the X server which drives your video hardware – those are available in other package.

XFree86-75dpi-fonts – (Version 3.3.2, 1,060K)   The 75dpi fonts used on most Linux systems. Users with high resolution displays may prefer the 100dpi fonts available in a separate package.

XFree86-8514 – (Version 3.3.2, 3,402K)   X server for older IBM 8514 cards and compatibles from companies such as ATI.

XFree86-AGX – (Version 3.3.2, 3,570K)   X server for AGX based cards such as the Boca Vortex, Orchid Celsius, Spider Black Widow, and Hercules Graphite.

XFree86-I128 – (Version 3.3.2, 3,799K)   X server for the #9 Imagine 128 board.

XFree86-Mach32 – (Version 3.3.2, 3,534K)   X server for cards built around ATI's Mach32 chip, including the ATI Graphics Ultra Pro and Ultra Plus.

XFree86-Mach64 – (Version 3.3.2, 3,647K)   X server for ATI Mach64 based cards such as the Graphics Xpression, GUP Turbo, and WinTurbo cards. This server is known to have problems with some Mach64 cards which newer versions of XFree86 (which were only available as BETA releases at the time of this release) may fix. Look at http://www.xfree86.org for information on updating this server.

XFree86-Mach8 – (Version 3.3.2, 3,412K)   X server for cards built around ATI's Mach8 chip, including the ATI 8514 Ultra and Graphics Ultra.

XFree86-Mono – (Version 3.3.2, 3,658K)   Generic monochrome (2 color) server for VGA cards, which works on nearly all VGA style boards with limited resolutions.

XFree86-P9000 – (Version 3.3.2, 3,589K)   X server for cards built around the Weitek P9000 chips such as most Diamond Viper cards and the Orchid P9000 card.

XFree86-S3 – (Version 3.3.2, 4,031K)   X server for cards built around chips from S3, including most #9 cards, many Diamond Stealth cards, Orchid Farenheits, Mirco Crystal 8S, most STB cards, and some motherboards with built in graphics accelerators (such as the IBM Value-Point line).

XFree86-S3V – (Version 3.3.2, 3,782K)   X server for cards built around the S3 Virge chipset.

XFree86-SVGA – (Version 3.3.2, 4,555K)   X server for most simple framebuffer SVGA devices, including cards built from ET4000 chips, Cirrus Logic chips, Chips and Technologies laptop chips, Trident 8900 and 9000 chips. It works for Diamond Speedstar, Orchid Kelvins, STB Nitros and Horizons, Genoa 8500VL, most Actix boards, the Spider VLB Plus. It also works for many other chips and cards, so try this server if you are having problems.

XFree86-VGA16 – (Version 3.3.2, 3,583K)   Generic 16 color server for VGA boards. This works on nearly all VGA style graphics boards, but only in low resolution with few colors.

XFree86-W32 – (Version 3.3.2, 3,447K)   X server for cards built around the ET4000/W32 chips, including the Genoa 8900 Phantom 32i, Hercules Dynamite cards, LeadTek WinFast S200, Sigma Concorde, STB LightSpeed, TechWorks Thunderbolt, and ViewTop PCI.

XFree86-devel – (Version 3.3.2, 7,632K)   Libraries, header files, and documentation for developing programs that run as X clients. It includes the base Xlib library as well as the Xt and Xaw widget sets. For information on programming with these libraries, Red Hat recommends the series of books on X Programming produced by O'Reilly and Associates.

XFree86-libs – (Version 3.3.2, 1,858K)   This package contains the shared libraries most X programs need to run properly. They are in a separate package to reduce the disk space needed to run X applications on a machine w/o an X server (over a network).

C.12.9   gnome

This section contains packages that are related to the GNOME desktop environment.

gnome-libs – (Version 0.13, 1,240K)   Basic libraries you must have installed to use GNOME.

GNOME is the GNU Network Object Model Environment. That's a fancy name but really GNOME is a nice GUI desktop environment. It makes using your computer easy, powerful, and easy to configure.

gnome-libs-devel – (Version 0.13, 1,287K)   Libraries, include files, etc you can use to develop GNOME applications.

xinitrc – (Version 1.4, 3K)   This package contains the basic X windows startup script used by the "startx" command.

D

General Parameters

This appendix is provided to illustrate *some* of the possible parameters that may be needed by certain drivers. It should be noted that, in most cases, these additional parameters are unnecessary.

Please keep in mind that if a device you are attempting to use requires one of these parameters, and support for that device is *not* compiled into the kernel, the traditional method of adding the parameter to the LILO boot command will not work. Drivers loaded as modules require that these parameters are specified when the module is loaded. The Red Hat Linux installation program gives you the option to specify module parameters when a driver is loaded.

For more information concerning the device support compiled into the kernel used by the Red Hat Linux installation program, please refer to Section 2.7 on page 25.

One of the more commonly used parameters, the hdX=cdrom parameter, *can* be entered at the boot prompt, as it deals with support for IDE/ATAPI CD-ROMs, which is part of the kernel.

D.1 CD-ROM parameters

Hardware	Parameter
Mitsumi CD-ROM	mcd=*port,irq*
Sony CDU 31 or 33 CD-ROM	cdu31a_port=*base_addr* cdu31a_irq=*irq*
Aztech CD268	aztcd=*port*
SB Pro or 16 compatible	sbpcd=*io_addr,sb_pro_setting*
ATAPI/IDE CD-ROM Drives	hd*x*=cdrom

Examples of the above would be:

Configuration	Example
non-IDE Mitsumi CD-ROM on port 340, IRQ 11	mcd=0x340,11
Sony CDU 31 or 33 at port 340, no IRQ	cdu31a_port=0x340 cdu31a_irq=0
Aztech CD-ROM at port 220	aztcd=0x220
ATAPI CD-ROM, jumpered as master on 2nd interface	hdc=cdrom
Panasonic-type CD-ROM on a SoundBlaster at port 230	sbpcd=0x230,1

Please Note: Most newer Sound Blaster cards come with IDE interfaces. You do not need to use sbpcd parameters, only use hd*x* parameters.

D.2 SCSI parameters

Hardware	Module	Parameters
Seagate ST0X	seagate.o	controller_type=1 base_address=*base_addr* irq=*irq*
F. Domain TMC-8xx	seagate.o	controller_type=2 base_address=*base_addr* irq=*irq*
F. Domain TMC-3260	fdomain.o	setup_called=1 port_base=*base_addr* interrupt_level=*irq*
AHA-2920	fdomain.o	setup_called=1 port_base=*base_addr* interrupt_level=*irq*
Trantor T128	t128.o	t128=*base_addr,irq*
NCR-5380 Based	g_NCR5380.o	ncr5380=*base_addr,irq,dma_channel*
AHA 152x	aha152x.o	aha152x=*base_addr,irq,scsi_id,reconnect,parity*
AHA 1542	aha1542.o	bases=*base_addr*
Buslogic	BusLogic.o	buslogic=*base_addr*
PAS-16 SCSI	pas16.o	pas16=*base_addr,irq*
Zip Parallel Port	ppa.o	ppa_base=*base_addr*
Always In2000	in2000.o	setup_string="ioport:*base_addr* noreset nosync:*x* period:*ns* disconnect:*x* debug:*x* proc:*x*"

Some examples would be:

Configuration	Example
Adaptec AHA1522 at port 330, IRQ 11, SCSI ID 7	aha152x=0x330,11,7
Adaptec AHA1542 at port 330	bases=0x330
Future Domain TMC-800 at CA000, IRQ 10	controller_type=2 base_address=0xca000 irq=10

When a parameter has commas, make sure you do not put a space after a comma.

D.3 Ethernet parameters

Most ethernet drivers accept parameters to specify a base IO address and an IRQ as follows:

```
io=base_addr irq=irq
```

For example, for a 3com 3c509 ethernet card located at IO address 210 (IO addresses are usually in hexadecimal) and IRQ 10, use the following parameters for the 3c509 driver:

```
io=0x210 irq=10
```

You can use multiple ethernet cards in one machine . If each card uses a different driver (e.g., 3c509 and a DE425), you simply need to add aliases (and possibly options) for each card to /etc/conf.modules; for example:

```
alias eth0 3c509
options 3c509 io=0x210 irq=10
alias eth1 de4x5
options de4x5 io=0
```

See Section 9.6 on page 128 for more information.

However, if any two ethernet cards use the same driver (e.g., two 3c509's or a 3c595 and a 3c905), you will need to compile a custom kernel with the ethernet driver built in. In that case, you can use the "classic" LILO boot: parameters of the form:

```
ether=irq,base_addr,interface
```

For example:

```
LILO boot: linux ether=10,0x210,eth0 ether=11,0x300,eth1
```

(For more information about using more than one ethernet card, see the *Multiple-Ethernet* mini-HOWTO.)

Red Hat Linux Frequently Asked Questions

E.1   Introduction

This is the Official Red Hat Linux FAQ. It answers as many common questions as possible about Red Hat Linux.

It is maintained by `mailto:faq-maintainer@redhat.com;` all comments or suggestions for this FAQ should be sent to that address. To get a more recent version of this FAQ see E.4 (Resources Section).

E.2   Errata

The single best source of information, especially with respect to bugs or problems with the Red Hat Linux distribution are the errata pages available at `http://www.redhat.com/errata` and look for both the General Errata and the platform-specific Errata for your version of Red Hat Linux. (See also E.4 (Resources Section) for other ways to get the Errata).

It may seem strange that we list this as the very first item, but the errata pages are perhaps the best resource for fixing 90% of the common problems with Red Hat Linux. Security holes for which there is a solution are generally on the errata page 24 hours after Red Hat has been notified.

You should *always check there first.*

E.3   Contacting Red Hat Software

Our primary addresses are:

- **General:**

```
Red Hat Software
4201 Research Commons, Suite 100
79 TW Alexander Dr.
PO Box 13588
Research Triangle Park, NC 27709
USA

http://www.redhat.com
ftp://ftp.redhat.com
mailto:redhat@redhat.com
```

- **Sales:**

```
tel: +1-888-RED-HAT1  (toll-free)
tel: +1-919-547-0012  (toll call)
fax: +1-919-547-0024
http://www.redhat.com/products
```

- **Support:**

```
support@redhat.com
http://www.redhat.com/support
```

- **Bugs:**

```
bugs@redhat.com    (Please see the Errata first)
```

- **Suggestions and requests for new features:**

```
suggest@redhat.com
```

E.4 General Resources List

There are a large number of resources for users of Red Hat Linux available. Some are provided by Red Hat Software, and some are provided by other sources. Also, a large number of questions about Red Hat Linux are generic to Linux or even Unix.

- **Red Hat Linux Web Pages:**

    - Main Red Hat Page `http://www.redhat.com`
    - Errata Pages `http://www.redhat.com/errata`
    - Technical Support `http://www.redhat.com/support`
    - Technical Support HOWTO
      `http://www.redhat.com/support/support-howto.html`
    - Supported Hardware `http://www.redhat.com/hardware`
    - Mailing List Information `http://www.redhat.com/mailing-lists`
    - Red Hat User's Guide: `http://www.redhat.com/manual`

- **Generic Linux Web Pages:**

    - Official home of Linux `http://www.li.org`
    - Generic information on a number of topics
      `http://www.redhat.com/linux-info`
    - Excellent general Linux resource `http://www.linuxnow.com`
    - Technical questions and more mailing lists `http://www.linuxhq.com`

- **Email Addresses:** (You can get documents from the following automated reply addresses)

    - Latest fixes for newest Red Hat release `mailto:errata@redhat.com`
    - Hardware list `mailto:hardware-compat@redhat.com`
    - How to get support `mailto:support-howto@redhat.com`
    - This FAQ document `mailto:faq@redhat.com`
    - Tips on getting PPP to work `mailto:ppp-tips@redhat.com`

- **FTP servers:** (There are also many Red Hat mirrors. Please see E.12.1 (Appedix list of mirrors.))

    - Red Hat FTP server `ftp://ftp.redhat.com`
    - RPM FTP server `ftp://ftp.rpm.org`

- **Usenet newsgroups:** For these newsgroups, pick **one**; crossposting is considered harmful.

    - For answers:
        * `news:comp.os.linux.announce`
        * `news:comp.os.linux.answers`

– For questions:

* news:comp.os.linux.advocacy
* news:comp.os.linux.development.apps
* news:comp.os.linux.development.system
* news:comp.os.linux.hardware
* news:comp.os.linux.m68k
* news:comp.os.linux.misc
* news:comp.os.linux.networking
* news:comp.os.linux.prog
* news:comp.os.linux.setup
* news:comp.os.linux.x

E.5   General Questions

E.5.1   How do I get new updates to Red Hat as they happen?

Keep your eye on the Red Hat Linux Errata. (See E.2 (errata).)

Also check the contrib directory on our FTP mirrors for packages that users have contributed.
We also make periodic announcements to the redhat-announce-list with updates.

E.5.2   How do I report a bug?

Send email to mailto:bugs@redhat.com.

E.5.3   Does Red Hat Linux include source code?

Yes. We include the exact source that was used to build the distribution. From release 2.0 on,
Red Hat Linux is built with a packaging system called RPM that ONLY uses pristine source (the
same as what you'd find at the author's site) and possibly a patch by Red Hat.

To install a source RPM, use the following command:

```
rpm -iv packagename-n.nn-r.src.rpm
```

RPM installs sources under the redhat source tree, which is /usr/src/redhat by default (you
can configure the directory using the topdir command in /etc/rpmrc). Spec files
(packagename-n.nn.spec) are installed in /usr/src/redhat/SPECS, while source archives
and patch files go in /usr/src/redhat/SOURCES.

To unpack the source once it is installed, change to /usr/src/redhat/SPECS and use the following command:

```
rpm -bp packagename-n.nn.spec
```

RPM unpacks the source into /usr/src/redhat/BUILD/packagename-n.nn and applies any patches listed in the spec file.

For more information, please read the RPM manual page and the complete RPM information at: http://www.rpm.org/.

E.6   Installation

E.6.1   I have a blank hard drive and would like to install DOS or Windows 95 and Linux onto it. What is the best method of doing this?

It is recommended to install the other operating system first, before installing Linux. This allows the other OS to "get comfortable" with the hardware and possibly write values to the MBR that it would just over-write if Linux was installed first.

You will probably need to do this in a several step method, however. First start the install, but if the operating system partitions the entire drive for itself, see if you can "bail out" early and use the native fdisk to create a primary partition of the size you want to leave for the OS (150-500 megs seems to be usual depending on your needs). Then reboot and go through the install again and normally the OS will just use the space that you just set aside. Once the install is finished, you can begin the Linux installation.

E.6.2   I do not have a cdrom that will work with Linux and I can not install from the network. Is there another method?

If you are going to need to do a hard drive install due to some problem with your cdrom, you will need to follow these steps.

Have a DOS partition that is formatted in FAT16, and create a directory called \RedHat. From there you will need to copy the items from the cdrom over to the hard-drive.

```
mkdir C:\RedHat
mkdir C:\RedHat\base
mkdir C:\RedHat\RPMS
copy E:\RedHat\base C:\RedHat\base
```

```
copy E:\RedHat\RPMS C:\RedHat\RPMS
```

If you do not have enough disk space for copying the entire RPMS directory tree over to your hard-drive, you will need to look in the file `\RedHat\base\comps` file for the RPMS that are needed in the base and any other sections you feel you need.

Once you have done this, you can start the install and choose a Hard-Drive install. You will be asked to insert the supplemental floppy and a progress meter will "pop-up" to show you what is happening. Once the supplemental disk has been loaded, you will be presented with the next screen on the install.

E.6.3   For whatever reason, I need to make new floppies. What can I do?

We are sorry for the problem. The cdrom contains all the data to make new boot and supplemental floppies for your system. To make new floppies under DOS, Win95, or NT (over-writing any data on the 1.44 Megabyte floppies):

- 1. Boot DOS and change directory to the CD-ROM #1.
  2. Enter the dosutils directory and run rawrite.

```
cd \dosutils
rawrite.exe
```

  3. When prompted, for a disk, for the boot image enter:

```
..\images\boot.img
```

  4. Then change floppies, and run 'rawrite' again. When prompted enter:

```
..\images\supp.img
```

If you are in Linux or another Unix, you can mount the CD-ROM and use dd to write the data to floppy. With Linux, you could do the following:

```
dd if=/mnt/cdrom/images/boot.img of=/dev/fd0 bs=72k
dd if=/mnt/cdrom/images/supp.img of=/dev/fd0 bs=72k
```

E.6.4   I have an IDE system, and I am confused by how Linux sets up drives in comparison to DOS. Can you explain this?

Linux sets up the drive system in a very different pattern than DOS, and this can be rather confusing. Instead of calling the first hard drive NT, it will be usually be a combination of letters signifying what kind of BUS (sd for SCSI, hd for IDE) and on which sequence it was detected. Finally a number is tagged onto the end to specify which partition on the drive is being referenced.

For IDE hard drives the layout depends on which IDE channel the drive is on and whether it is the master or slave on that channel.

```
Channel           Jumper           hdx
===================================
ide0              master           hda
ide0              slave            hdb
ide1              master           hdc
ide1              slave            hdd
ide2              master           hde
ide2              slave            hdf
ide3              master           hdg
ide3              slave            hdh


ide0 = primary
ide1 = secondary
ide2 = tertiary
ide3 = quarterary
```

The partition number follows an old PC standard that there are a limit of 4 primary partitions per hard drive, but one of those partitions can be designated as an extended partition. Inside of this extended partition, logical partitions can be specified (for most drives you can have 12 logical drives in the extended partition for 16 partitions all together).

The numbering scheme is broken into the following:

- 1-4 primary partitions

- 5-16 logical partitions

E.6.5   My cdu31a/33a cdrom is not recognized. What can I do?

It has been found that the options for a cdu31a need some tweaking in the install. Instead of auto probing for the cdrom, select "specify options". A screen like the following should appear.

```
+---------------| Module parameters |---------------+
|                                                   |
| Module options:                                   |
|                                                   |
|   IO base, IRQ, PAS?:      cdu31a=_____ |
|                                                   |
|   Miscellaneous options:   _____        |
:                                                   :
+---------------------------------------------------+
```

Erase the complete first input line (cdu31a=) and entered the following as `Miscellaneous` options:

```
cdu31a_port=0x360 cdu31a_irq=0 sony_pas_init=0
```

If your cdrom is on a Sony PAS

```
cdu31a_port=0x360 cdu31a_irq=0 sony_pas_init=1
```

With these input everything should work perfectly. Auto probing the CD-ROM drive will usually not be successful, but this might be caused by the not- too-usual port address setting of the CDU33A.

E.6.6   I am having trouble getting linux setup on my Laptop computer.

The following web pages contains a great deal of information regarding installing linux on a laptop computer:

```
http://www.cs.utexas.edu/users/kharker/linux-laptop/
```

E.6.7   I am trying to upgrade my earlier Red Hat system to 5.x, but it complains that it can't find a valid RPM data base. What do I need to do?

The problem is that a very few earlier versions of rpm would write the database in a way that seems corrupted to later versions. Rebuilding the database fixes the install problems. We will need to upgrade rpm on your system to the one on the installation cdrom, and rebuild the databases.

First thing to do is mount the 5.0 CD on the system.

```
mount /mnt/cdrom
```

After doing this upgrade 'rpm' off the CD like so:

```
cd /mnt/cdrom/RedHat/RPMS
rpm -Uvh --nodeps --force rpm-*rpm
```

When the new RPM is installed, rebuild the database.

```
rpm --rebuilddb
```

This will now put the database in a format that the installation RPM can use (since they are the same.)

E.6.8 I have an Adaptec 2920. During the install I do not see a choice for it, why and what do I do? or I have a Future Domain TMC-3260, but when I specify options for it to be probed, it can't find it during the install.

The Adaptec 2920 does not use an Adaptec chip set, but actually uses the Future Domain TMC-3260. If the card is not found with an auto-probe, you will need to specify options for it. When the installation menu asks you about SCSI, choose "options" and enter the following :

```
setup_called=1 port_base=<io base> interrupt_level=<irq>
```

An example of this would be

```
setup_called=1 port_base=0xd000 interrupt_level=9
```

In case you do not have the port_base or the interrupt_level of the card, you can do the following. If you have reached the 2nd stage of the install (meaning the install has found the cdrom), you can ALT-F2 over to the root console, and cat /proc/pci to see what Linux found on the PCI bus. Otherwise, you will need to boot into rescue mode, and say no to having any scsi devices in the system. Then at the # root prompt, cat /proc/pci and write down the values for the card. Then restart the machine with a CONTROL-ALT-DELETE and fill in the values for the card during the install.

If the above options do not work, your card may have a newer BIOS that we can't probe correctly. We are working on the problem, but do not have a time for when it will be resolved.

E.6.9   I have an Adaptec SCSI card with the `aic7xxx` chipset (2940, 2840, 2740, 3940, etc). It is pretty common, so why is it not fully supported by Red Hat Linux?

Unfortunately, Adaptec has not actively supported the development of a driver for the AHA2940 SCSI adapter and AIC7xxx SCSI chipset.

Specifically, Adaptec continues to release new BIOSes and chip set revisions without making the specifications available to the authors of the Linux driver. Consequently, some AHA2940 adapters work well with Linux, because they have compatible chip sets, while other AHA2940s have different chip sets that the developers haven't seen and do not work well with Linux. Until the authors of the Linux drivers are able to make the driver work with all the different AHA2940 BIOSes, we cannot put this hardware on the supported list, but instead provide a driver in an "AS IS" form. If it works, great, and if it doesn't, you can try the following:

- 1. The AHA-2940 is, like most Adaptec cards, extremely sensitive to termination issues (having active termination on BOTH ends of the bus can help a lot)
  2. SCSI Hard drives that have on-drive termination seem (as a general rule) to supply _active_ termination whereas SCSI CD-ROM drives and SCSI tape drives that can be configured for on-drive termination seem (as a general rule) to supply only _passive_ termination
  3. If a SCSI-based system doesn't work when you have sync negotiation and disconnect enabled for your SCSI devices, but _DOES_ work OK when you disable sync negotiation and/or disconnect for your SCSI peripherals, then suspect bad cables and/or bad (or less than adequate) termination, and
  4. HP C3725S SCSI drives do not work at all well with AHA-2940AU and Redhat 4.2, perhaps due to a problem with the drive, but just as likely due to some problem/problems with the AHA-2940 driver in the Linux 2.0.30 kernel.
  5. For some large drives you have to disable the default option in the Adaptec-SCSI BIOS: "Extended BIOS translation for DOS drives > 1 GByte". This option causes the BIOS to use a translation scheme of 255 heads, 63 sectors per track. LILO does not like this. After disabling, everything works OK (windows95 installation, Linux and LILO installation, dual-boot).
  6. Make sure that on a SCSI chain that the drive you are installing to is SCSI ID 0 (or 1 if you have no IDE drives in the system.)
  7. Others have found that using the conservative/slow settings "no tagged queuing", "5MB/s" etc, fixes problems.

E.6.10   During the install, I get a fatal signal 11 or signal 7. What does this mean and what can I do?

Signal 11's and signal 7's are errors indicating a hardware error in memory or on the bus. This can be due to problems in executables or with the hardware of the system. The Linux kernel uses a lot more capabilities of the CPU, Cache, and memory, and is more prone to faulting on marginal hardware.

The first thing to do is check to see if you have the latest installation and supplemental floppies from Red Hat. Check the errata for updates and also the FTP site to see if newer versions are available. If the latest images still fail, it may be due to hardware. Common suspects are memory or CPU-cache. Try turning off the CPU-cache in the BIOS and see if the problem goes away. Also try swapping memory around in the motherboard slots to see if it is either slot or memory related.

More information is available at `http://www.bitwizard.nl/sig11`.

E.6.11 During the install, I am having problems with Linux working with my Ultra DMA IDE drive and motherboard controller, what can I do?

Ultra DMA support in the Linux kernel is rather limited in kernels before 2.0.34 For some motherboards it works well, and others not at all. When interfacing Ultra DMA drives with these motherboards, you may need to set the BIOS to use PIO mode 2 versus PIO mode 4 transfers.

E.6.12 I have a PCI Ultra DMA controller in my machine. Can I install Linux on my machine?

Due to various problems, most Ultra DMA controllers that are not built onto the motherboard will not work with the stable Linux kernel series 2.0.xx. Due to these problems, these cards can be a pain to install Linux onto. The following mini-HOWTO describes has more information on these controllers and possible ways to install Linux on them.

`http://www.redhat.com/linux-info/ldp/HOWTO/mini/Ultra-DMA.html` by Brion Vibber, `brion@pobox.com`

The important parts are included below, but we recommend reading the rest of the HOWTO for why this works (and what to do if this doesn't work).

Under Red Hat 5.0, use the installation boot floppy, and at the boot prompt type `rescue`. It'll load some stuff, prompt you for the supplemental disk, ask you about your monitor and keyboard, and finally put you into a command prompt. Then, do `cat /proc/pci`, write down the numbers as above, and reboot from the boot disk. This time, type `linux ide2=(this is where you put the numbers like shown above) ide3=(more numbers)`. It should now be able to install onto your hard disk without difficulty.

Thanks to Gadi Oxman for the following information on getting the interface settings:

```
If we can access the console with the installation disk, we can
also use "cat /proc/pci" to display the Promise interface
```

```
settings:

RAID bus controller: Promise Technology Unknown device (rev 1).
   Vendor id=105a. Device id=4d33.
   Medium devsel.  IRQ 12.  Master Capable.  Latency=32.
   I/O at 0xe000.   (a)
   I/O at 0xd804.   (b)
   I/O at 0xd400.   (c)
   I/O at 0xd004.   (d)
   I/O at 0xc800.   (e)
```

and pass "ide2=a,b+2 ide3=c,d+2" as a command line parameter to the kernel.

Note that the numbers probably aren't the same as what you'll have. Just as an example, the parameters to use for the above set of numbers would be:
ide2=0xe000,0xd806 ide3=0xd400,0xd006. You may or may not also need to include the IRQ, which would make it:
ide2=0xe000,0xd806,12 ide3=0xd400,0xd006,12. If you're only using the first channel on the Promise controller (for instance, if you only have one drive, or two if they're master and slave on the same channel, on the Promise), then you won't need to specify ide3.

E.6.13 I have NT and would like to install Linux, but I have heard there are problems with the booting both OS's. How can I avoid this.

The best instructions on dual-booting NT and Linux are to be found in the howto, Linux+NT-Loader. The latest version can be found at the HTTP site:
http://sunsite.unc.edu/LDP/HOWTO/mini/Linux+NT-Loader and a possibly earlier one can be found on the cdrom in /doc/HOWTO/mini/Linux+NT-Loader

E.6.14 I can not install Linux below the 1023 cylinder in my system, what can I do?

You will need to have the kernel below this limit, and use a different bootloader than LILO. The BIOS may not be able to reach it for one of the following reasons:

- The kernel is above the 1023 cylinder of the hard drive.
- The kernel is on a drive the BIOS can't boot to (not on Primary IDE or SCSI chain)
- Other esoteric kernel/BIOS problems.

经济舱 ECONOMY CLASS

承运人 CARRIER

航班 FLIGHT
BR 856

日期 DATE
03FEB

登机口 GATE

座位号 SEAT NO.
36A ⊕XX

登机时间 BOARDING TIME
1605

出发地 FROM
HONGKONG

目的地 TO
TAIPEI

姓名 NAME
HONG／JACK

登机号 BOARDING NO.
001

← 请 沿 箭 头 方 向 插 入   PLEASE ENTER THIS WAY

- You have hardware that can only be initialized in DOS (Plug and Play, etc)

You will probably need to use the LOADLIN boot loader that is provided on the cdrom in \dosutils. You will need to copy this directory over to your DOS hard drive partition and edit the autoboot.bat file to point to its new position and remove the initrd= line. If your system is a SCSI system, you will need to go into rescue mode and copy the /mnt/boot/initrd.img from the hard drive over to the dos partition, and use it for booting.

E.6.15   For whatever reason, I want to remove LILO from the Master Boot Record (MBR) of my machine. How do I do this?

There are several methods to removing LILO from the master boot record of the machine. Inside of Linux, you can replace the MBR with an earlier saved version of the MBR using the /sbin/lilo command:

```
/sbin/lilo -u
```

In DOS, NT, and Windows 95 you can use the fdisk command to create a new MBR with the "undocumented" flag /mbr. This will ONLY rewrite the MBR to boot the primary DOS partition

```
fdisk /mbr
```

E.6.16   For whatever reason, I want to remove Linux from my harddrive. I tried using DOS's fdisk, and it shows non-DOS partitions, but it can't remove them. What do I need to do?

If you need to remove linux from a hard drive, and have attempted to do this with the default DOS fdisk, you are having the "Partitions exist but they don't exist" problem. The best way to remove non-DOS partitions is with a tool that understands partitions other than DOS.

You can do this with the installation floppy by doing the following. Start the installation, select install (versus upgrade) and when it comes to partitioning the drive, choose fdisk. In fdisk type p to print out the partition numbers, and remove the Linux partitions with the d command. If satisfied with the changes you have made, you can quit with a w and the changes will be saved to disk. If you deleted too much, type q and no changes will occur.

Once you have removed the Linux partitions, you can reboot the box with Control-Alt-Delete instead of continuing with the install.

E.6.17 I have installed Linux without errors but on a reboot, I get only an L, LI, and some other items. What is happening and how can I recover?

If you have rebooted the system and have gotten a L, LI, or a combination of this and a lot of scrolling numbers, this indicates that LILO is having a problem bootstrapping itself due to one or more problems.

Write down the error codes that are being printed and what letter it stopped on (L, LI, LIL, etc). If you can access the cdrom (from DOS floppies or another machine), you can cd to (assuming DOS) \live\usr\doc\lilo-0.20\README and check to see what the error seems to indicate.

Most of the time, the LILO failures are due to the BIOS and the hard-drive mismatching geometries or something similar:

- First the kernel (or parts of it) are above the 1023 cylinder so the BIOS can not bootstrap the information. If your BIOS has the capability to use LBA (Linear Block Addressing) mode and it isn't already enabled, you should enable it and then re-run lilo (either by reinstalling or using rescue mode). In most cases, you will probably have to repartition after enabling LBA.

- If you can reinstall and add more partitions, create a /boot partition and place it entirely below the 1023 cylinder.

- You have placed the kernel on a drive the BIOS can't access. This can be an IDE drive that is not on the primary chain (IDE0 hda, hdb) or if you have placed Linux on a SCSI drive it is because the SCSI ID is not 0 (or 1 if you have NO IDE drives in the system).

If you need to gather more information for someone else (either for official support or from the mailing lists, news groups, friends, etc) you can use the rescue mode

Insert the installation floppy, and at the boot prompt type:

```
linux rescue
```

After a couple of screens that ask about hardware you will get a root prompt (#). You will need to mount the linux root partition like is done in this example which has the / partition as /dev/hda5

```
mkdir /mnt
mount /dev/hda5 /mnt
```

Then do the following:

```
lilo -v -r /mnt
```

Record the output of the command. You can add more -v's if you need more information. If errors still occur, you can send that output to the appropriate support group.

E.7   Using Red Hat Linux

E.7.1   I can't run any of the programs I compile because I get a "command not found" error message. I see the command in the directory, but it doesn't run.

The problem is that, according to the computer shell, the program isn't there. The computer shell (the part of the OS that runs your commands) finds programs using a very strict path setting that figures out where items are. If you type the following, you will see what your PATH variable is set to:

```
echo $PATH
```

One of the items that should not be there is the current working directory [cwd] (sometimes called the present working directory) which is called . in Unix and DOS terms. So to execute commands in the cwd, you need to either add the directory to your path, or type something like the following:

```
./command
```

E.7.2   How come I don't see colors when I run ls?

In order to allow the color option, you must edit .bashrc. This line must be placed in the file:

```
alias ls='ls --color=auto'
```

E.8   X Windows

E.8.1   I hear there is a new version of XFree86 available, how do I install it? or I need to install the latest version of XFree86 because the older version does not support my video card. How do I install it?

Before upgrading to a newer version of XFree86, you should make sure that you have the latest fixes from Red Hat's ftp site. Check with ftp.redhat.com/pub/redhat/updates to see if anything extra has been added by Red Hat.

As of the April of 1998, and the 5.0 release, the current fixes were available.

```
ftp://ftp.redhat.com/pub/redhat/updates/5.0/i386/ \
                            Xconfigurator-3.26-1.i386.rpm
ftp://ftp.redhat.com/pub/redhat/updates/5.0/i386/ \
                            xserver-wrapper-1.1-1.i386.rpm
```

The latest XFree86 is available at:

```
ftp://ftp.redhat.com/pub/home/wanger/XFree86/i386/
```

You'll find these files that pertain to XFree86:

```
XFree86-100dpi-fonts-X.X.X-Y.i386.rpm
XFree86-X.X.X-Y.i386.rpm
XFree86-75dpi-fonts-X.X.X-Y.i386.rpm
XFree86-8514-X.X.X-Y.i386.rpm
XFree86-AGX-X.X.X-Y.i386.rpm
XFree86-I128-X.X.X-Y.i386.rpm
XFree86-Mach32-X.X.X-Y.i386.rpm
XFree86-Mach64-X.X.X-Y.i386.rpm
XFree86-Mach8-X.X.X-Y.i386.rpm
XFree86-Mono-X.X.X-Y.i386.rpm
XFree86-P9000-X.X.X-Y.i386.rpm
XFree86-S3-X.X.X-Y.i386.rpm
XFree86-S3V-X.X.X-Y.i386.rpm
XFree86-SVGA-X.X.X-Y.i386.rpm
XFree86-VGA16-X.X.X-Y.i386.rpm
XFree86-W32-X.X.X-Y.i386.rpm
XFree86-devel-X.X.X-Y.i386.rpm
XFree86-libs-X.X.X-Y.i386.rpm
```

(Note: X.X.X represents the current version of XFree86, while Y represents the packages revision. Where ever you see this, replace it with the appropriate numbers. As of April 1998, the latest release of XFree86 was 3.3.2 and the latest package revision was 5.)

You need at least these:

```
XFree86-X.X.X-Y.i386.rpm
XFree86-75dpi-fonts-X.X.X-Y.i386.rpm
XFree86-100dpi-fonts-X.X.X-Y.i386.rpm
XFree86-libs-X.X.X-Y.i386.rpm
XFree86-VGA16-X.X.X-Y.i386.rpm
```

as well as XFree86-XF86Setup-X.X.X-Y.i386.rpm
from /pub/contrib/hurricane/i386

If you want to build X apps (if you are not a programmer, I doubt you will), you want XFree86-devel-X.X.X-Y.i386.rpm as well.

You will also need one of the other, card-specific servers. Exactly which one you need will depend upon which server supports your card. There are several ways you can figure out which server to use. First, you need to know what type of video card you have. If you don't know this, check your documentation. If that doesn't work, you can open the system up and look at the card, or use the SuperProbe program, located in /usr/X11R6/bin/.

You can then use the XFree86 FAQ, located at /urlhttp://www.xfree86.org/FAQ/, as well as the release specific information at /urlhttp://www.xfree86.org/X.X.X/index.html to help you determine which server to use. You can also check the documentation that is included in the XFree86-X.X.X-Y.i386.rpm and placed into /usr/X11R6/lib/X11/doc/. Note, you will have to install the XFree86-X.X.X-Y.i386.rpm before you can read this documentation, so you may end up ftping to ftp.redhat.com several times.

Download all of the packages to a temporary directory, such as /tmp. Please be sure to use binary mode in ftp. You can check the packages with rpm -K -nopgp *.rpm – that will tell you if they got corrupted during the transfer.

You can then install everything like this:

```
rpm -Uvh --force XFree86*
```

Once that's done, run Xconfigurator or XF86Setup and you should be able to get things going from there.

If you use XF86Setup to configure X (you may have to, since Xconfigurator doesn't know how to configure some of the newer cards that XFree86 supports), you may have to fix some of the symbolic links by hand. Here's how it should work, assuming you have installed xserver-wrapper (like you are supposed to):

/usr/X11R6/bin/X should be a symbolic link to xserver-wrapper and /etc/X11/X should be a symbolic link to the card specific X server that you use, for example XF86_SVGA.

Here's an example of how you might create these symbolic links, as root:

```
ln -sf /usr/X11R6/bin/xserver-wrapper /usr/X11R6/bin/X
ln -sf "../../usr/X11R6/bin/XF86_SVGA" /etc/X11/X
```

XF86Setup doesn't know to do this, so you may need to do this manually after running XF86Setup to create an /etc/X11/XF86Config file.

E.8.2   When I try to start X with with the `startx` command I get errors that no server was installed and I am back at a prompt. What could be wrong?

When you get an error about no servers installed, you should check to see if first the correct X server was installed and that the correct links were set up.

If you are using the latest Red Hat packages, you will be using the xserver-wrapper as a method to protect against various security problems.

/usr/X11R6/bin/X should be a symbolic link to xserver-wrapper and /etc/X11/X should be a symbolic link to the card-specific X server that you use, for example XF86_SVGA.

Here's an example of how you might create these symbolic links, as root:

```
cd /usr/X11R6/bin
ln -sf xserver-wrapper ./X
cd /etc/X11
ln -sf "../../usr/X11R6/bin/XF86_SVGA" ./X
```

This should set up the symbolic links correctly for your system.

E.8.3   When I start X, all I see is a grey background and a X cursor.

One of the most common reasons is that you are not using the correct command to start the X server. The best command to start the X windows system is

```
startx
```

If you are using this command, and only the gray screen is coming up, there can be some other explanations. First, are you waiting long enough? Due to either the speed of the processor, the amount of memory (less than 16 megs of ram), or network problems it may take up to 6 minutes before X windows is fully operational. In most cases this is an indication of a problem that can be solved (faster CPU, more memory, or finding out what is broken in networking).

Another problem can be that the starting scripts are not able to execute some command. You can try to get around this by creating a very simple ~/.xinitrc and running startx. You may also check /var/log/Xerrors for errors that might help you troubleshoot the problem.

E.8.4 How do I customize the X window manager?

To customize any of the default window manager settings, add or remove programs from the menus, and/or change which programs start up automatically, you will need to change the files in /etc/X11/AnotherLevel. Please see the man page for xinit, startx, AnotherLevel, fvwm2, FvwmM4, and wmconfig for more details.

E.8.5 I don't like the Windows 95 like configuration, how can I change it?

If you really don't like the look or feel of the default window manager setup, you can select a different style from the Preferences menu, and then clicking on WM Style menu.

If you are interested in changing to other window managers, you will want to check out this web page:

/urlhttp://www.plig.org/xwinman/

E.8.6 I get an error about errno=111. What does it mean and what can I do?

Whenever the XFree86 Xserver crashes, dies, ceases to exist or is inaccessible for any reason, you will see the error message _X11TransSocketUNIXConnect: Can't connect: errno = 111 or one similar to it.

It is a message from an X-client (any program running on your XFree86 Xserver, for example the window manager) telling you that it tried to connect to the Xserver, but failed to do so for "some" reason.

To further debug this issue, you will need to look into the server output for what got this error. Normally you should see the real error message (why the server stopped to work) a few lines before the error 111 message. If you still can't make head or tail from all those messages, make sure to quote the FULL server output in your problem report (to either technical support or a mailing list).

It is impossible to provide you with any help if you just mention the error 111, as so many people do. Obtaining the full server output is normally accomplished by redirecting both standard output and standard error to a file while starting the server. You can do this by running X like this:

```
startx &> startx.out
```

Other useful information to check are the symbolic links of X, the .xinitrc (if one exists) or what commands were running when the error occurred.

E.8.7   My keyboard mappings don't work correctly in X. What can I do?

If you are using Metro-X you will need to do the following

```
cd /usr/X11R6/lib/X11/xkb/keymap
cp xfree86 metro
```

This will solve many of the problems experienced. However it isn't a full solution due to the fact that some of the XFree86 mappings are out of date with modern keyboards. If you still experience problems with the keyboard settings, you will need to use the xmodmap and xev commands to correct the problems. Please send these corrections to bugs@redhat.com and bugs@xfree86.org so that they can be corrected in the main distributions.

E.8.8   I get an error message that libX can't be opened. or I can't compile X apps due to missing libraries.

More than likely, the needed libraries are not installed. You will (re)install the packages to get them.

Insert installation cdrom.

```
mount /mnt/cdrom
cd /mnt/cdrom/RedHat/RPMS
rpm -Uvh --force XFree86-devel* XFree86-libs* Xaw3d*
```

This should install most of the X libraries that you might need. If you still get the error, it may be due to the fact that the requested library is part of a package we do not provide (qt, xforms, motif, etc).

E.8.9 I have an AGP graphics card. Is it supported?

AGP cards were not supported in XFree86 before version 3.3.2. If you have 3.3.2 installed on your system, then Xconfigurator should show which AGP cards are supported. Note that Red Hat Linux 5.1 and later versions have XFree86 version 3.3.2 (or better) already.

If you do not already have 3.3.2, you may want to consider upgrading to this release. Please see their web page at /urlhttp://www.xfree86.org/ for more details.

E.8.10 My computer has a NeoMagic graphics card chipset, how can I get X to work?

The NeoMagic cards are currently not supported by Red Hat Linux's X servers. XFree86 can't support them since NeoMagic requires a non-disclosure agreement before they will release programming information and this precludes any source code release.

Xi Graphics' Accelerated X has support for the NeoMagic chips in their laptop specific X server. See /urlhttp://www.xig.com/ for more information on their server.

E.8.11 I upgraded from 4.1 (or earlier) and now when I use startx, the machine seems to hang at a grey screen.

The problem is that releases prior to 4.2 installed (.Xclients) in every users home directory, which calls:

```
fvwm95-2 -cmd 'FvwmM4 -debug /etc/X11/TheNextLevel/...'
```

as their window manager, which doesn't exist in 5.0. The proper workaround for this problem is to:

```
rm -f ~/.Xclients
```

(A more drastic work workaround available to the root user):

```
rm -f /home/*/.Xclients
```

E.8.12   When I run netscape, the colors don't seem right, or When I run netscape, I get error messages and warnings about colors.

This problem often comes with the error:

```
Cannot allocate colormap entry for default background.
```

The reason is that X has run out of colors to allocate to applications (this shows up a lot on 16 and 256 color applications) To solve this problem you can try the following:

- 1. run netscape with -install switch. This can be **ugly** in that you get large color flashes.
  2. run X in 15bpp or higher. To obtain a higher bpp than 8 (default) run startx like:

    ```
    startx -- -bpp 16
    ```

    If it doesn't work, consult your X driver manuals, Xconfigurator or upgrade your videocard.

E.8.13   I have a Microsoft serial mouse, and Linux doesn't want to work with it. What can I do to fix it?

It has been found that the 2 button Microsoft Mouse of version 2.1A or greater is a "smart" mouse. It has been speculated that it is looking for wakeup signals from Windows, or it will not respond back to the computer.

This causes X and/or gpm to not work with Linux because the mouse is not responding in a way these programs are expecting. To "reset" the mouse to work with these programs, you can follow one of several methods. Use mouseconfig to set things up before running X.

```
mouseconfig --kickstart --device cuaX
```

where X is either 0 (for com 1) or 1 (for com2)

Another solution is to get gpm-1.13, run as gpm -t pnp -R, and configure XFree86 for MouseSystems Protocol with /dev/gpmdata as the device.

E.9   System Administration

E.9.1   When I create users with usercfg, they can't login.

If when using usercfg the password is never encrypted when typed in or only one asterisk is placed in the password field, it is a usercfg bug. We are working to fix this bug, but currently we have this work around.

Click the button to the left of the entry field and choose change, then type the password TWICE in the entry field (follow it with a return each time).

Another alternative is to set their password using the command line passwd program.

E.9.2   What is PAM? Why use it?

PAM is a standard adopted by other unices such as Solaris 2.6. For more information on PAM please read: /urlhttp://www.redhat.com/linux-info/pam/

E.9.3   How can I setup Secure Shell (SSH) on my linux system?

Due to United States of America export restrictions on munitions, Red Hat Linux can not distribute ssh. The site ftp.replay.com has set up various downloads of ssh and PGP.

E.9.4   Why does Linux only see part of my RAM?

There are a couple of things that could be causing Linux to not see all your memory. On some 386's you need to compile your kernel with 'Limit memory to 16M?" enabled.

On most systems, the reason is that the BIOS has a limit of how much memory it will tell the OS is present in the machine, even though the board can have more. Common limits seen with this problem are 16M, 32M, 64M, and 128M. To get around this, we need to explicitly specify the amount of memory to the kernel at boot time via the mem=< actual memory goes here > flag.

In the following example, we have a 32M machine but only 16M are being seen by Linux. At the LILO prompt, we type

```
LILO: linux mem=32M
```

After the machine boots, we use the free command to see if the larger amount of memory was recognized by the kernel. If so, we can add an append line to the /etc/lilo.conf file and rerun lilo to make it happen permanently. The example from above could look like the following:

```
boot=/dev/sda
map=/boot/map
install=/boot/boot.b
prompt
timeout=50
image=/boot/vmlinuz-2.0.32
        label=linux
        root=/dev/sda1
        initrd=/boot/initrd-2.0.32.img
        read-only
        append="mem=32M"
```

Do not forget to run lilo after editing the file.

E.9.5   I have over 64 Megs in my pentium or greater machine, however it seems sluggish when doing anything. If I tell Linux to use only 64Megs with the mem=64M machine, it seems to speed up. What is going on and can I do anything about it?

This problem is a problem with hit rates and memory. A few motherboards do not use the external cache at all if the machine tries to access memory more than 64M in size. This will cause a noticeable slow down, and there is not much that can be done about it. Most other problems is that the CPU is not using the External Cache if you only have 256K cache and more than 64Megs of ram. Increase the Motherboard cache to 512K to 1Megabyte and you may see the sluggishness go away.

E.9.6   I have Red Hat 5.0 and have upgraded to the Id.so RPM package listed in the errata, but my libc5 applications still seg fault. What is wrong?

The problem with crashing libc5 applications can be due to several items.

- 1. Before/after the upgrade, there was installed another version of libc that didn't get obsoleted by the Upgrade process or placed libc5 libraries in a place that causes conflict.
  To find out if this is the case, do this:

  ```
  rpm -qa | grep libc
  ```

  It should produce the following output:

  ```
  glibc-devel-2.0.5c-12
  ```

```
libc-5.3.12-24
glibc-debug-2.0.5c-12
rpm-2.4.10-1glibc
rpm-devel-2.4.10-1glibc
glibc-profile-2.0.5c-12
glibc-2.0.5c-12
```

If you see items like libc-debug-5.3.12-18 or libc-5.4.44-2, you will need to remove these packages (rpm -e libc-debug) and run ldconfig -v

2. Your /etc/ld.so.conf file has been changed from an optimal setting. For optimal loading, set your /etc/ld.so.conf file in the following order:

```
/usr/i486-linuxaout/lib
/usr/i486-linux-libc5/lib
/usr/openwin/lib
/usr/X11R6/lib
```

E.9.7   When I run fstool, I get a message that says a partition seems to have been deleted and asks if I want to remove it from /etc/fstab.

The fstool program is not working properly with current versions of tcl and shouldn't be used. It should have been obsoleted, but slipped through the cracks.

First we will have to fix the /etc/fstab file since fstool may have corrupted it. The areas that seem to be changed by fstool are usually the cdrom and swap. Here are sample lines (you will need to change the partitions to match your system.)

```
/dev/sda2          swap          swap  defaults     0 0
/dev/cdrom         /mnt/cdrom    iso9660 noauto,ro   0 0
```

You should now remove the fstool program using rpm.

```
rpm -e fstool
```

Please use cabaret which is a functional working alternative. This program is located in /usr/sbin/cabaret and can be executed from the command line.

E.9.8   How do I configure my Jaz drive under linux?

Documentation on using Jaz with Linux can be found on the cdrom in doc/HOWTO/mini/Jaz-Drive and on the system in /usr/doc/HOWTO/mini/Jaz-Drive.

E.9.9   How do I use my parallel port zip drive?

Here's something you can try: edit `/etc/conf.modules` and add the following line to the others

```
alias scsi_hostadapter ppa
```

If you need to send the ppa driver any options about which LP is being used etc, you would add the line

```
options ppa ppa=<options go here.>
```

For more information, check `www.torque.net/paraport`

E.9.10   I'm having problems getting my IDE zip drive to work.

First check and make sure there is a disk in the drive. Also, make sure you are mounting it as partition 4 instead of 1. An example would be hdc4. The supposed reason for it being partition 4 is that Mac SCSI uses this partition as it primary partition.

E.9.11   Some of my older applications get the incorrect time.

Some libc5 apps want `/usr/lib/zoneinfo`, so you can either recompile them for libc6 or provide a symlink so that things will work.

```
ln -s ../share/zoneinfo /usr/lib/zoneinfo
```

Please see also check the Red Hat errata (`www.redhat.com/errata`) for other items.

E.9.12   I have all the latest updates installed, but my programs still get the incorrect time.

If you have installed all the latest updates and you programs still get the incorrect time, try checking the settings in `/etc/sysconfig/clock`. They probably look something like this:

```
UTC=true
ARC=false
```

This means that Linux will assume that your BIOS clock is set to the UTC or GMT timezone. More than likely, the clock is set to your local timezone, and you need to change the UTC line to be

```
UTC=false
```

E.9.13 During the install, I was not asked to use the 2nd cdrom. When I use the X program glint on it, it reports that there are no rpms, but when I look at the directories, I see lots of them. What is going on?

The 2nd cdrom in the Red Hat Linux boxed set contains the source code rpms (SRPM) for all of the Open Source applications that are on the first cdrom. From these source rpms, you can build all the Open Source applications we have in the distribution.

The reason that glint does not see source rpms is due to that SRPMS are not stored in any of the RPM databases. This makes it almost impossible to tell if you have installed an src.rpm before or are over-writing an older version. Thus you will need to use the plain rpm command to install these items.

`rpm -ivh < filename >` will install the source code into the directory that the maintainer of that SRPM used. The data in src.rpms packaged by Red Hat are installed into `/usr/src/redhat` by default.

Rebuilding and improving on rpms is beyond the scope of this answer. The book Maximum RPM and the man pages are good sources of information on this.

E.9.14 Linux recognizes my CDROM, but when I try to mount it, I get "mount failed" What do I do?

If your system was installed properly, simply typing `mount /mnt/cdrom` should work. If it does not, you must edit your `/etc/fstab` file. Here is an example of entry in `/etc/fstab`:

```
/dev/hdc          /mnt/cdrom       iso9660 noauto,ro 0 0
CD-ROM device)   (directory)      (filesystem type and options)
```

To find out what the CD-ROM device is, type `dmesg | less` and scan it for information regarding your CD-ROM. If you wish to mount the CD-ROM without adding this to your `/etc/fstab`:

```
mount -t iso9660 /dev/hdc /mnt/cdrom
```

E.9.15   I have Linux installed on an IDE drive, and for whatever reason I need to boot from floppy. How can I boot my system from the install floppy?

If you have installed Linux onto an IDE hard-drive, you can boot from the installation floppy using the following method.

Insert the installation floppy and restart the machine. At the boot: prompt type the following:

```
vmlinuz root=/dev/hdXY
  [Example: vmlinuz root=/dev/hdb5 ]
```

Where X = is the Linux drive letter and Y is the partition on the drive you installed the root (/) partition to.

E.9.16   I can't get my Plug and Play card to work.

The 2.0.xx kernels do not directly support the Plug and Play (PNP) protocol. You will need to either disable PNP on the card (via jumpers or card setup tools). You can also change your boot method to use Loadlin.exe from Windows (as windows would then have set up the PNP hardware).

Finally you can try using the isapnptools programs. First, type this:

```
pnpdump > /etc/isapnp.conf
```

This will create a configuration file that you will need to edit to choose the settings used for each card. Then type isapnp /etc/isapnp.conf to set up the devices.

See /urlhttp://www.roestock.demon.co.uk/isapnptools/ for more information.

E.9.17   When the system boots up, I see a message that says I have unknown PCI hardware. What does this mean?

The error "unknown PCI device" can occur for several reasons. The first and most harmless one is that PCI isn't responding to Linux's queries in a way it understands, but Linux is able to keep going. The more common occurrence is that the system hangs on querying PCI bus cards and cannot get any further.

Since this is a hardware problem in the kernel, there is not much that RedHat can do except point you to the maintainer of that section of the kernel. They may be able to let you know what is going on, and may want to look at what hardware you do have in your system so they can better handle it in the future. The maintainer can be reached at:

```
linux-pcisupport@cck.uni-kl.de
```

Please include the following information:

- /proc/pci

- your exact hardware description. Try to find out which device is unknown. It may be your main-board chip set, PCI-CPU bridge or PCI-ISA bridge.

- If you can't find the actual information in your hardware booklet, try to read the references of the chip on the board.

E.9.18 Currently when the machine boots, LILO defaults to running Linux. I would like it to boot my other operating system. How can I accomplish this?

To change the default OS that Linux boots into, you will need to edit the /etc/lilo.conf file and change the order of the OS's that LILO looks at. In the following example we change the order of booting so that DOS gets booted by default instead of Linux.

```
pico /etc/lilo.conf

# here is the old version

boot=/dev/hda
map=/boot/map
install=/boot/boot.b
prompt
timeout=50
image=/boot/vmlinuz-2.0.31
        label=linux
        root=/dev/hda2
        read-only
other = /dev/hda1
        label = dos
        table = /dev/hda

# change it to the following:
boot=/dev/hda
map=/boot/map
install=/boot/boot.b
prompt
```

```
timeout=50
other = /dev/hda1
        label = dos
        table = /dev/hda
image=/boot/vmlinuz-2.0.31
        label=linux
        root=/dev/hda2
        read-only
```

Save your changes to the file and leave the editor. Run the command

```
/sbin/lilo -v
```

and the updated lilo will be written to the boot device. On a reboot, the machine will boot into
DOS as default now instead of Linux, with a 50 second delay to give you time to choose linux
at the boot prompt if you wish to boot to Linux.

E.9.19   For whatever reason, I need to use the rescue mode to edit a file. The editors complain about unknown window type. How can I edit files after I have booted from the rescue disk?

After selecting rescue mode and answering a few questions, you will get a root prompt (#). You
will need to mount the Linux partition like is done in this example. The partitions below are an
example only. You should change them to be appropriate for your system (sda1,sdb1,hda5,
etc)

```
mkdir /mnt
mount /dev/sdb1 /mnt
cd /mnt/etc
export TERMCAP=/mnt/etc/termcap
vi filename
```

or, if you wish to use a different editor, such as pico, you may want to chroot /mnt.

E.10   Network Administration

E.10.1   Linux isn't detecting my NE2000 compatible network card.

It has been found that some NE2000's that worked with earlier kernels, do not work with the later 2.0.X kernels. For some, the following work around will enable them to work.

You can try to get the card to work by doing this:

```
insmod 8390
insmod ne io=0xXXXX irq=Y
```

(Note: Replace XXXX and Y with your IOAddress and IRQ. Most common values for th IOAddress are 0x300 and 0x310. The IRQ may be anything.)

After this, use ifconfig or netcfg to configure the card. Sometimes, even though the card is recognized, there have been reports of the card still failing to transfer TCP/IP packets. This is being looked into.

If the above works, add it to /etc/conf.modules. It should look something like this:

```
alias eth0 8390
alias eth0 ne
options eth0 io=0xXXXX irq=Y
```

E.10.2   I have installed Linux, and it seems to initially start booting. However it gets down to something called sendmail and then the machine seems to hang. What is happening and what should I do?

If after the install the machine seems to hang when it reaches certain processes like sendmail, apache, or SMB there is probably a network problem. The most common cause is that Linux can not look up the name of the machine you have called the box (if you set up networking to have a machine name). The machine is currently paused waiting for the network timeout of DNS lookups, and will eventually bring up the login prompt. Login in as root and check the usual culprits for a problem.

If you are directly on a network with a DNS server, check the file /etc/resolv.conf has the correct values for your machines DNS server. Check with your systems administrator that the values are correct.

If you are using Linux on a network without a DNS server (or this box is going to be the DNS server :)), then you will need to edit the /etc/hosts file to have the hostname and IP address so that the lookups will occur correctly. The format of the /etc/hosts file is like the following example:

```
127.0.0.1                    localhost localhost.localdomain
192.168.200.1                mymachine mymachine.mynetwork.net
```

Where the example machine is called mymachine.

E.10.3 I have upgraded to 5.0, and sendmail is no longer relaying email like it used to. What is going on?

Due to various email spammers using unknowing Red Hat boxes as email relayers and some other problems, we have turned this off by default in 5.0

You can add the names of systems that you want to be allowed to relay mail to the file /etc/relay_allow. The web site /urlhttp://www.informatik.uni-kiel.de/%7Eca/email/check.html for more details on this.

If you are having problems with sites sending you UBE (Unsolicited Bulk Email), you can also deny them access to your machines with the new features of sendmail. Add the sites to the file /etc/mail/deny and then make a hash table for it.

The following command can be used to create the hash database version of this file:

```
makemap -v hash /etc/mail/deny < /etc/mail/deny
```

E.10.4 I have installed Linux, recompiled my kernel, and now I get errors when the network comes out about various net-pf modules not found. What is happening and what should I do?

This means that Linux was unable to find modules for various network protocols. The most common ones are net-pf-4 (IPX) and net-pf-5 (appletalk). It looks like that during a kernel recompile these were not included and some service is looking for it during the boot.

First check to see that you are not running a service that is wanting it (mars-nwe, netatalk, etc). If you are you will need to recompile the kernel with these items or turn off the service.

If you still get net-pf errors you can fix it by following these directions:

```
cd /etc
vi conf.modules
```

Add to the file:

```
alias net-pf-3 off
alias net-pf-4 off
alias net-pf-5 off
```

This should turn off the messages upon boot as it tells linux that these are OFF and should not be looked for.

E.10.5   How can I configure my dialup PPP Internet connection?

These sites have excellent current PPP information..

```
http://www.redhat.com/support/docs/rhl/PPP-Tips/PPP-Tips.html
http://www.redhat.com/support/docs/rhl/Dialup-Tips/Dialup-Tips.html
```

In addition, The control-panel in X windows has a tool called netcfg that will allow configuration of your modem.

To configure PPP, via the control-panel bar:

- Click 'Network Configuration'

- Click 'Interfaces' (at the top bar section of the screen)

- Then click 'Add'

- Click 'Ok' for PPP

- type in "#", "name" and "password"

- Click 'Customize'

- Go into 'Networking' and select 'defaultroute' if you have a 'dynamic IP', otherwise type in your IP information

- Then click 'Done' to save configuration.

- it should show up in your interface table following this setup procedure

The ppp-list@redhat.com is also useful.

E.10.6   How can I allow non root users to start ppp connections?

Have netcfg setup ppp for non-root users. Then as the non-root user use the command

```
/usr/sbin/usernetctl ifcfg-ppp0 up
```

E.10.7   My system keeps losing its network routing information.

The problem that you are describing may be due to the fact that the gated program is running on your system. In a proper configuration it will bring interfaces up and down when needed. Unless you have configured its startup scripts and are running a router, it should be disabled (we are sorry it was shipped enabled, and future versions will not have it enabled.) To turn off gated, please do the following:

```
/usr/sbin/ntsysv

disable gated

quit ntsysv
```

Then, for best consideration, please reboot as gated may have left the network in a bad condition. If that is not possible, please do the following

```
/etc/rc.d/init.d/gated stop
/etc/rc.d/init.d/network restart
```

E.11   Printer Administration

E.11.1   I am having trouble setting up my printer. My printer is not listed in the printer configuration tool.

Due to licensing problems, we can not ship the latest ghostscript. It is however available for download in the directory (having been contributed by another Red Hat user):

```
http://www.users.dircon.co.uk/~typhoon/
```

This later version of ghostscript supports many more printers.

E.11.2   I have a Canon BJC printer and it isn't printing properly.

If you have a Canon BJC printer and it is not working with 5.0, you may want to try editing /var/spool/lpd/lp/postscript.cfg. Commenting out the line:

```
COLOR=-dBitsPerPixel=1
```

has been effective for some users with Canon BJC printers.

E.11.3   When I print, lines from my printout get truncated.

Some printers truncate ASCII lines when printing a page. This is how the printer handles lines that are too long. The text must be run through something that will format the text, like pr or mpage before sending it to the printer.

E.12   Appendix [*sic*]

E.12.1   The Red Hat FTP site is slow. Are there mirrors?

There are many mirrors of Red Hat Software's FTP site. An up-to-date list can always be found at ftp://ftp.redhat.com/pub/MIRRORS.html.

Index

Symbols

A

B

C

S

Index of Packages

Y

Z